Your Undergraduate Dissertation

→SAGE Study Skills

Your Undergraduate Dissertation

The Essential Guide for Success

Nicholas Walliman

2nd Edition

Los Angeles | London | New Delhi
Singapore | Washington DC

Los Angeles | London | New Delhi
Singapore | Washington DC

SAGE Publications Ltd
1 Oliver's Yard
55 City Road
London EC1Y 1SP

SAGE Publications Inc.
2455 Teller Road
Thousand Oaks, California 91320

SAGE Publications India Pvt Ltd
B 1/I 1 Mohan Cooperative Industrial Area
Mathura Road
New Delhi 110 044

SAGE Publications Asia-Pacific Pte Ltd
3 Church Street
#10-04 Samsung Hub
Singapore 049483

Editor: Katie Metzler
Production editor: Nicola Marshall
Copyeditor: Gemma Marren
Proofreader: Kate Harrison
Indexer: Author
Marketing manager: Catherine Slinn
Cover design: Wendy Scott
Typeset by: C&M Digitals (P) Ltd, Chennai, India
Printed and bound by CPI Group (UK) Ltd,
Croydon, CR0 4YY

Library of Congress Control Number: 2013935324

British Library Cataloguing in Publication data

A catalogue record for this book is available from the British Library

ISBN 978-1-4462-5318-2
ISBN 978-1-4462-5319-9

To my wife, Ursula

Brief Contents

Contents

About the Author

Nicholas Walliman is a qualified architect and senior lecturer in the School of Architecture at Oxford Brookes University and a researcher associate in the Oxford Institute for Sustainable Development. After many years of practice in architecture in the UK and abroad, he returned to academic life to do his PhD. This experience raised his interest in research theory and methods, and he was subsequently asked by the university to write a distance learning course to guide postgraduate students embarking on research degrees. He has subsequently published several other books on research theory and methods for students and practitioners at various levels of expertise.

He is currently conducting research with a team of architects and environmental scientists as part of the Oxford Institute for Sustainable Development. They are engaged in nationally and internationally funded projects on a range of aspects of building technology, such as energy saving building envelope design, mitigation of the effects of floods on buildings and advanced construction methods. He has published numerous research papers on aspects of architectural technology. He is also supervising several PhD and Masters students. Despite this emphasis on science and technology, his work with research students covers many other aspects of architecture and its relationship to society, such as vernacular architecture, the effects of westernization, architectural education, conservation, administration and sustainable design.

Acknowledgements

My grateful thanks go to the many people that have given me support in writing this book. I would particularly like to acknowledge my wife, Ursula, who gave me much needed impetus and encouragement at crucial times. I have also been inspired by the enthusiasm and willingness to overcome difficulties encountered by my students at Oxford Brookes University. They have clarified for me some of the problems that students face as they tackle a major piece of academic work. I have greatly appreciated the guidance and help afforded by the editorial team at Sage: Katie Metzler, Anna Horvai, Nicola Marshall and Catherine Slinn to mention just a few. I could not have written this book without consulting the expertise of many other authors. These are cited in the list of references and reading lists. Although most of the anonymous artists of the copyright-free illustrations used in this book must have passed on by now, I salute their skill and artistry, and often also their humour.

Introduction

Oh no, not another book to read! After all, I've got a dissertation to write!

I understand your concern, but I intend this to be not just another book. In fact, if you read this book, writing your dissertation should be quicker, easier and you're more likely to get a good grade. The main consideration is that you will be doing a research-based written exercise of this scale for the first time. This means that there is a lot to learn and not much time to learn it. What's more, you have little room for making errors or miscalculations; you cannot postpone the deadline. You will need to learn about how to set up a dissertation project successfully, find out what will get you good marks, organize and do all the work, and hopefully make the process as enjoyable as possible. That is where this book will be of invaluable use to you. In fact, it could help you avoid having to read lots of other books to glean all this necessary information from here and there; textbooks on research methods are generally a heavy read!

I have kept the chapters short (that is why there are so many of them) in order to focus on answering one particular question at a time. You should then easily be able to pick out whichever question interests you at the moment. It is, therefore, not necessary to read through from the beginning to the end. However, I have tried to put the questions into the same general sequence as they appear when you progress through the project, so you should find navigating the process easy enough. This also results in some elaboration later on in the book of topics that were raised earlier, consistent with your growing understanding of the issues.

Some books provide lots of exercises to do in order to practice what you have read and to test yourself on whether you have understood the main points made. I have generally avoided these, as I believe that exercises are rarely completed and often seem remote from your subject, which is the reason for reading the book in the first place. It is difficult to find illustrative examples that will resonate with everyone. Instead, I urge you to reflect constantly on what you are reading, how this influences your thoughts in relation to your own dissertation topic, what you will do and how you will do it. In this way, you will be able to decide what is relevant to your own work and where you will need to follow up the issues in more detail in other literature. In order to prompt you to make some decisions at the end of each chapter, I have added a section on 'what to do next'. Again, what you do will be directly linked to your own topic, so you will not waste any time doing generalized academic exercises. I have also provided short lists of books where you can find more on the topics discussed if you need to. A list of references cited is given at the end of the book.

Use this book as a guide, just as you would a travel guide. Extract what you find useful (which I hope is most of it) and leave aside the parts that are not relevant. Once you have decided on your topic and the methods that you will use to explore the research problems or answer the research questions, you will be able to judge just what information you need to complete the work.

Don't expect this book to provide you with all the answers. I have written it in order to give a basic introduction to the main factors in writing an under-graduate dissertation – in almost any subject. This is where the rub is. Because of the diversity of topics and different approaches, you will almost certainly have to get further information on specific research methods selected for your own project. The chapters that are essential reading for all subjects are Chapters 1–11 and 15–19. Chapters 12–14 need to be read selectively, depending on the type of research that you will be doing. There is no point in me listing subjects and what you should read in each case. The main distinctions are whether you are investigating ideas, people or things, and what combination of these. You will probably have to skim through Chapters 12–14 in order to decide what is most relevant, though I have given some indications at the beginning of these chapters.

What this book will also help you to do is to decide just what further infor-mation you require. Of course, background and specific information about your subject will need to be gathered independently by you, irrespective of which research approach you take.

I hope that you find doing your dissertation is not just hard work, but also a useful experience, where you learn a lot about a subject in which you are interested and end up getting the good marks you deserve.

1

What's It All For?

1.1 Why do I have to do a dissertation? The point of independent study

The dissertation is commonly the last component of a degree course, or a module taken towards the end of the undergraduate course. After having, over the years, been fed with lots of information, guided step by step through various assignments and been tested on your knowledge and understanding in examinations, you undertake the dissertation as an exercise in independent study. It tests your abilities to educate yourself, to demonstrate your expertise in collecting and analysing information, and to come to conclusions based on solid argument. It also gives you an opportunity to show how well informed you are, how well organized you can be, and how you can make a clear presentation of your work for effective communication.

FIGURE 1.1   You will be doing this on your own

The big difference between this and your previous work is that you will be doing the dissertation on your own. You will probably receive some general guidance, but most of the decisions about what you do and how you do it will be yours. This not only gives you a lot of freedom to pursue a particular interest, but also enables you to put your own individual talents to their best use. This will inevitably require some soul-searching and evaluation of where your strongest talents lie. It is really up to you to make yourself shine in your best light!

What you are required to do can be termed 'research', as it is about finding out new things (even if they are only new to you), making sense of these, and presenting your findings in an organized and well-argued way. As with any research project, there must be stated aims at the outset, and some kind of achievement of these by the end.

This type of work obviously presents lots of opportunities, but also some dangers. The point of this book is to guide you through the process of doing a dissertation, and to explain and discuss the options you might have at each stage. It will help you to make informed decisions that you can build on in order to produce a successful outcome. It should not be all hard slog, but it will present some serious challenges in terms of your knowledge and understanding of your subject matter, and of your abilities to organize and motivate yourself. In fact, it can be one of the most satisfying processes to go through – and come out of at the other side.

FIGURE 1.2   Lots of opportunities, but also some dangers

1.2 The main components of a dissertation

Although dissertations come in many shapes and sizes, there are some aspects that are shared by most of them. Of course, the subject and how it is dealt with will have an enormous influence on the form and appearance of the finished work. However, as all dissertations are an exercise in academic research, there will be certain components that are regarded as essential for them to have academic credibility. A standard type of dissertation in, say, the social sciences or education will probably have the following components.

Preambles

- A title – this provides the briefest summary of the dissertation.
- An abstract – a slightly longer summary of the dissertation outlining the main issues, methods of investigation and conclusions.

- Acknowledgements – an expression of thanks to all those people and organizations that have helped you in the preparation and writing of the dissertation.
- A list of contents – the guide to the various sections of the work.
- Lists of figures, tables, appendices – as appropriate.

The main section

This is usually a series of chapters or sections. A typical example contains separate sections consisting of:

- An introduction to the dissertation.
- Some background to the research that reveals the issues to be researched and the work already done on the subject.
- A statement of the research problem and an explanation of how the research work was carried out (i.e. the methods used).
- The results of data collection and analysis.
- Some conclusions based on the results.

FIGURE 1.3   An expression of thanks

The add-ons

At the end are sections that provide important information on aspects of the work:

- A list of references – fuller details about all the publications and other sources that you have cited in the text.
- Perhaps a bibliography – other literature that is relevant to the study but has not been referred to directly in the text.
- Possibly some appendices (supplementary information such as questionnaire forms, letters, related information, pictures, etc.). These give examples of your methods of working and/or further background information about issues that are important to your work, but not so central as to warrant being included in the main text.

FIGURE 1.4   Some kind of illustrations or diagrams

I don't know about you, but I always like to see some kind of illustrations or diagrams in things that I read. Not only do these enliven the appearance of the page, but they also can encapsulate ideas or issues in an incredibly compact manner. Not all subjects lend themselves easily to this, but some demand it. (I studied architecture – picture books galore!)

1.3 What will impress? Seeing it from the examiner's point of view

In order to be awarded a really good grade, it is obviously useful to understand exactly what the examiner will be looking for when giving marks. The following list will indicate the main areas that gain marks in any dissertation, regardless of the subject. These areas will be discussed in detail in the following chapters of this book, with many handy hints to help you achieve the best possible result. The list is not presented in any order of priority. It will help you to understand the particular requirements of your own course if you read through the instructions for your dissertation extremely carefully. Make a note of the issues mentioned and compare these with the comments below. There may even be a breakdown of how the marks will be allotted. If not, read between the lines to see if there are any hints. Don't hesitate to take any opportunity you may get to discuss the requirements with your tutor or supervisor.

Here is the list of main assessment areas and the sorts of questions that the examiner will be asking him/herself.

First impressions

Presentation How does it look? A neat cover, practical binding and well-designed page layout all give a favourable impression to start with. Remember that your dissertation will be on a pile with all the rest, so comparisons can easily be drawn with the others. Your examiner will be naturally better disposed to the more attractive submissions.

Organization A brief scan through the dissertation should give an immediate impression of how the work is organized. This means clearly headed sections, easily spotted chapter divisions, and a logical arrangement of the sections of the study. The examiner will feel much more comfortable with work that is easy to navigate. A clear structure is a strong indication of clear thinking – a markable aspect of the work.

Length This should conform to the requirements. A report that looks too thin or too thick immediately rings alarm bells for the marker. The former will be difficult to award sufficient marks and the latter will be a daunting task to wade through.

FIGURE 1.5   On the pile with all the rest

Quick review

Abstract Though not always a requirement, this is so useful as a brief introduction that it should not be left out. Summarize your whole dissertation in 150–200 words, including main conclusions. Not an easy task but good practice, and again demonstrates clear thinking.

List of contents Situated near the front of the dissertation, this gives a simple overview of not only what is in the text, but how it is organized. It will also provide a useful navigation tool for later on to find the page numbers of the different sections.

Main conclusions One of the main points of doing a dissertation is to come to some conclusions based on the research. The final chapter should spell out the conclusions extremely clearly so that they can be picked out by the examiner by simply scanning through the pages. He or she will check that the conclusions relate exactly to the research problem or question.

Reference list This will be a measure of your background reading, both in depth and in scope. You will impress your examiner if the relevant books are cited, but won't if your list is padded with numerous extraneous references.

Detailed reading

Relevance and quality of background study You will not be reinventing the wheel. Whatever the subject you are tackling, there will be numerous other writers and experts who have worked in the same area. The examiner will look to see if you have discovered the main

FIGURE 1.6   The foundation stone of your dissertation

ones relevant to your study and have understood what they have written. This will provide the context for your own research and will enable you to pinpoint the particular issue that you will tackle in your study. It will also provide precedents of how the research might be carried out.

Clarity of the research problem or question It is essential to be clear, not only in your own mind but also in your writing, about the exact problem or question that you are tackling. This is the foundation stone of your dissertation and produces the main aims of the research. The research problem or question will be elaborated and dissected during the course of your study, but it remains the linchpin of all your research efforts. It should be possible throughout the dissertation for the examiner to relate the writing to the stated aims derived from the research problem or question.

Selection of methods for data collection and analysis One of the main aims of doing a dissertation is to discover and implement basic research methods. The choice of methods is huge, so you will be marked both on the discussion about possible methods and on the appropriateness of your choice.

Use of research methods Each method has its own rules and procedures, so you need to demonstrate that you have understood these and implemented them correctly.

Solidity of argument to support findings and conclusions You could see the whole dissertation as a piece of detective work, with the report being the evidence and argument that leads to your conclusions. Do you have a watertight case? The examiner will dissect the logic of your argument and weigh the strength of your conclusions based on the evidence you bring forward.

Quality of referencing Your work will inevitably be based on the research and writings of others; after all, that is how we learn about most things. It is therefore essential that you acknowledge the source of your information and ideas by consistent use of a citing and referencing system. Marks are specifically allotted to this aspect of the work.

Quality of writing The main form of your communication is the written word. Correct spelling and grammar are basic requirements (your word processor will help to some extent). Proper sentence and paragraph construction are also essential; these will be partly dependent on your personal style. You should aim at clarity throughout. The examiner will have limited time to read your work, so make it easy for him or her: you will be rewarded for this. If you are not writing in your first language, it is a good idea to find a native English speaker to read through your work and correct it as necessary.

1.4   Chapter summary

In this chapter I have discussed the reasons for doing a dissertation, which are to demonstrate that you can do a piece of independent work and that you understand the basics of research.

The main components of a dissertation are: the preambles – consisting of a title, abstract, acknowledgements and lists of contents, figures, tables, etc.; the main section – consisting of an introduction, background, research problem, methods, data collection and analysis and conclusions; and the add-ons – such as list of references, bibliography and appendices.

The examiner will be looking for clear presentation, good organization and the correct length. The quality of the main components of the dissertation will also be checked, particularly for evidence of reading of the relevant literature, identification of the research problem and questions, appropriate use of research methods, and the solidity of the argument that leads to your conclusions.

1.5 What should I do now?

Even if you do not know yet exactly what you are going to choose as a subject for your dissertation, it is a good idea to go and look at the work of students from previous years. Your department or your university/college library should keep copies of all the dissertations. Find out where they are. You will probably be impressed by the sheer number of them, so how do you start looking to find something useful? Here is a good way to do it.

Find out what order they are in on the shelves. If they are in some kind of subject order, then choose four or five on the subject area that you are interested in. If not, any recent dissertations from your course will do. If you can only get them by request from the library catalogue, then choose some from the list. Ideally, choose dissertations that have been completed according to the regulations and instructions that you have to follow.

Don't sit down and try to read them! First, compare the following features:

- format (size and shape)
- design of cover
- type of binding
- design of page layouts
- printing fonts and styles and text layout
- number and type of illustrations.

Now that you have got a general impression of a range of designs (note how important these are in the initial impact), it is time to look more carefully at the components and structure of the dissertations. Check each for the following:

- Title – length and clarity. Can you understand what it is about just by reading the title? Is it too long and complicated? Is it too short and general?
- Preambles – are these clearly labelled and set out? Check what they consist of: title page, acknowledgements, abstract, list of contents with page numbers, lists of figures and tables, anything else (e.g. statement of individual work, dedication, etc.). Look at the layout and design of each of these.
- Chapters or sections – how many, how long and in what sequence? Does the sequence of chapter titles show you how the dissertation is structured? One example might be: introduction, background, research problem, research methods used, data collection, data analysis, conclusions. There are, however, several different ways of structuring dissertations, depending on the type of research undertaken. Compare those that you have selected.

Now go to the end of each dissertation and compare the add-on sections. Note:

- length and format of the list of references
- number and type of appendices.

Now, if you want to, you can read a few sections of the text to see what the written style is like. Note the use of technical words, the method of citing references and the style of the writing. Check the length of paragraphs and sentence construction. Are they short and precise, or long and complex? Explore how the illustrations are used to complement the text. Whatever you do, don't try to read all the way through. Rather, if you have the time, pick a few more examples of dissertations and repeat the exercise. You will soon get a feel of the difference in quality and style, which will help you to form preferences on which to base your own work.

The length and complexity of the dissertations might be rather daunting, particularly when you consider that you will have to produce something similar within a few months or even weeks. Don't get too worried. Although there will be a lot to learn and plenty to write, if you can choose a subject in which you are really interested, then despite the hard work it should be a pleasurable and rewarding exercise, and something to be proud of when you have finished.

1.6 References to more information

As mentioned above, a good place to start is to look at previously completed dissertations in your subject. This will not provide you with instructions on how to proceed, but will give you plenty of food for thought, and help to stimulate your own critical faculties about the quality of the work presented. This will be important when it comes to reviewing your own work later on.

Most books on this subject cover the whole sequence of preparing and writing essays and dissertations, much like this one. But hardly any actually discuss why you should do a dissertation, and what the examiners will be looking for. Despite this it is interesting, if you have time, to compare the advice given at this stage of the process. The approaches vary, depending on the level of essay or dissertation aimed at, and in some, the specific subject area catered for. Only look at the preliminary advice given in the first few pages of the books and scan the contents page to see if there is anything else of interest further on. You can probably do this in the library without even taking the books out on loan.

Here are a few books that I have found, and I have given notes on what to look for in them. They are in no particular order as each gives a slightly different view of the issues, so refer to as many as possible. Consult your own library catalogue for these and any similar ones that are available. When you locate them on the shelves, look at the contents list of promising books for relevant chapters.

Further reading 📖

Redman, P. (2011) *Good Essay Writing*, 4th edition. London: Sage/Open University. Chapter 2 discusses what tutors look for when marking essays.

Mounsey, C. (2002) *Essays and Dissertations*. Oxford: Oxford University Press. See Chapters 1 and 10.

Blaxter, L., Hughes, C. and Tight, M. (2010) *How to Research*, 4th edition. Buckingham: Open University Press. The first chapter gives an entertaining review of what research is about.

Swetnam, D. (2009) *Writing Your Dissertation: How to Plan, Prepare and Present Successful Work*, 3rd edition. Oxford: How To Books. See Chapter 1.

2

What Types of Studies Are Suitable for a Dissertation?

Chapter contents

2.1 Your choice

In any discipline, if you are granted a degree of freedom to decide, there will be a range of subjects that you will be able to choose from. The subject matter of your choice will have a direct bearing on the sort of study you will undertake and the type of dissertation that you will write. The character of possible studies ranges from highly scientific and technical to abstract philosophical and artistic, with a whole medley of social, economic, natural and psychological options in between.

One way of looking at different approaches to doing a dissertation is to list the five broad generic areas within whose boundaries almost all research falls (Leedy and Ormrod, 2010: 86). These headings concentrate on the objects of investigation, and you can ask yourself whether you are particularly interested in any one of these:

- People – social, medical, religious, political and all other subjects that include how people exist, act, interact and behave individually and in society.
- Things – biological, geological, chemical and all other subjects that look at the condition and behaviour of the things around us, from the scale of the microbe to that of the universe.
- Records – studies of archives and any written documents, reports, recordings and archaeological remains, and even works of art and music manuscripts.
- Thoughts and ideas – philosophy and religion, political theory, language and semantics and all other subjects that deal with the products of human intellectual argument.
- Dynamics or energy – studies of causes and effects in diverse fields such as astronomy, physics, chemistry, biology, sociology, politics and industry, and other disciplines where forces and reactions are present.

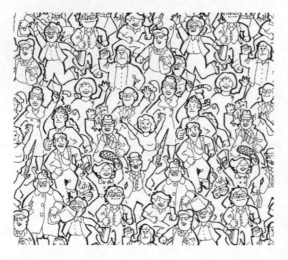

FIGURE 2.1　People

In fact, if you consider your degree subject, it might even be based on dealing almost exclusively with one of these particular aspects of study.

Another way is to look at doing a dissertation from the point of view of the kind of approaches you might take. Investigation in any of the above areas requires different approaches, some of which you might be more attracted to than others. In order to give an indication of what may be involved in the different types, I have started by dividing choice between theoretical and practical approaches, and built up a diagram of some of the offshoots of these. Following this diagram is a short account of the characteristics of some of the main activities and the skills you need to carry them out. This might help you to decide what kind of research you will be interested in doing. In all the cases below, it is unlikely that you will be able to concentrate solely on one type, as there is invariably a cross-fertilization between one and another.

2.2 Practical investigations versus theoretical studies

Do you prefer to spend your time organizing and getting involved in real-life activities, or would you rather search through the library shelves and pore over the thoughts and theories of others? This is a pretty unrealistic question, as any useful research must have a sound theoretical basis and most theories have a basis in reality: hence you will probably have to spend some time in both camps. Nevertheless, there is always some weight in one direction or the other, and you can choose to put the stress either way (or even balance the two equally).

FIGURE 2.2 Theoretical

FIGURE 2.3 Practical

Figure 2.4 extrapolates beyond the simple descriptions above to show some of the branches of investigation that might follow on from particular approaches. It is quite possible, indeed likely, that you will venture down more than one path, as it is usually very difficult to completely isolate aspects of a problem. But it will be necessary to limit yourself to a manageable task; so having a strong emphasis on one approach is necessary, any other related aspects should be considered only enough to feed into your main focus of effort. In all the subjects I can think of, there will be an option of both practical investigations and theoretical studies. Let us look in more detail at what sort of activities may be involved in each of these branches of research.

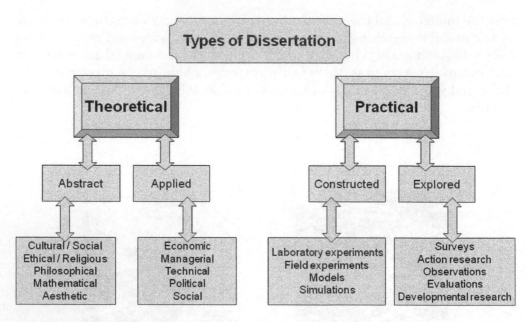

FIGURE 2.4   Types of dissertation

2.3 Practical investigations

The accent here is on doing rather than philosophizing, though you will still have to do some thinking to make sure you are doing the right things! There are two main categories of practical investigation: work in controlled conditions (such as a laboratory experiment), and work in uncontrolled conditions (such as fieldwork for a scientific or social survey). In both cases, the accent may be on an attempt to verify or test an existing belief or theory, or an attempt to formulate a new theory. It is unlikely that you will be able to achieve the latter within the scope of an undergraduate dissertation.

Experiments

The essence of these is the control that you have over as many as possible of the factors (or, technically speaking, the variables) that are present in the process. It is not necessarily the case that experiments have to take place in a laboratory, or that they are limited to natural science subjects. The main point of experimentation is that you observe the influence of specific factors on a situation, so it is necessary to isolate the important elements in order that you can manipulate them and exclude as many extraneous influences as possible.

In order to do this successfully, you will have to be very clear about exactly what you want to test, and to devise or adopt a reliable way of doing this. You will probably need to have specific equipment in order to carry out the test, and you will have to be well organized in order to carry it through and record the results. It is also essential that you give yourself enough time to analyse the results of the experiments, as a long list of raw data is of no use to anyone.

You do not have to be a boffin in a white coat to do experiments. However, personal attributes and enthusiasms needed for this are: a clear, logical thinking ability; practical DIY skills; good organization and timing skills; and, if you are dealing with human subjects, good diplomacy and social gifts.

Fieldwork

This usually means getting out and about. The big distinction is probably whether you are doing investigations that involve people or things. The techniques you use will be very different in each case, though even when investigating things, people are invariably involved in some way or another (e.g. in order to get permissions, to locate sites, to provide transport, etc.). You might have to contend with bad weather, unforeseen circumstances, practical and social difficulties and even dangers. The point about fieldwork is that you are entering into an existing situation (that you want to observe without changing it), so your control over events is usually weak.

FIGURE 2.5   Getting out and about

As with experimentation, you will have to be well prepared as to exactly what you want to find out and how you are going to do so practically. The methods you use should be tried and tested, and applied in an ethical and rigorous manner. It often requires some resourcefulness to get your own way, and persistence and patience are needed when everything does not go as planned, or if results are not immediately forthcoming. You will probably not need to devise specialist equipment to carry out fieldwork; often, good pairs of ears and eyes and quick recording skills are sufficient.

You do not have to be a train-spotting anorak to do field research. You do, however, need to be enthusiastic and to have: a capacity for clear, logical thinking; practical organization skills; patience and resourcefulness to get over unexpected difficulties; methodical observation and recording skills; and again, if you are dealing with human subjects, good diplomacy and social gifts. You should also be pretty resistant to adverse weather conditions if you are doing your fieldwork outdoors.

2.4 Theoretical studies

Ideal for bookworms and eggheads, you might think! Yes, but you could also be a revolutionary or a guru. Theoretical studies might be abstract, but they are not always divorced from real life. After all, actions (apart from the most instinctive and animalistic) are based on theories, even if these are not overtly recognized. Also, our understanding of virtually everything is founded on concepts and theories: this is the way we make sense of the world around us.

Abstract

Whatever subject you are studying for your degree, you will have encountered abstract concepts and theories that underpin the thinking about the subject. Examples of these are feminism, aesthetics, sustainability, social contract, capitalism, subsidiarity and so on. Spend a few moments thinking of the theoretical terms that appear over and over again in your subject. There is usually plenty of argument about the exact definition of these concepts and theories and about how they are relevant to the particular subject.

These arguments can be studied on an intellectual level, and conclusions can be drawn from the discourse arising. Subjects such as philosophy, sociology and psychology are obvious areas where theoretical debate is rife and an important aspect of the discipline. But most other subjects also have a theoretical base that is contentious and open to discussion and examination. Architecture and design, education, healthcare, management – all subjects that have very practical applications – rely on theoretical foundations. For example, all of these require ethical issues to be addressed, economic priorities to be set, and equal rights to be considered, apart from theoretical matters uniquely connected with their individual characteristics.

You can define your study to examine these theoretical issues at an abstract level, weighing up arguments, contrasting positions, comparing approaches and verifying implications.

Applied

In most subjects, the underlying theory is a foundation for action. For example, the theory of sustainability is becoming influential in many aspects of life, whether in the built environment, social development or industry. How these theories are applied in the real world, how they work and how useful they are, are excellent subjects for a dissertation study. Again, consider your own degree subject. You will be able to think of many theories that are influential in how the subject is studied and applied. Some theories may be strongly based on scientific evidence that would need expert knowledge to challenge, but others are more philosophical and institutional and thus more open to general critical examination. What their implications are and whether they deliver what is claimed can be studied by examining actual case studies. In this way, theoretical issues and their effects can be a focus for your dissertation.

This kind of research combines investigation and understanding of theory – a literature-based activity, perhaps combined with consultations with influential

FIGURE 2.6   Practical applications rely on theoretical foundations

thinkers, and with practical field-based activities, to study the application and effects of the theories. This type of study will involve you with a really interesting and varied set of activities, particularly suitable if you are the type who wants to combine thinking with doing.

2.5 Another way of looking at types of dissertation

Another way to review the choice of dissertation types is to consider what is the main technique of enquiry that you will use when doing the research. Here are seven that I could think of.

FIGURE 2.7   History of events or people

Tracking through time This is the study of the history of events or people. The actual time element can be anything between a few seconds or millions of years, depending on what you are studying, e.g. the first fractions of a second after the Big Bang, or the development of dinosaurs.

Describing Finding out what things are like. This involves identifying particular features, classifying, measuring sizes and quantities, examining constituents and organizations. The things can be objects, living beings, organizations, systems or even ideas.

Comparing This can be comparing like with like, or like with unlike. In both cases the aim is to identify differences and similarities. Aspects studied might be performance, organization, methods and techniques, appearance, attitude and so on.

Correlating Searching for relationships between objects and events, and sometimes tracking influences and causes. This technique often uses statistics to record the behaviour of two or more phenomena and judges the likelihood and strength of relationships. Other non-statistical methods can be used in some cases.

Evaluating This is examining something and judging it against a set of criteria. Questions like how successful, profitable, quick, efficient, etc. are answered. It is necessary to set up a basis for judgement before you start the evaluation.

Intervening By making changes to a system, evaluations can be made as to whether the change is beneficial or not, or to gauge other effects on the system's performance. It is often difficult to predict in theory what will happen when changes are made, so this technique is used, often on a small scale at first, to help development efforts.

FIGURE 2.8   A controllable microcosm of the phenomenon

Simulating This is the technique of making a controllable microcosm of the phenomena that you want to study. It always involves simplification of the real-life situation, sometimes miniaturization or expansion, and possibly abstraction. Experiments and models are the typical medium for this kind of study.

Of course, these techniques can and often must be combined. The introduction to a dissertation will commonly give some historical background; description is normally the necessary first step in carrying out the other techniques. It is, however, useful to be aware of these different techniques, as one or more can be used as the basis for your study.

2.6 Chapter summary

You are free to choose your dissertation subject and have a choice whether you do a practical investigation that might include doing some experiments or fieldwork, or a theoretical study that may be abstract in character or applied to life.

Another way of looking at types of dissertation is by the activities involved in the research, such as tracking through time, describing, comparing, correlating, evaluating or simulating.

2.7 What should I do now?

Consider what you have read in this chapter and think about what sort of activities and interests attract you the most. Do you like the company of people and are you not afraid of talking to strangers, or are you more retiring and do you prefer to observe from the background or to manipulate inanimate things? Are you interested in abstract ideas, or do you only see the point in something if you can go out and do it? Are you more fascinated by how things became what they are, or would you prefer to explore how things might be changed in the future? Are you a specialist, better at concentrating in a narrow field of study and in great depth and detail, or are you more a generalist, who likes studying the wider context and is adept at making cross-disciplinary connections?

Use the answers to these questions to help you decide the direction your study should take and the activities that you will enjoy doing. Keep in mind that you will write a much better dissertation if you enjoy the activities involved. I know it won't all be easy-going and entertaining, but it will take much less effort to motivate yourself if you actually quite like doing the main tasks.

Make a list of the activities you will enjoy doing best and relate them to the dissertation types above. This will give you an indication of the sort of dissertation that you want to write. You could draw up a sort of specification for the work. Now you can go on to the next chapter to consider how this can be used to home in on the actual title of your dissertation.

FIGURE 2.9   Enjoy the activities involved

2.8 References to more information

Most books on 'doing research' have a section on the different types of theses or dissertations. If you want to add to what is given here, it would be a good idea to look for books that concentrate more closely on your subject area. Do a search in your library in your own subject area, but be careful that you do not get bogged down in books that are all about specific research methods. Look for books that are aimed at doing undergraduate dissertations. Here are a few examples that I found of books in this genre arranged by subject area. Generally, as in this book, the issue of what choices you have in your research will appear near the beginning of the book.

Further reading

For business students:

Horn, R. (2012) *Researching and Writing Dissertations: A Complete Guide for Business and Management Students*, 2nd edition. London: Chartered Institute of Personnel and Development.
Fisher, C. (2010) *Researching and Writing a Dissertation: An Essential Guide for Business Students*, 3rd edition. Harlow: Pearson Education.

For education students:

O'Hara, M., Dewis, P., Kay, J. and Wainwright, J. (2011) *Successful Dissertations: The Complete Guide for Education, Childhood and Early Childhood Studies Students*. London: Continuum Publishing.
Thomas, G. (2009) *How to Do Your Research Project: A Guide for Students in Education and Applied Social Sciences*. London: Sage.
Walliman, N. and Buckler, S. (2008) *Your Dissertation in Education*. London: Sage.

For psychology students:

Cone, J.D. (2006) *Dissertations and Theses from Start to Finish: Psychology and Related Fields*, 2nd edition. Washington, DC: American Psychological Association.
Forshaw, M. (2013) *Your Undergraduate Psychology Project*, 2nd edition. Malden: John Wiley & Sons.
Sullivan, C., Gibson, S. and Riley, S.C.E. (2012) *Doing Your Qualitative Psychology Project*. London: Sage.

For health and social care students:

Walliman, N. and Appleton, J. (2009) *Your Undergraduate Dissertation in Health and Social Care*. London: Sage.

Glasper, A. and Rees, C. (2012) *How to Write Your Nursing Dissertation*. Oxford: Wiley-Blackwell.

Carey, M. (2009) *The Social Work Dissertation: Using Small-Scale Qualitative Methodology*. Buckingham: Open University Press.

For politics students:

Silbergh, D.M. (2001) *Doing Dissertations in Politics: A Student Guide*. New York: Routledge.

And a few other options:

Herbert, T. (2009) *Music in Words*. New York: Oxford University Press.

Naoum, S.G. (2007) *Dissertation Research and Writing for Construction Students*, 2nd edition. Oxford: Butterworth Heinemann.

Borden, I. and Rüedi, K. (2006) *The Dissertation: An Architecture Student's Handbook*, 2nd edition. Oxford: Butterworth Heinemann.

Gilbert, N. (ed.) (2008) *Researching Social Life*, 3rd edition. London: Sage.

Parsons, T. (2004) *How to Do Your Dissertation in Geography and Related Disciplines*, 2nd edition. Abingdon: Routledge.

3

What Will It Be About?

3.1 What really interests you?

In most subjects, students have a choice about the subject that they will write about for their dissertation. Sometimes, this amounts to so much freedom that it is really difficult to know where to begin. If you are in this situation, or if you don't know how to make a choice between suggested titles or themes, the following thoughts will help.

As mentioned in the last chapter, it is always easier to write an extended piece of work if you are interested in the subject and when the research involves activities that you enjoy doing. Moreover, greater interest inevitably means a greater thirst for knowledge, and this enthusiasm is bound to show in the final product. So, how can you weave your favourite topic or pastime into the dissertation? You might need to indulge in some creative thinking to achieve this, depending on the subject you are studying.

Most dissertation subjects are a combination of a background subject discipline, e.g. sociology, architecture, education, physics, etc., and a particular situation, activity or phenomenon, e.g. countryside, sport, poverty, etc. You will have to take the subject discipline you are studying as a given, as that is presumably the label of what you are studying for your degree. The freedom lies in what you choose to investigate within this context.

A few examples of subjects and study titles will be useful here, some pretty obvious, some less so:

- Physics and surfing – 'Surfboard size and shape for different waveforms and height: a calculated approach to board design for greater performance'. (No doubt lots of field-work tests could be arranged here!)
- Education and fantasy games – 'Transferable skills and playing fantasy games: a pain-less way to learning?'
- Sociology and pop music – 'Pop trends and ageing: do rockers stay rockers forever?' ('Does enthusiasm for hip-hop last until the hip op?')
- Publishing and surfing the web – 'Interactive websites of paper-based magazines. Opportunities and pitfalls: a critical appraisal'.
- History and thoroughbred dogs – 'Dogs and the aristocracy: fashion and utility'.
- Geography and getting rich quick – 'Wealth hotspots: the influences of location and climate'.
- Real estate management and sailing – 'Marinas and the jet set: value enhancement of redundant harbours and seaside resorts'.

FIGURE 3.1   History and thoroughbred dogs

You might come up with a list of several interests and favoured approaches. Try to devise a connection between each interest and your main study subject and to formulate titles such as I have done above. You will need to be aware of the diversity inherent in your main subject in order to spot promising connections: for example, sociology covers pretty well all human interactions, and geography spans physical, human and economic aspects of life on earth. Almost all disciplines have a history, and provide pointers to the future. Even purely technical subjects such as engineering or chemistry have applications that impact on everyday life.

If you find it difficult to pin down what your main interests are, you could try answering the following questions:

1. What do you do when you are not 'working'? You may be doing something very useful, but you regard it as an enjoyable activity rather than 'work'. If it is something as general as watching the television, what programmes do you watch most? Wherein lies this fascination?

2. If you are together with like-minded friends, what do you enjoy talking about most?

3. Is there any activity, subject or skill that you have always wanted to find out more about, but have never had the time or incentive? This may just be the opportunity to get to grips with it.

4. What do you like reading? Newspapers, comics, romantic fiction, crime or historical novels? Analyse what it is that fascinates you and drives you to read these.

5. Where do you like to go when you have time off? What do you like to see? Are you an avid gallery visitor or would you rather scale the highest peaks? Even the sun, sand and sex holiday has potential research value in relation to some subjects (e.g. hospitality, tourism, planning, sociology, healthcare, architecture, media studies and many others).

6. What do you like about things? Are you design conscious? Are you fascinated by miniaturization or by mega-projects? Do you look for simplicity or thrive on complexity? Do you prefer artificial or natural materials? Are you the type that likes to think about things as abstract concepts or are you a nuts and bolts practical type?

When you have devised one or perhaps several promising dissertation subjects, it is time to look more carefully at the practical implications of these. At this stage you will not be able to go into details, but you will definitely be able to make a preliminary assessment so that really impractical ideas are rejected. Several issues need to be examined.

Scope of the subject

You will need to limit the 'width' and 'depth' of your study to keep it manageable. There is so much information on every subject, and so many implications can be followed up that link to a wider field, that it is easy to lose your direction and end up with an unfocused piece of work. Think about where you will draw the line, where you will say 'this goes beyond my field of study'. Delineation can be achieved, for example, by stipulating a time frame (e.g. in a historical study), location, size, type (e.g. of building, commercial transaction, treatment, social segment, etc.), and level of detail.

Individuality

Is what you are planning just a repeat of what has been done before, or is there something different or new that can be learned from the outcomes? You do not have to achieve a scientific breakthrough or a new direction in thought. What is needed is an individual stamp on the work, some personal contribution that makes your project unique. This is gained by adding your own perspective to the study, your own collection of data (perhaps surveys or observations), and your own interpretation of some data, yours or from elsewhere. At this stage it is worth assessing your own capabilities in relation to the task: can you see yourself being able to do it?

Timing

You will only have a limited time in which to complete your work. How fast a worker are you, and how much do you already know about the topic, and how much time will you be able to dedicate to the project? If you are planning to travel as part of the work, or need to observe particular events, make sure that these can be reliably programmed into your allotted time. At this stage it will be difficult to devise a reliable programme of work, but you will be able to get a feel for how much time might be involved in getting prepared, collecting information, sorting and analysing it, and writing it all up and presenting it.

Resources

Many dissertation projects involve getting specific information and/or using particular pieces of equipment, or even meeting certain people. Does your subject imply the necessity for these? If so, what is the likelihood of you gaining the required access? You will need to establish alternatives if things do not work out as expected. There is also the question of money. Calculate the likely cost implications of pursuing your topic(s), and whether you can afford it. You will incur basic costs anyway in the production of your dissertation (printing, photocopying, binding, etc.).

FIGURE 3.2   Using particular pieces of equipment

3.2 Regulations and supervision

Important aspects of your dissertation are bound to be governed by the regulations of your university or college, and also by more detailed instructions issued by your course administration. The principal matters covered are the maximum and minimum length (word count), format and presentation, quality of work, marking criteria and expected outcomes, approvals for subject choice, supervision arrangements, deadlines, extent of group or individual working, and so forth.

It is essential that you are fully informed about these issues, so if you do not have a copy of both the general regulations issued by the university or college, and the course-specific instructions, get hold of them now and read them carefully. Your work will be judged on the basis of compliance with these, so you can save yourself a lot of time and grief by getting it right from the beginning!

Although the point of doing a dissertation is to challenge you to produce a piece of work devised and organized by yourself, you are not really expected to do this without any help. You should be allocated a tutor or director of studies whose duty it is to guide and advise you during the project. Do make use of him or her, both to check on your progress and as a source of ideas and advice. Ask what format has been arranged for consultations: is there a weekly prearranged meeting, or do you have to book a slot when they become available? The onus will probably be on you to ensure that you get regular tutorials.

FIGURE 3.3   Regulations

The regulations are likely to be quite specific about the approval required for the choice of your dissertation topic, so early consultation with your tutor is essential. He or she will quickly be able to comment on the suitability of your title or titles. It is best if you can give a short explanation of how your topic relates to your main area of study (your tutor might not be familiar with your particular interest) and how it will develop your knowledge and skills in the subject. Once you get the initial approval of the title and subject, you will be able to start to develop a greater understanding of the tasks ahead. A good way to get a feel for the requirements of the whole project is to look at examples of completed dissertations.

3.3 Previous examples

As already mentioned in Chapter 1, most courses will keep copies of all their previous dissertations and they should be available for you to consult. They might be held in the central library or in your own department: you should know by now where they are! You should look at them rather differently now from the last time. One of the really useful aspects of looking at completed dissertations is to be able to gauge the size and content of the finished works. The danger, however, is that you become intimidated by the scale and detail provided, especially if they deal with subjects unfamiliar to you. Don't worry, they managed and so will you!

It is best to look at several dissertations. Perhaps you will find one or two that deal with subjects near to your own. What should you look for when reviewing these dissertations? Just as the last time, you will certainly not want to read them all. Here are a few points to consider:

- Visually compare the different styles of presentation, i.e. the use of fonts, illustrations and graphs, colour, chapters and headings, indexes and lists of references, etc. Which do you find more attractive and immediately informative?
- Look to see how the subject title is broken down into different aspects to make it easier to investigate. A clue to how this is done is to look at the chapter headings.
- Scan through the whole collection to get an idea of the range of topics covered. Are there any similar to your chosen title? If so, have a quick look at them to get an idea of the approach and content. Again, chapter headings will reveal a lot quickly. Spot the

differences and similarities to your own thoughts about your approach. Again, make a note of those that might serve as a model. If there are no titles anything like the one you have devised, you might be either way off the mark or brilliantly innovative.

- Compare the scope of the work of several examples. Some will look at a wide subject but not in much depth; others will concentrate on one narrow aspect but delve deeply; and others will fall somewhere in between. Observe how the styles differ. Reflect on where your subject lies within this spectrum.
- Examine how the work was done. Did it involve careful measurement and calculation on a scientific basis, or was it more an interpretation of events or opinions that could not be accurately measured? Consider your own subject and ponder what sort of approach might be suitable. Sometimes a combination of both is required.

You will probably want to refer to previous examples later in your work, when you are faced with specific problems of method, organization or presentation. So do make a note of those that you think could serve as good examples so that you will easily be able to find them again.

If you cannot get to see previous examples from your course, then you will have to look elsewhere, perhaps at those from a different course. But be aware that the requirements may have been different, and you will not have much help from the range of subject choices. Even so, issues of organization and presentation will still be worth investigating. Here are a few dissertation titles of previous years from the School of the Built Environment at Oxford Brookes University for you to peruse:

Architecture afloat

From rural life to urbanization: the role of the architect in a developing community

Nineties minimalism: a return to early modernism?

A comparison of six residential companies

Alternative design methods for the construction of large diameter piles in Weald clay

A semiotic analysis of New College cloister

A study into student accommodation

Enhancing development by reducing vulnerabilities: a Jamaican study

Housing policy and tenant participation: a case study

Investigation into the tensile strength of bonded-in rods in forming timber connections

Is property still a good investment?

Opening the mind to sensory perception

Serge Chermayeff: a critical biography

The future role of rail in our society

The high street and its rivals

The spatial concepts of Japan

Traditional rural buildings in south-west England

Unsophisticated applications of sophisticated lending techniques

What determines the after-use of quarry sites?

Women in construction

3.4 Getting background information

A title is only a germ of an idea. In order really to understand the implications of it, you need to investigate what has been done on the subject already, what information is available to inform your study, and what gaps in your knowledge need to be filled. This is called doing a background study.

The main aim of doing this background study is to make sure that your subject idea is not just 'pie in the sky'. I am sure that you based your selection on some considerable knowledge of both your main subject and your enthusiasm. But what you probably are not so informed about is what other people have done in this field, and how they have done it. When, shortly, you will devise the research proposal that gives a rationale for your project, you will need to argue that the subject is relevant to your studies and fits within the remit of the main subject. There is no better way of doing this than to cite work that has already been done in this field and to identify the gaps that still need to be filled.

Your title will give indications of where to look for information. Take for example the first on the list given earlier: 'Surfboard size and shape for different waveforms and height: a calculated approach to board design for greater performance'. Information will be required on the geometry of a wave and how to calculate it and perhaps how to model it as it changes. Similarly, surfboards are made of curves, which will need to be calculated. The dynamics of surfboarding will need to be studied – drag, acceleration down slopes, wave speed, the effects of weight distribution, buoyancy, etc. Perhaps research on hull design generally will establish the basic principles involved. Wave dynamics have probably been studied in relation to sea defences and oilrigs. The practical knowledge of surfers is also likely to be a valuable guide to performance and wave type, e.g. under what conditions surfers change to a long-board.

Every title will have a series of connections to related information and research. Greater familiarity with the issues will in turn lead on to further

FIGURE 3.4

relevant fields. There is a danger here of getting overwhelmed by the amount of information available and there is the problem of sorting out what is useful. A quick way to check that you have not missed anything important after you have done some initial investigation is to talk with experts in the field – those in your department or in other parts of the university or college. Just a few words will suffice, so don't be shy to contact them by email or letter.

Where will you find the required information? The quickest and easiest option is the Internet, doing a search using key words to see what comes up; try not to get bogged down or waylaid by the sheer volume of material. The next step is your university library. You should be pretty good at doing searches by now. Try using some selected key words to search for books in the main library catalogue. For more specialist issues, a search through the relevant databases of journal articles should be productive. Ask your librarian for help if you get stuck or do not seem to be finding the right kind of information. More advice on searching for secondary (published and stored) information is given in Chapter 8, and on how to organize your note taking in Chapter 9. The secret is to know when to stop. At this stage you are only testing the feasibility of your suggested title and getting a feel of the nature of the project.

These first steps in collecting information will form a useful foundation for your work, and help you to decide on the nature and scope of your study. Now is the time to change your mind if you see that things are not working out how you wish. Explore alternative approaches; or if you develop a real distaste for the prospect of work in that subject, abandon it and choose an alternative. In the latter case, you will have to move quickly to establish a new direction and get approval for your new subject; it is important not to lose too much time at the outset of the project.

Just remember that your best work will be done when you are really interested in what you are doing. But also remember that learning new things is always tough: there is no really easy way.

3.5   Chapter summary

The motivation for your work should come from you doing what really interests you. You might be able to combine your academic subject with one that fascinates you in your everyday life. However, it is important to keep the scale of the study to something manageable within the time and resources you have available and make sure that it is not a repeat of what has been done before.

Check on the regulations and instructions relevant to your dissertation, and make use of previous examples of dissertations for gauging the formats and styles that have been successful. When you have chosen a subject, you should read as widely as possible to investigate what has been written about the various aspects that you are interested in. This will help you to clarify the issues that are important, and to test whether you are really interested in that subject. Don't, at this stage, get lost in the mass of information – try to be selective in what you read and keep focused on the relevant issues.

3.6 What should I do now?

If you have followed the advice above, you will already have done a lot! If you are still dithering, now is the time to examine your options and to make decisions. If you do not make your mind up about your subject, it is impossible to make any real progress in your work, as you cannot know where to focus your research.

Here is a checklist of things that have been suggested so far in this chapter:

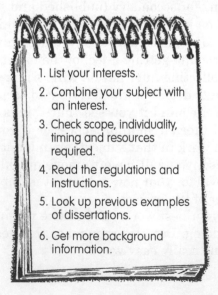

1. List your interests.
2. Combine your subject with an interest.
3. Check scope, individuality, timing and resources required.
4. Read the regulations and instructions.
5. Look up previous examples of dissertations.
6. Get more background information.

If you are really lost for ideas, or have got hopelessly bogged down, make an appointment with your tutor and explain what you have done so far and ask for advice. If you have taken any of the steps recommended above, you will be some way towards getting started, and will probably be aware of where your problem lies. This may be because, for instance, you are daunted by the complexity of the task, or you cannot decide between several options, or you are not confident that your choice is feasible, etc. It will be best if you can identify specific problems before seeing your tutor, rather than turning up and saying simply, 'I don't know what to do!'

To get yourself well organized, make a list of the sources of background material that you have found useful. Then write a short text in the form of bullet points indicating the main issues that this material has raised. This text should indicate:

- the sort of information that you will be likely to need, and where you might obtain it
- the sort of techniques you might need to use or to learn in order to obtain the information and to analyse it
- the equipment that might be needed
- the people and places you might need to see
- any timing considerations that need to be taken into account (e.g. waiting for special events).

When you are clear about these, and they seem achievable, it will give you confidence that the project is 'doable' and free you to proceed with defining and planning the project in greater detail.

3.7 References to more information

The guidance given above should be sufficient to put you on the right road (your road) to working out what your dissertation will be about. However, if you have time and want to compare advice, or need further inspiration, there are other books like this one that have a section with advice on how to decide what to do as a dissertation, or in many cases, a postgraduate thesis. It may help you to compare the different approaches. As mentioned in the previous chapter, specific guidance on topics in a particular subject can be gained from books dedicated to one particular discipline. Explore your own library catalogue for both general and subject-related guides to dissertation writing. But do be careful not to get bogged down in technicalities: peck like a bird at the juicy pieces of use to you now, and leave the rest. The list below is in order of detail and complexity – the simplest first.

Further reading 📖

Ajuga, G. (2002) *The Student Assignment and Dissertation Survival Guide: Answering the Question Behind the Question!* Thornton Heath: GKA Publishing. See pp. 46–55. Do you want to become the teacher's pet?

Mounsey, C. (2002) *Essays and Dissertations*. Oxford: Oxford University Press. Chapter 2 looks at ways to develop research questions.

Swetnam, D. (2009) *Writing Your Dissertation: How to Plan, Prepare and Present Successful Work*. 3rd edition. Oxford: How To Books. See Chapter 1 for simple guidance on how to get started.

Blaxter, L., Hughes, C. and Tight, M. (2010) *How to Research*, 4th edition. Buckingham: Open University Press. A much bigger book, but see Chapter 2 on how to get started.

The following books, in date order, are aimed more at postgraduate research, but again, selective reading of the preliminary chapters will provide further hints about getting started.

Glatthorn, A.A. (2013) *Writing the Winning Dissertation: A Step-by-Step Guide*, 3rd edition. Thousand Oaks, CA: Corwin.

Murray, R. (2011) *How to Write a Thesis*, 3rd edition. Buckingham: Open University Press.

Rudestam, K.E. and Newton, R. (2007) *Surviving Your Dissertation: A Comprehensive Guide to Content and Process*, 3rd edition. Thousand Oaks, CA: Sage.

4

How Do I Get Started?

Chapter contents

4.1 What's the problem?

Writing a dissertation is not like writing a novel: you cannot just sit down and start writing from out of your head. You need to do some preparation work first – you will have already begun this if you have followed the book to this stage. By now you will have decided the subject area and done some background reading to get information and explore aspects of the subject. Now it is time to build on this and to focus more clearly on the direction of your intended study. To start with, it is best to define your research problem as clearly as possible in order to provide a focus for all your subsequent work. It sounds easier than it actually is, so don't worry if you agonize over it for a few days and alter your ideas several times over. Only by grappling with the issues can you forge some clarity in your thinking.

The purpose of the dissertation task is to get you to do some individual research. To do research you need to identify a problem or an issue that you will focus on in your investigations. After selecting your subject area and deciding on the issues that are of the greatest interest to you, the next step is to define the research more closely so that it can be expressed as a specific *research problem*. You will get to the point, when you are clear and decided, that you can explain the nature of your research problem in one or two sentences.

It can be quite difficult to decide on and to define your research problem. So what should you look for in your subject in order to generate a focus for your dissertation?

It is not as if problems are hard to find: in fact, we are surrounded by problems. Many are connected with society, the built environment, education, etc., and can readily be seen and read about. Take for example social problems such as poverty, crime, unsuitable housing and uncomfortable workplaces; or technical problems such as design deficiencies; or organizational problems such as business failures and bureaucratic bungles. In many subjects there may be a lack of knowledge that prevents improvements being made, for example, the influence of parents on a child's progress at school, or attitudes in the relationship between designers and clients.

FIGURE 4.1   It is not as if problems are hard to find

40

However, don't think that real-life problems are the only subjects to choose. Many issues are worthy of investigation but present no threat to anyone. How about investigating the little known works of a forgotten writer or artist, a historical study of a custom or area, or the use of language in particular contexts? The possibilities are endless. The difficulty lies more in devising a specific research problem that will be suitable in scale and character as the subject of a dissertation.

So, what are the necessary features of a dissertation research problem?

- It should be of great interest to you. You will have to spend many weeks or even months investigating the problem. A real interest in the subject is a great incentive to keep you going. If you have some choice in the subject you choose, then do yourself a favour and investigate something you wanted to find out about anyway.
- The problem should be significant. It is a waste of time and effort investigating a trivial problem or repeating work that someone has already done. Although you are not obliged to break new ground and extend the boundaries of knowledge, you will at least be expected to throw some new light on existing knowledge.
- It should be delineated. You do not have much time, even if it seems that you do at first. As you have to learn so many things in order to complete a good dissertation, you will take longer than you might think to do the necessary tasks. Hence the topic must be kept manageable, with restricted aims. Work out how much time you have got to complete the study, taking into account all the other commitments you have. How much detail do you need to go into? You can cover a wide field only superficially, and the more you restrict the field, the more detailed the study can be. Also consider the cost of necessary travel and other expenses.
- You should be able to obtain the information required. Obviously, you cannot carry out research if you cannot collect the relevant information needed to address your problem. Can you get access to relevant documents or other sources, and/or can you obtain the co-operation of individuals or organizations essential to your project?
- You should be able to draw conclusions related to the problem. The point of asking a question is to find an answer. The problem should be one to which the research can offer some solution, or at least the elimination of some false 'solutions'.
- You should be able to state the problem clearly and concisely. A precise, well thought out and fully articulated sentence, understandable by anyone, should normally clearly be able to explain just what the problem is.

For this search you need to have an enquiring mind, an eye for inconsistencies and inadequacies in current ideas and practice, and also a measure of imagination. It often helps to pose a simple question, for example, 'Does the presence of indoor plants affect a person's frame of mind?', or 'How can prevention measures reduce vandalism?', or 'What makes a successful young children's play area?' At this stage, the nature of the question will give some indication of the type of research approach (or approaches) that could be appropriate. Will it be a historical study, a descriptive inquiry, an analysis of correlations or an experimental exercise, or a combination of more than one of these (see Chapter 2)?

Note, though, that seemingly simple questions are riddled with ambiguities that must be cleared up by careful definition. For example, in the above questions, what does 'frame of mind' mean, what sort of 'prevention measures' are envisaged, and are all types of 'young children's play area' included? It is likely that the problem is too broad if you can state it in less than half a dozen words. A few additional questions posed against each word can help to delineate the problem: where, who, what, which, when? Break the problem down into short sentences, not worrying at this stage about the overall length of the problem statement. It is a useful trick to put each sentence on a separate slip of paper, so that they can be ordered in different sequences. When the best logical progression from sentence to sentence is achieved, the statement can be edited into a more elegant form.

Most research problems are difficult, or even impossible, to solve without breaking them down into smaller problems. The words used during the problem formulation period can give a clue to the presence of *subproblems*. Does one aspect have to be researched before another aspect can be begun? For example, in one of the research questions asked above, concerning the kinds of prevention measures that can be used against vandalism, how they can be

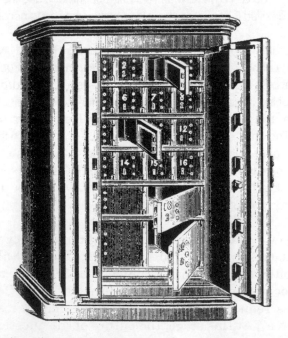

FIGURE 4.2   Breaking them down into smaller problems

employed, and for what types of vandalism they are suitable, will all have to be examined. By defining the subproblems, you will be able to delineate the scope of the work.

4.2 Second review of literature

Once you have defined a research problem, you will be able to make a much more focused review of the literature. You will be able to learn more about existing research on aspects of your research problem, and how it has been carried out. You will also be able to make more in-depth investigations into the factors that are important in your subject. Look for the following information in order to help you get started on your own research:

- results of previous research, which can form a springboard for your own investigations
- concepts, indicators and variables used (see below for details of these)
- ideas on how to gather data
- data presentation techniques
- methods of data analysis
- instrumentation which has been used
- methods of argument and the drawing of conclusions
- success of the various research designs of the studies already undertaken.

This exercise should not take too long, as you will be able to home in on the relevant research quite quickly using the key words from your research problem and question(s). Do reference everything relevant that you find, and make notes with comments about how the information relates to what you are intending to do (see Chapter 9 for specific instructions on note taking and referencing). This will be really useful stuff to put into your research proposal and the introduction and background section of your dissertation, to demonstrate that you have really investigated the present situation of research into your particular topic.

The words you use in your problem statement are loaded with meaning. You must have carefully chosen them from many other words to precisely indicate the main components of your investigation. Let us now look more closely at these words, or concepts, and how they are used.

4.3 What are the main concepts?

First, what is a concept? It is a general expression of a particular phenomenon, e.g. cat, human, anger, speed, alienation, socialism, etc. Each one of these represents an idea, and the word is a label for this idea.

FIGURE 4.3   A particular phenomenon – cat

We use concepts all the time as they are an essential part of understanding the world and communicating with other people. Many common concepts are shared by everyone in a society, though there are variations in meaning between different cultures and languages. For example, the concept 'respect' will mean something different to a streetwise rapper than to a noble lord. There are other concepts that are only understood by certain people such as experts, professionals and specialists, for example, dermatoglyphics, milfoil, parachronism, anticipatory socialization, etc. Sometimes, common phenomena can be labelled in an exotic fashion, often in order to impress or confuse, for example, a 'domestic feline mammal' instead of a 'cat'. This is called jargon and should be avoided.

Any kind of enquiry requires a set of concepts that communicate the elements being studied. It is important to define concepts in such a way that everyone reading the work has got the same idea of what is meant. This is relatively easy in the natural sciences where precise definition is usually possible, e.g. acceleration, radio waves, elements. In the social sciences this may be much more difficult. Human concepts such as fidelity, dishonesty and enthusiasm, and even more technical concepts such as affluence, vagrancy and dominance, are difficult to pin down accurately, as their meanings are often based on opinions, emotions, values, traditions, etc. Hence the importance of carefully formulated definitions when using concepts that are not precise in normal usage.

You will be able to find definitions of the concepts that you are planning to use in your investigations from your background reading. Because definitions for non-scientific and non-technical concepts can vary in different contexts, you may have to decide on which meaning you want to give to those concepts. Rarely, you might even have to devise your own definition for a particular word.

4.4 What about indicators?

As you can see, many concepts are rather abstract in nature, and difficult or even impossible to evaluate or measure. Take 'anger' as an example. How will you detect this in a person? The answer is to look for indicators – those perceivable phenomena that give an indication that the concept is present. What might these be? Think of the signs that might indicate anger: clenched fists, agitated demeanour, spluttering, shouting, wide-open eyes, stamping, reddened face, increased heartbeat, increased adrenaline production, and many others. Again, you can see what indicators are used in previous studies – which is much easier and more reliable than trying to work them out for yourself. For more technical subjects, indicators are usually well defined and universally accepted, for example, changes of state like condensation, freezing and magnetism.

FIGURE 4.4   Signs that might indicate anger

4.5 What are the main variables and values?

If you want to gauge the extent or degree of an indicator, you will need to find a measurable component. In the case of anger as above, it would be very difficult to measure the redness of a face or the degree of stamping, but you could easily measure a person's heartbeat. You could even ask the subject how angry he or she feels. The values used are the units of measurement. In the case of heartbeat, it would be beats per minute; level of anger felt could be declared on a scale from 1 to 10. Obviously the precision possible will be different depending on the nature of the variable and the type of values that can possibly be used. Certain scientific experiments require incredibly accurate measurement, while some social phenomena, e.g. opinions, might only be gauged on a three-point scale such as 'against', 'neutral', 'for'.

To summarize then, there is a hierarchy of expressions, going from the general to the particular, from abstract to concrete, that make it possible to investigate research problems. The briefest statement of the research problem will be the most general and abstract, while the detailed analysis of components of the research will be particular and concrete. The terms introduced are linked as follows:

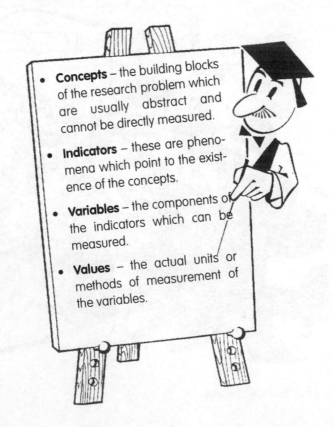

- **Concepts** – the building blocks of the research problem which are usually abstract and cannot be directly measured.

- **Indicators** – these are phenomena which point to the existence of the concepts.

- **Variables** – the components of the indicators which can be measured.

- **Values** – the actual units or methods of measurement of the variables.

Note that each concept may have several indicators, each indicator several variables, and each variable several values. To clarify these terms consider the following, which gives only one example of each term:

- Concept – poverty.
- Indicator – poor living conditions.
- Variable – provision of sanitary facilities.
- Values – numbers of people per WC.

Try to think of more indicators, variables and values related to the concept of poverty.

Being aware of these levels of expression will help you to break down your investigations into manageable tasks. This will enable you to come to overall conclusions about the abstract concepts in your research problem based on evidence rooted in detailed data at a more concrete level.

4.6 Ways of stating your research problem

You have a choice of how to state your research problem. How you state it will provide some indication of how you will go about your investigation. Here are some of the most common ways of presenting the research problem with examples to show how they work.

Question or questions

The method of investigating the problem may be expressed through asking a question or a series of questions, the answers to which require scrutiny of the problem from one or more directions. This is a very direct and open-ended way of formulating your investigations. Your aim is to provide some answers to the questions. It is your judgement, and that of the examiner's, whether your answers are sufficient and based on enough evidence. Here is an example of this form of presentation:

- The subject of this dissertation is 'Representation of contemporary art in the media'.
- The main research question is 'How is contemporary art represented in the media?'
- Three interrelated research subquestions are raised:

  1. What are the characteristics of the representation of contemporary art issues in the media?
  2. How does this representation differ in coverage presented in different types of media, e.g. television, magazines, newspapers?
  3. What role do specialist journalists, and specifically art correspondents, play in shaping this representation?

Obviously, the question or questions should be derived directly from the research problem, give a clear indication of the subject to be investigated and imply the methods that will be used. As above, the form of the questions can be a main question, divided into subquestions that explore aspects of the main question. The main question is very general: you could probably devise other subquestions to explore different aspects of this question. But by being so specific in your choice, you can limit your research to only those issues that you think are important, or that you have interest in pursuing.

Hypothesis

The use of hypotheses is the foundation of the hypothetico-deductive approach to research, so it is important to know what makes good hypotheses and how they can be formulated. When used in a rigorous scientific fashion, there are quite strict rules to follow. Important qualities distinguish hypotheses from other forms of statement.

According to Kerlinger and Lee (2000), a hypothesis:

1. is an assertion (not a suggestion)
2. is limited in scope
3. is a statement about the relationships between certain variables
4. contains clear implications for testing the relationships
5. is compatible with current knowledge
6. is expressed as economically as possible using correct terminology.

The objective of the method is either to reject the hypothesis by finding evidence that contradicts it, or to support it (you will not be able to prove it) by presenting evidence that underlines it. It might also be possible to modify the hypothesis in the light of what you have found out.

Actually, hypotheses are nothing unusual: we make them all the time. They are hunches or reasonable guesses made in the form of statements about a cause or situation. If something happens in our everyday life, we tend to suggest a reason for its occurrence by making rational guesses. For example, if the car does not start in the morning, we might hypothesize that the petrol tank is empty, or that the battery is flat. For each hypothesis, a particular action taken could support or reject it. If the petrol gauge indicated 'full', then the hypothesis of an empty petrol tank could be rejected, and so on. When a particular hypothesis is found to be supported, we have got a good chance that we can take the right action to remedy the situation. If, for example, we hypothesized that a wire to the starter motor had become loose, and then we find such a loose wire, fixing the wire might result in the car starting

FIGURE 4.5   Limit your research to only those issues that you think are important

again. If this was not the result, further hypotheses would be needed to suggest additional faults. Although these examples may seem banal, many of the greatest discoveries in science were based on hypotheses: Newton's theory of gravity, Einstein's general theory of relativity and a host of others.

In order to formulate a useful researchable hypothesis, you need to have a good knowledge of the background to the subject and the nature of the problem or issue that you are addressing. A good hypothesis is a very useful aid to organizing the research effort. It specifically limits the enquiry to the interaction of certain variables; it suggests the methods appropriate for collecting, analysing and interpreting the data; and the resultant confirmation or rejection of the hypothesis through empirical or experimental testing gives a clear indication of the extent of knowledge gained.

You need to formulate the general hypothesis on a conceptual level, in order to enable the results of the research to be generalized beyond the specific conditions of the particular study. This is equivalent to the general research question. Then, you normally need to break down the main hypothesis into two or more subhypotheses. These represent components or aspects of the main hypothesis and together should add up to its totality and are equivalent to the subquestions. It is one of the fundamental criteria of a hypothesis that it is testable. However, a hypothesis formulated on a conceptual level cannot be directly tested: it is too abstract. It is therefore necessary to convert it to an operational level. This is called operationalization. The operationalization of the subhypotheses follows four steps in the progression from the most abstract to the most concrete expressions by defining in turn the concepts, indicators, variables, values. Each subhypothesis will suggest a different method of testing and therefore implies different research methods that might be appropriate. The various research methods for collecting and analysing data are explained in some detail later in this book.

Although the term 'hypothesis' is used with many different meanings in everyday and even academic situations, it is advisable to use it in your research only in its strictest scientific sense. This will avoid you being criticized for sloppy, imprecise use of terminology. If your research problem does not lend itself to being formulated in a hypothesis, do not worry: there are plenty of alternatives, many of which involve a completely different research approach to that of the hypothetico-deductive method.

Proposition

Focusing a research study on a proposition, rather than on a hypothesis, allows the study to concentrate on particular relationships between events, without having to comply with the rigorous characteristics required of hypotheses. Consider this example:

- The title of the research is 'Public sector housing for young single people'.
- The main research problem is formulated in the form of three interrelated propositions:

  1. Public sector housing specifically provided for young single people to rent has been, and continues to be, designed according to the recommendations and standards in the design guidance for single persons' housing.
  2. The relevant design guidance is not based on accurate perceptions of the characteristics of young single people.
  3. From these two propositions follows the third: there is a mismatch between the public sector housing specifically provided for young single people and their accommodation requirements.

Statement of intent to critically investigate and evaluate

Not all research needs to answer a question or to test a hypothesis. Especially in undergraduate dissertations or in smaller research studies, a more exploratory approach may be used.

You can express the subject and scope of the exploration in a statement of intent. Again, this must be derived from the research problem, imply a method

FIGURE 4.6   A more exploratory approach may be used

of approach and indicate the outcome. Here are four examples of this form of research definition:

1. The intention of this study is to identify the main aspects of recent developments in government organization and procedures for local taxation in Switzerland and Bulgaria, and then to assess the extent to which, or whether, features of the Swiss organization and implementation of local taxation can be adopted to improve the system of the administration of local taxation in Bulgaria.
2. This study examines the problems in career development of women lawyers in the British legal establishment. It focuses on the identification of specific barriers (established conventions, prejudices, procedures, career paths) and explores the effectiveness of specific initiatives that have been aimed at breaking down these barriers.
3. In this study it is intended to consider whether relevant US standards for food safety as applied to hotels and restaurants could be transferred to hotels and restaurants in Nigeria.
4. This thesis provides a reassessment of Engelbert Humperdinck's early career and travels up to 1978. It aims to explore the musical foundation of Humperdinck's career and analyse his early compositions in order to provide a basis for a more objective reassessment of his music.

4.7 Definition of research objectives

When you have successfully formulated the various detailed research problems, questions, statements, etc., you will need to indicate what measures you will take to do the investigation. You can do this by defining the research objectives and indicating how the research objectives will be achieved. This is a first step to planning your project and will enable you to check back to see if the objectives fall in line with your preferences for the type of research that you were interested in doing.

The example below indicates how it is proposed to provide an adequate assessment of the relationship between the design of security systems in computer networks and the resulting restrictions on the wide accessibility of these systems to the general public. The research problem previously highlighted a lack of such methods of assessment.

To overcome this problem it is necessary to:

1. Propose a method of measurement by which the extent of incorporation of security systems can be assessed. This will enable an objective comparison to be made between alternative design proposals in terms of the extent of incorporation of security features. There is a need to identify and categorize the main security systems advocated in past studies of publicly accessible computer networks in order to establish the general applicability of the methods of measurement proposed.
2. Propose a method of measurement by which the extent of public accessibility to computer networks can be assessed. This will enable an objective comparison to be made between computer networks in terms of the extent of their accessibility in use. In order to arrive at a method of measurement, a more comprehensive interpretation of accessibility needs to be developed so that the measures proposed will not be confined to any one particular computer system type.
3. Assess the extent of accessibility achieved after the incorporation of security systems, by a study of actual computer networks in use. To achieve this a number of publicly accessible networks needs to be examined.

Notice how there is an argument behind the build-up of the research problem and the definition of objectives. Briefly, it goes like this:

*   According to the background research there is a problem, or a lack of information, or an unanswered question about such-and-such.
*   The important aspects to be studied are this, this, etc.
*   In order to investigate these it is necessary to do such-and-such.

Pretty obvious really, but it is important that it makes logical sense. In fact, there is usually a choice of things you could do, so it may be necessary to limit the scope of the problem/question to make the necessary investigations more inevitable. Once you have got this far, you will have a good idea of what you are planning to undertake. Do you think you will be able to manage it?

4.8 Chapter summary

Defining a research problem is the first step in doing your dissertation. Make sure that it interests you, that it is manageable in scope, and that you are able to access the necessary information to investigate it. You will need to clearly define that problem and be able to draw conclusions related to it as a result of your research. A second review of the literature will be required at this stage in order to refine the issues considered and to find out what relevant research has already been done, and how.

In order to investigate your chosen problem, you will need to identify what are the main concepts and the indicators that provide a way of detecting them. The variables and values should then be determined to enable you to measure the concepts in different ways.

You have several choices in how you state the research problem in a succinct way in order to form a strong basis for your research project. You could pose a question or set of questions that require an answer. Alternatively, by stating a hypothesis, you have something to test whether it stands up to scrutiny. The same is the case for a proposition. More directly, you could state what you want to investigate and evaluate, or make a list of aims and objects that you will fulfil. Remember, however you express it, the research problem should be the constant focus of your dissertation.

4.9 What should I do now?

Now is the time to make some decisions about how you will formulate your research problem(s) so that you can make the first steps in embarking on planning your dissertation. If you take the following steps, you will form a good foundation for all the work ahead:

- Once you have decided on the particular research problem you will focus on, test it against the list of necessary features given in Section 4.1. If it conforms to all of these you can be assured that you have got a good one!
- Consult the notes you have made during your background reading, or delve back into the books that are relevant to your research focus. Now search for what has already been done in this field, how it was carried out, and what were the main components of the work. Look at what terminology has been used, what factors have been studied and what methods have been used. This will help you enormously in deciding on what you could do, and in expressing your intentions in the appropriate language.
- In order to do this you should decide how you will state your research problem. Will you pose a question, formulate a hypothesis, suggest a proposition or make a statement of intent? Perhaps try out more than one way to see which works the best. Formulate it as succinctly as possible.

FIGURE 4.7   Do you think you will be able to manage it?

Now you should be in the situation where you will be able to put down in writing just how you will tackle the research problem. Break it down into 'doable' components, and clarify just what your objectives will be. Check that you will actually be able to reach the objectives; be practical, as it is you that has to do it! Check also, when you have written it down, that the argument you make is sound (read more about argument in Chapter 10).

4.10 References to more information

Again, most books that provide an introduction to research and advise how to do dissertations have a section on how you get started. Apart from the ones that have been listed in the previous chapters, here are a few more in case you want to check them out. I have listed them in order of what I think are useful, though a quick look through them in the library or bookshop will help you to judge for yourself. It really depends on what aspects you are particularly interested in; so again, just look at the relevant bits, finding them with the help of the contents list and perhaps the index at the end of the book.

Further reading

O'Leary, Z. (2009) *The Essential Guide to Doing Your Research Project*, 2nd edition. London: Sage.

Thomas, G. (2009) *How to Do Your Research Project: A Guide for Students in Education and Applied Social Sciences*. London: Sage.

Allison, B. and Race, P. (2004) *The Student's Guide to Preparing Dissertations and Theses*. London: RoutledgeFalmer.

Greetham, B. (2009) *How to Write your Undergraduate Dissertation*. London: Palgrave Macmillan.

And some books with a more subject-oriented approach:

Polgar, S. (2007) *Introduction to Research in the Health Sciences*, 5th edition. Edinburgh: Churchill Livingstone.

Pennings, P., Keman, H. and Kleinnijenhuis, J. (2005) *Doing Research in Political Science: An Introduction to Comparative Methods and Statistics*. London: Sage.

Wilson, J. (2010) *Business Research Methods: A Guide to Doing Your Research Project*. London: Sage.

Horn, R. (2012) *Researching and Writing Dissertations: A Complete Guide for Business and Management Students*, 2nd edition. London: Chartered Institute of Personnel and Development.

Saunders, M. and Lewis P. (2012) *Research Methods for Business Students*, 6th edition. Harlow: Pearson Education.

Punch, K. (2009) *Introduction to Research Methods in Education*. London: Sage.

5

What's All This About Philosophy?

Chapter contents

5.1 Can I believe what I see? Do I see what I believe?

You might well ask, 'Why a chapter about philosophy? After all, I'm doing a degree in education, nursing, social science, geography, etc.?' The simple answer is, that your whole life is determined by your philosophical approach, whether you realize it or not. Everyone is a philosopher – everyone has his or her own concept of the world.

> The alternative to philosophy is not no philosophy but bad philosophy. The 'un-philosophical' person has an unconscious philosophy, which they apply to their practice – whether of science, politics or daily life. (Collier, 1994: 16)

The research work involved in doing your dissertation requires you to take a conscious stance with regard to the nature of knowledge, its acquisition and analysis, and the quality and certainty of the conclusions that can be reached

FIGURE 5.1   Your position will not necessarily be shared by your reader

from it. You cannot assume that your position will necessarily be shared by your reader, so you will have to make clear to the reader what your philosophical approach is.

So, what is it that makes up this philosophical approach, and how can one recognize its nature? The best way is to look at some of the debate about different approaches to knowledge and enquiry – the sorts of issues that are inherent in the process of producing a dissertation. There is a wide spectrum of attitudes in the debate about research, with two opposing camps, the positivists and the relativists, at the extremes, and a range of intermediate stances. I will briefly compare these divergent attitudes.

5.2 Positivism

On the one hand, the positivists maintain that in order to know something it should be observable and measurable. The observer must stand apart and take a detached and neutral view of the phenomenon. For example, an engineer testing the strength of a beam will make careful measurements of loading and deflection, and careful observations of cracks and signs of failure. It should not make any difference if the engineer's dog had died that morning and he or she was feeling really low. Any other engineer doing the same test elsewhere would come up with identical results and knowledge about that beam.

This is simple enough to understand when dealing with controllable inanimate material and forces. But extreme positivists would go further. They would say that any observable phenomenon can be understood and explained in a logical way, if only enough was known about all the complexities of the situation. Hence, for example, the development of life on earth will be fully explained when enough information is gained and enough experiments are carried out to successfully test the theories about the process.

Inherent to this way of thinking is a set of assumptions. It is these that underpin the positivist approach and form the basis of scientific method that has brought us so many advances in science and technology. The main assumptions are as follows.

Order There is a conviction that the universe has some kind of order, and because of this, it is possible that we should be able to achieve some kind of understanding of it. Consequently, we can find out the links between events and their causes and thus understand 'the rules of the game'. This then allows us to make predictions. Admittedly, some phenomena are so complicated that it is very difficult to possess enough information and understanding to make reliable predictions (e.g. long-range weather forecasting).

External reality This maintains that everyone shares the same reality and that we do not all live in different worlds that follow different rules. Although there is much philosophical debate about the nature of reality, the positivists rely on the assumption that knowledge is shareable and verifiable: that is, you see the same as I do when, say, looking down a microscope. A theory built upon observations can therefore be tested by any observer to see if it is reliable, in order that the theory can achieve general acceptance.

FIGURE 5.2   Find out the links between events and their causes

Reliability Human intellect and perceptions are reliable. You can depend on your senses and methods of thinking. Despite the dangers of deception and muddled thinking, careful observation and logical thought can be depended on. The accuracy of memory is also an important feature of this assumption.

Parsimony This maintains that the simplest possible explanation is the best. Needless complexity should be avoided. Einstein's formula $E = mc^2$ that sums up his momentous theory of relativity, is a good example of this.

Generality It is no good if the results of one experiment are only relevant to that one case, at that particular time, in that particular place. It must be possible to generalize from particular instances to others, e.g. from the performance of one tested beam to the predicted performance of other similar beams. It is impossible to see every instance of a phenomenon, e.g. water boiling when it is heated, but it is possible to maintain that any water will boil if heated sufficiently.

When society is organized in a 'scientific' way, logical methods can be applied to all aspects of life, so as to share all the increasing benefits equally and to ensure that people themselves act rationally.

5.3 Relativism

FIGURE 5.3   We are all encumbered by our own experiences and viewpoints

On the other hand, the relativists maintain that we humans are inextricably bound up with the events of the world, and that it is impossible for anyone to stand aside and observe it impartially, as it were, 'from on high'. We are all encumbered by our own experiences and viewpoints, and are enmeshed in our society. However well established they are, facts are human interpretations of reality, and may well change with time or be understood quite differently by different cultures.

This approach is particularly relevant when studying anything to do with human society. Scientific method is poorly equipped to track the inconsistencies, conflicts and subtleties of beliefs, ideals and feelings that form such an important part of human life.

But even in what is regarded as pure scientific research, for example astronomy, physics and biology, the mindset of society, referred to as the current paradigm, is an enormously powerful force that distorts thinking away from idealistic detachment and channels it into socially (and sometimes religiously) 'acceptable' routes. A striking example of this in the past was the complicated solutions devised to explain the movement of the heavenly bodies to conform to the belief that the earth was the centre of the universe. Commercial pressure can also distort scientific efforts, for example, in the development of particular drug treatments where heavy investment almost 'requires' that it be shown that the treatment works.

In order to understand this basically different approach to understanding reality it is revealing to compare the relativists' attitudes to the previously listed assumptions that underlie the positivist position.

Order The creation of some kind of order in our understanding of the world is based on our own human perceptions of the world. As time passes, our ordering of the world changes, not because the world has changed but because our attitudes to life, society and beliefs have changed. However much knowledge is gained, we will never reach a definitive understanding of the world order. The 'rules of the game' are constructed by our intellect which is irrevocably bound up in our society and individuality.

External reality Our perceptions of the world are uniquely individual. The world we actually perceive does not consist of a series of stimuli that we interpret through our senses and make sense of logically in a void. Rather, we already have a picture of the world, and what we perceive is interpreted in relation to our feelings and understanding – our reality. Admittedly, we might share reality by using the same meanings of words in language (even that is debatable), but this sharing is only a tiny part of our individual experience. We look on the world from within it, and from within ourselves.

Reliability Can we believe our senses? Does our memory always fool us? We will answer 'not always' to the first and 'quite often' to the second, if we believe that human nature is inevitably bound up in its culture and past experiences. These lead us to a personal interpretation of our perception and memorizing of events in our surroundings. Our senses can be tricked in many ways, and our memory is far from perfect, so researchers cannot rely on these to give a definitive record and measurement of the work. However, our skills of reasoning must be taken as a reliable method of organizing data and ideas, even though there may be several ways of interpreting data.

Parsimony Life and society are not so simple and uniform that a simple explanation is possible. Hence simplification usually implies oversimplification. Although needless complexity should be avoided, it is rarely possible to sum any situation up in the form of a neat formula.

FIGURE 5.4 Our senses can be tricked in many ways

Generality Relativists tend to reject the importance, or even possibility, of categorizing individuals and events into classes.

> Owing to the uniqueness of each person and the uniqueness of each event it is very difficult to predict what may happen in the future under similar conditions; it is dangerous to generalize from studied cases.

The function of language becomes an important issue in this debate. Actually, this issue is widened into the subject of communication, which goes beyond just the spoken and written message. We communicate by all sorts of gestures; we assume roles and follow conventions. Consider how difficult it is to gauge people's meanings and feelings when you are in a strange country where different social rules apply, even if you understand the language. This subject of communication is called 'discourse'. How things are communicated is often as important as what is communicated – remember Marshall McLuhan's (1976) phrase, 'the medium is the message'? (McLuhan and Fiore, 1976). Discourse analysis recognizes these important factors and stresses that there is no 'neutral' way of communication.

5.4 How do these attitudes affect your dissertation?

You will need to think about this. Your own philosophical approach to how we can see and understand the world around us will be a fundamental factor in your investigations. There are many ways in which any situation can be

FIGURE 5.5   You will need to think about this

analysed. Each approach will have a tendency to be based on a particular philosophical line that influences what you look at, the data you collect and the types of conclusions that you aim at. This is best explained using an example.

Suppose that you have decided to carry out some research into children's playgrounds in cities. You could base your research on official statistics about how many playgrounds there are in relation to population figures, their sizes, facilities and locations, and records of vandalism and child crime. Or you could arrange interviews with children and parents to find out what they felt about different playgrounds. You could also observe the playgrounds from above and plot children's playing patterns in the form of geometrical shapes; or you could observe from nearby and record how the children used each piece of equipment. You could also make measurements of how much force is exerted by children playing on the equipment, test its strength and measure rates of corrosion, in order to ensure that it is safely built. Each of these approaches involves basic theoretical as well as methodological decisions.

Accordingly, you will have to decide which philosophical standpoint(s) to adopt when carrying out your research. This is not to say that any approach is better or more true than any other. Your research approach will depend on the characteristics of your research problem and your own convictions about the nature of research. It is even possible to take different approaches to different aspects of your research topic. Your decisions will help you to determine the nature of your enquiry, the choice of appropriate research methods, and the characteristics of the outcomes that you can expect.

5.5 Chapter summary

Being aware of your philosophical or theoretical standpoint is an important aspect of your research. The assumptions made at the heart of your investigation have a large bearing on how you approach your subject and investigate the aspects of interest. The opposite poles of approach are positivism – the belief that there is an inherent order in the universe which can be discovered if we possess enough information; and relativism – that as human beings within a culture, we can only understand the world from our own perspective, which could be different from that of other humans in other cultures.

The concepts of order, external reality, reliability, parsimony and generality are all understood differently in positivism and relativism. In positivism, facts can be established that are immutable so certainties can be achieved, while in relativism, it is understanding that is aimed at, that might be 'true' only in certain situations and cases.

5.6 What should I do now?

In the light of what you have read in this chapter, how does your thinking about your dissertation topic fit in with the different philosophical approaches? Are the assumptions of positivist thought acceptable in your research approach, or is a more relativist basis appropriate?

In order to examine what might be an appropriate philosophical stance to the issues of your research, first look carefully at the subject of your dissertation. Now ask yourself the following rather general questions.

- Is your study concerned with things or people, or does it include a study of both, perhaps of their interrelationships?
- Can your problem be analysed and explained in terms of forces or inner physical processes, or rather in terms of meanings and subjective forces?
- Are notions of causation an important aspect, or are you seeking to find explanations in order to reach an understanding of a situation?
- Will knowledge be gained through impartial observation and/or experimentation, or will you have to immerse yourself in the situation and make subjective interpretations or value-laden observations?
- Are you trying to find solutions to a perceived problem, explain reasons for events, investigate to discover new knowledge, or compare and criticize the work of others?

If you are going to look at things themselves and their properties and performance, e.g. the performance of certain materials in certain situations, or you are going to look at processes or procedures in their manufacture or use, then a positivist approach is quite suitable for either option, as the uncertainties of human interaction, feelings and habits are not an issue.

FIGURE 5.6   You might investigate personal relationships

FIGURE 5.7   Causation has a sort of inevitability about it

If it is people that you are going to study, you might look at trends in soci-ety, i.e. taking an overview of large groups or classes of people, or you might investigate personal relationships within small groups or between individu-als. The large amounts of quantitative data involved in the former also imply that taking a positivist approach is possible if you think that there are 'natural' or inevitable forces and laws that determine social events on a large scale. If you believe that the uncertainties of human reactions and beliefs operate even at this large scale, then a more relativist stance is appropriate.

The latter, examining individuals and small groups, is more likely to be approached in a relativist manner as your own background and attitudes make it difficult to see the situation from a purely neutral stance. Even so, if you were a psychologist or neurologist, you might disagree: there might be a purely scientific biological basis for all our actions.

In many cases, the technical and organizational aspects of the subject will be influenced by the human aspects. Hard science will need to be adapted to cater for the abilities, feelings and habits of people. You will need to adapt your approaches to these different aspects.

Causation has a sort of inevitability about it, as if it follows certain rules: 'If these certain events take place, then they will cause this other event to happen'. In the natural sciences the role of human relative values plays little part, e.g. the rules of aerodynamics can be harnessed to make a plane fly even without a pilot. A positivist approach is appropriate here. When the issues have a more human perspective, then certainties are more elusive, e.g. what are the causes of war? Understanding and explanations will be more subjec-tive and relativistic.

Do remember though, when thinking about the philosophical attitude you have developed in relation to the subject of your project, that the extreme stances described above are crude formulations of the range of intermediate approaches one could take. What may be appropriate for one aspect of your study might be inappropriate for another. The main thing is to be aware of your attitudes, and to question your assumptions when you formulate the design of your research activities. It is a good exercise to explain your motivations for choosing your particular topic: this might quite clearly reveal your attitudes towards the subject.

5.7 References to more information

You could spend an awful lot of time reading about philosophy and its impact on enquiry and research. If you get interested in this subject, beware of getting bogged down and spending too much time exploring. You could carry on for a lifetime! Still, you can follow up all the interesting aspects after you have finished your dissertation.

If you are doing a topic that involves social research, i.e. with people and society, then it might be worth having a look at these, in order of complexity (simplest first) for more detail.

Further reading

David, M. and Sutton, C., (2004) *Social Research: The Basics*. London: Sage. Chapter 4 has a very clear description of philosophy of methods, paradigms and methods.

Seale, C. (ed.) (2012) *Researching Society and Culture*, 3rd edition. London: Sage. Chapter 2 deals with the philosophy of science and can be accessed for free online at www.uk.sagepub.com/upm-data/45990_Seale.pdf (accessed 10 April 2013).

Hughes, J. (1990) *The Philosophy of Social Research*, 2nd edition. Harlow: Longman.

Jarvie, I. and Zamora-Bonilla, J. (2011) *The SAGE Handbook of the Philosophy of Social Sciences*. London: Sage.

6

How Do I Write a Proposal?

Chapter contents

6.1 What is a proposal?

A proposal is a careful description of what your dissertation will be about and how you intend to carry out the work involved until its completion. It is a really useful document that challenges you to think very carefully about what you are going to do, how you will do it and why. It will be required in order to inform your supervisor of your intentions so that he or she can judge whether:

1. The subject and suggested format conform to the requirements of the course.
2. It is a feasible project in respect to scope and practicality.

3. You have identified some questions or issues that are worth investigating.
4. Your suggested methods for information collection and analysis are appropriate.
5. The expected outcomes relate to the aims of the project.

Not only is this the main opportunity to crystallize your thoughts before you embark on the project, it is also a sober consideration of how much you will be able to actually achieve within the few weeks/months allowed. You will not be able to sit down and write your proposal without referring to your background research. A good proposal will indicate how your chosen topic emerges from issues that are being debated within your subject field, and how your work will produce a useful contribution to the debate. At this level of research you do not have to make any earth-shattering discoveries, but it is necessary to produce some useful insights by the appropriate application of research theory and methods.

FIGURE 6.1   Several redrafts will be needed

The proposal must be quite short (usually not more than two sides of A4 paper), and therefore a lot of thought needs to be put into its production in order to cover all the matter to be conveyed, in an elegantly dense manner. Several redrafts will be needed in order to pare it down to the limited length allowed, so don't panic if you cannot get it all together first time. A really informative proposal will not only impress your supervisor, but also give you a good guide to the work, and help to get you focused back on the important issues if (probably, when) you get diverted up branching paths of investigation later on in the project.

There is a fairly standardized format for writing proposals which, if followed, ensures that you cover all the important aspects that must be included. The advice under the following headings will help you to focus on the essential matters and to make the hard choices required at this early stage in the project.

6.2 The subject title

The subject title summarizes in a few words the entire project. You will probably not be able to formulate this finally until you have completed the proposal, but you will need something to be going on with in order to focus your thinking.

A title should contain the key words of the dissertation subject, i.e. the main subjects, concepts or situations. Added to these are normally a few words that delineate the scope of the study. For example:

> Temporary housing in the suburbs: the expansion of residential caravan sites in British cities in the 1970s.

Start, therefore, by summing up the core of your chosen subject by its principal concepts. To find these, refer to the background reading you have done. What words are mentioned in the book titles, the chapter headings and the content lists? These may be quite esoteric, but should represent the very heart of your interest. They should also, when linked together, imply an issue or even a question. For example:

> Obese and depressed, or fat and happy?

This part of the title will, by its nature, be rather general and even abstract. In order to describe the nature of the project itself, more detail will be required that states limitations such as the location, time and extent. Locations can be countries or towns, types of place or situations. Time might be historical periods, the present or during specific events.

FIGURE 6.2   Locations can be countries or towns

Examples of locations and time:

- in Brazil
- in market towns
- in one-to-one teaching lessons
- in the sixteenth century
- contemporary trends
- during the General Strike
- after motorway accidents
- high-altitude mountaineering.

6.3 The aims or objectives

The aims or objectives of the project should be summarized in three or four bullet points. This then provides a very succinct summary of the thrust of the research, and an introduction to the rationale that follows. If you find this difficult to write, then you have probably not thought sufficiently about what you are actually going to do. Some useful indicative words you can use are: to explore, to test, to investigate, to explain, to compare, to predict. Ensure that there is an indication of the limits of the project by mentioning place, time, extent, etc. Here is an example:

Vienna as represented in literature

Aims:

- to contrast some ways that writers have textualized cities
- to explore in detail three distinct readings of Vienna
- to compare and seek connections between these three readings
- to examine the connection between the myth and the reality of Vienna.

6.4 The background

Anyone reading your proposal for the first time needs to be informed about the context of the project and where it fits in with current thinking. Do not assume that the reader knows anything about the subject, so introduce it in such a way that any intelligent person can understand the main issues surrounding your work. That is one function of the background section. The other function is to convince your supervisor that you have done the necessary reading into the subject, and that you have reviewed the literature sufficiently. This is why it is necessary to have plenty of references in this section.

FIGURE 6.3   It requires quite an effort to get a lot of information across in a succinct manner

The references should refer to history, theories, relevant data, accepted practices, contentious issues, and recent research publications dealing with your subject of study.

It requires quite an effort to get a lot of information across in a succinct manner. Use the notes you have made from your reading. Check that the most important theories and writers have been mentioned. You will find these in the main publications about your subject. Expect to cite about 10–20 references in this section.

You could spend an enormous amount of time doing this, as the volume of previous work in the field could be extensive. Alternatively, you could worry that you have missed out on essential references, especially if your searches are not very productive. Just remember that at undergraduate level you are not expected to already know everything in your chosen subject. One of the points of doing a dissertation is to widen your knowledge and understanding. So stop as soon as you can provide enough background material to give a context to your project. Your supervisor should be able to tell you if you have missed out any crucial references.

6.5 Defining the research problem

Based on the issues explained and discussed in the background section, you should be able to identify the particular part of the subject that you want to investigate. Every subject could be studied for a lifetime, so it is important that you isolate just one small facet of the subject that you can manageably deal with in the short amount of time that you are given. Once you have explained the topic of your study, and argued why it is necessary to do work in this area, it is a good idea to state briefly the research problem in one or two clear sentences. This will be a direct reflection of your title, and will sum up the central question or problem that you will be investigating.

A clear definition of the research problem is an essential ingredient of a proposal; after all, the whole project hinges on this. The nature of the problem also determines the issues that you will explore, the kind of information that you will collect, and the types of analysis that you will use. The main research problem should grow naturally and inevitably out of your discussion of the background. You can state it clearly as a question, a hypothesis, etc., as explained in Chapter 4. Then explain briefly how it will be broken down into subproblems, subhypotheses, etc. in order to make it practicable to research. There should be a connection between these and the aims or objectives of the project: everything should link up neatly.

6.6 The main concepts and variables

Every subject has its own way of looking at things, its own terminology and its own methods of measuring. Consider the differences between analysing the text of a Shakespeare play and the data transmitted back from a space probe. You will certainly be familiar with some of the concepts that are important in your subject: just look at the title you have chosen for examples of these. It will probably be necessary to define the main concepts in order to dispel any doubts as to their exact meaning. There might even be some dispute in the literature about terminology: if so, highlight the nature of the discussion.

A mention of the indicators that are used to make the concepts recognizable will be the first step towards breaking down the abstract nature of most concepts. Then a description of the variables that are the measurable components of the indicators can be used to demonstrate how you will actually be able to collect and analyse the relevant data to come to conclusions about the concepts and their nature (see Chapter 4 if you have forgotten what indicators and variables are).

You do not need to write much here, just enough to convince the reader that you are not vague as to how you can investigate any abstract concepts that you might be dealing with, e.g. suitability, success, creativity, quality of life, etc. Even well-known terms might need to be broken down to ensure that the reader understands just how you will study them.

FIGURE 6.4   Every subject has its own way of looking at things

6.7 Methods

What exactly will you do in order to collect and analyse the necessary information? This is the practical part of the proposal where you explain what you will do, how you will do it and why. It is important to demonstrate the way that your research activities relate to the aims or objectives of your project and thus will enable you to come to conclusions relevant to the research problem. Different methods will be required for different parts of the research. Scan through Chapters 12–14 in order to get an idea of the range of research methods that are available. At this stage you need not know in detail just how you will implement them, but you should quite easily be able to choose those that seem appropriate for different aspects of your enquiry.

It is best to spell out what you intend to do in relation to each subproblem or subquestion when they require different methods of data collection and analysis. Try to be precise and add reasons for what you are planning to do, i.e. add the phrase 'in order to ...'. This methods section of the proposal can be in the form of a list of actions.

This whole process will need quite a lot of thought and preparation, especially as you will not be familiar with some of the research methods. But time spent now to make informed decisions is time well spent. It will make you much more confident that you can plan your project, that you have not over-reached yourself, and that you have decided on activities that you will quite enjoy doing.

Consider the following actions that you might need to take:

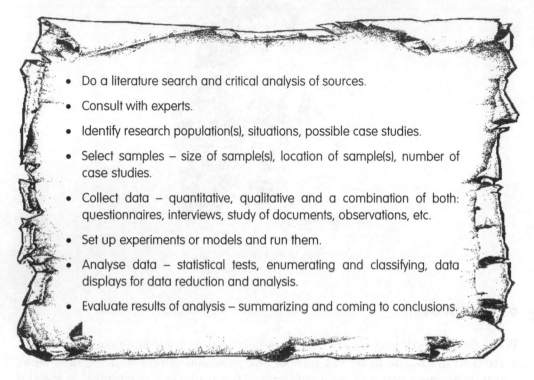

- Do a literature search and critical analysis of sources.
- Consult with experts.
- Identify research population(s), situations, possible case studies.
- Select samples – size of sample(s), location of sample(s), number of case studies.
- Collect data – quantitative, qualitative and a combination of both: questionnaires, interviews, study of documents, observations, etc.
- Set up experiments or models and run them.
- Analyse data – statistical tests, enumerating and classifying, data displays for data reduction and analysis.
- Evaluate results of analysis – summarizing and coming to conclusions.

6.8 Expected outcomes

It is a good idea to spell out to the reader, and to yourself, just what you hope will be achieved by doing all this work. Since the proposal is a type of contract to deliver certain results, it is a mistake to 'promise mountains and deliver molehills'. Although you cannot predict exactly what the outcomes will be (if you could, there would be little point in carrying out the research), you should try to be quite precise as to the nature and scope of the outcomes and as to who might benefit from the information. Obviously you should make sure that the outcomes relate directly to the aims of the research that you described at the beginning of the proposal. The outcomes may be a contribution at a practical and/or a theoretical level.

6.9 Programme of work

The next chapter deals in detail with how to plan your time, but you could even now, before reading it, make a stab at allocating your major future activities into your available timeframe. A simple bar chart showing the available time in weeks, and the list of tasks and their sequence and duration, will be sufficient. Don't forget to give yourself plenty of time to actually write up and present your dissertation. You will quickly spot if you have been too ambitious in your intentions, because the tasks just will not fit realistically into the time. If you see problems ahead, now is the time to adjust your proposal to make it more feasible. Reduce the scope of the investigations by narrowing the problem still further (you can do this by becoming more specific and by reducing the number of subproblems or subquestions), by being less ambitious with the amount of data to collect, and by simplifying the analytical stages.

6.10   Chapter summary

A proposal is a short description of what you intend to research, why, and how you will do it. The main ingredients are the subject title (containing the main concepts of the study), the aims or objectives (which give direction to the work), the background (which provides the context), definition of the research problem (which pins down the scope of the research), the main concepts and variables (the basic factors investigated), the methods (explanation of how you will collect and analyse data), the expected outcomes (what you hope to achieve by the study), and a programme of work (which maps out the list of activities required and their timing relevant to the submission date).

The formulation of the proposal is an essential first step to doing research. It provides a focus for your work and the very act of compiling it will force you to think carefully about the subject, its suitability for a dissertation with regard to scope and resources, and to find out about the context on which it is based.

6.11 What should I do now?

Write your proposal! Just follow the above recommendations and it should not be too difficult. The biggest danger is that you agonize for ages over what to do before you even write anything down. This is a mistake, for if you try to work out everything in your head you cannot realistically review it. Committing yourself to paper not only relieves your memory from having to retain all your decisions, but also forces you to construct an argument to structure your intentions. Once you have something written down, you can review it, build on it, add detail to it and alter it as required.

Using a computer to write gives you the opportunity to sketch out your ideas, perhaps as a series of headings or points, and you don't have to worry

FIGURE 6.5

too much what you write down, as it can so easily be altered, moved, expanded or even deleted. You can work like a painter who first sketches out a few indicative lines, then builds on these to produce, stage by stage, a finished picture. Assuming you have a good idea of the sort of problem you wish to address, you don't even have to start at the beginning. You could work back from the desired outcomes and create a rationale on how you would get there. Or you could select the activities that you enjoy doing most and explore how you could exploit these to devise a project. Once you have a framework that looks feasible, you can add the detail – work that will require rather more reflection and reference to further information.

The final version should be set out following the structure outlined in this chapter. You will also need to add a list of references that give the details about the publications cited in your text. Check with any coursework instructions you have been given to make sure that you are fulfilling the requirements. When you have finished, even if you are not formally obliged to do so, give a copy to your supervisor and request his or her comments. Be prepared to alter your proposal in response to any comments you receive, but first think carefully about the implications of these changes. The comments should help to make life easier for you, or clarify the implications of your proposals. It is also in the interest of your supervisor that you do well and enjoy the experience of writing your dissertation.

The proposal will form a firm foundation for your research work. You should refer to it from time to time during the next weeks when you get into the detail of your work, in order to check that you are not going astray, getting too bogged down on one particular aspect, or missing out on an essential detail.

6.12 References to more information

There are books that are solely dedicated to writing academic proposals of all kinds. The principles are the same for all of them; it is the extent and detail that vary. All are reasoned arguments to support a plan of action. If you want to read more, or find different approaches to proposal writing, you can explore some of these books. Some will be rather too detailed for your purposes, but you will undoubtedly find something useful. I have put them in order of complexity, simplest first, though you may want to look at a more subject-specific book first. Every book on how to do dissertations will also have a section on writing a proposal. Several have been mentioned in previous chapters.

Further reading

Denscombe, M. (2012) *Research Proposal: A Practical Guide.* Maidenhead: Open University Press.

Locke, L.F. (2007) *Proposals That Work: A Guide for Planning Dissertations and Grant Proposals*, 5th edition. London: Sage.

Coley, S.M. and Scheinberg, C.A. (2008) *Proposal Writing*, 3rd edition. London: Sage with the University of Michigan.

Punch, K. (2006) *Developing Effective Proposals*, 2nd edition. London: Sage.

Jay, R. (2000) *How to Write Proposals and Reports That Get Results.* London: Prentice Hall.

Denicolo, P. and Becker, L. (2012) *Developing Research Proposals.* London: Sage.

7

What About Working and Planning My Time?

Chapter contents

7.1 Motivation and discipline

This chapter is in danger of sounding patronizing in places, partly because it sometimes states the obvious, and partly because the idea of discipline evokes the picture of someone talking from on high and wagging a finger at you. But I know only too well (from writing this book) that motivation and discipline are two factors that play an important part in helping to actually get the work done. It is after all *self*-motivation and *self*-discipline that are the issue, not something imposed by a higher authority. So, to become aware of a few techniques which help to make life easier is no bad thing.

Ideally, if you have enough motivation, you are unlikely to need to impose much onerous discipline on yourself. In order to be motivated, it is pretty important that the project you have chosen really interests you. When you think of it, this is probably the first opportunity you have had since beginning your education to choose yourself what you will study for the next few months, so you should seize the opportunity to select something that will make this exercise enjoyable and rewarding. This point has already been made more fully in Chapter 3.

Even so, not every task can be interesting, and there are so many other enjoyable things to do and other deadlines to meet. There will also be several new skills to learn and others to develop, both of which require energy and dedication. You are only human, so it is worth considering how your efforts can be optimized by being in tune with your personality and mental and physical characteristics. Below are some ideas of how you can achieve this.

7.2 Moods

No one can be upbeat and raring to go all of the time. We are all subject to moods that have an important influence on our ability to concentrate and be creative. Philippa Davies (2002: 15) mentions two sets of opposite conditions – energetic/tired and calm/tense – which can be understood to contain a range of moods from mild to extreme. One cannot simply equate one or other state with being conducive to hard work or concentrated effort. It depends on your personality how you react to these moods. What is useful though is to be aware of how you are feeling, and also what sort of activities you can do best in which mood. For instance, some people need the tension of working to a deadline to get going, while others are only productive when they can mull over their work in a peaceful setting.

It is well known that people's mood varies during the course of the day. But they are not all the same: some are 'morning people', others 'evening people', while some fall between the two, or are even 'night people'. Take note of how you feel during the day. Do you find working easiest during the morning, or do you only get going in the evening hours? This is not just a psychological phenomenon, but also a physiological one (something to do with body temperature at different times of the day). If you can detect a pattern, then plan your activities to suit. Not all that you need to do requires intense concentration, so you can reserve the less demanding tasks for your 'weaker' periods. For women, the monthly cycle might also be taken into account.

Moods are also a form of information or feedback about your biomedical condition. Healthy living in the form of plenty of exercise, a balanced diet, and regular and sufficient rest, promote an upbeat mood. Conversely, a lack of sleep, poor diet, too much drink and smoking, and lack of exercise will tend to depress your mood. I know that these often feature largely in student life,

FIGURE 7.1 It depends on your personality how you react to these moods

but it is just as well to be aware of it, and know that a good meal and a night's sleep will actually make working easier. You can also do things to influence your mood. To avoid getting stuck in a boring and depressing routine, why not organize a shift of scene? Work somewhere different, visit different libraries, choose case studies or do other field research in different locations. Although you might not be in a position to make a study of exotic butterflies in the Amazon jungle, visits to new places can be a stimulating experience.

Ruminating about a subject for a long time can be a 'downer'. There is only so much that one can resolve in one's head. Thinking too long around a problem, without getting it down on paper or discussing it with someone, tends to lead to circular thinking and the feeling of being stuck. Only when the problem gets clearly laid out can you find ways to grapple with it, or even to let your subconscious work on it.

Make the best of when you are feeling great. At these times you will feel inspired, ideas will tumble into your head, you will see connections and have insights and have a strong urge to get it all down onto paper. Avoid getting interrupted, as it is difficult to pick up from where you left off. Put off other commitments and savour the moment: this is when you will be at your most productive. There are other times when you feel that you are running at half speed. Make use of these times for more menial tasks, such as tidying up, sorting out notes, drawing or scanning illustrations, making graphs and figures. You can also catch up on your reading.

Sometimes, having worked for some time you can get stuck, fed up or just tired. Peter Woods (2006: 16–18) has collected a few ploys that he and other well-known writers have used to reinvigorate themselves: Spend some time gazing out of the window (at a panoramic vista if there is one), drink numerous cups of coffee, pace the room, listen to the birds singing or to a piece of music, examine what is going on in the neighbourhood with a pair of binoculars, give an imaginary speech or hold a conversation with yourself, take a walk or go for a run, play the violin or a computer game or a game of snooker, go out and do some sport.

7.3 Being creative

One of the main points of getting you to do a dissertation is to force you to work independently, and this requires some creativity. Although you will get a certain level of support, it is really up to you to work things out and find solutions, and even to discover problems that need solving. Understanding complex situations also needs an open-minded approach. Creative thinking helps you to break out from habitual thought patterns and explore a wider range of possibilities. There are several easy-to-use techniques that can help you to think creatively. Here are a few exercises you might find useful.

Brainstorming You need a group of people for this (though you can do it on your own; it is then called brainwriting). First clearly define a particular problem you want to solve. List as many ideas as come into your heads of how to solve the problem. In a group, you can also feed off other people's suggestions, combine ideas and extrapolate or modify them. The main rule is not to criticize, however bizarre or ridiculous the suggestions may be. The evaluation of the ideas comes later. A typical brainstorming may produce about 50 different ideas (probably rather less for brainwriting) for solutions to a particular problem. These can then be classified and evaluated.

Checklists A bit like a shopping list. Make a list of things you need to consider, difficulties you might encounter, tasks you need to do, information you need to collect, etc. Again, you need to focus on one aspect of your project for useful results. You can also use checklists to look at alternative ways of doing things by using trigger words, e.g. combine solutions, reverse the problem (see it from a different perspective). Other trigger words are adapt, rearrange, substitute, magnify, minify, modify, put to other uses.

Analogies You can often draw parallels between two different problems or situations, where knowledge about one can help to explain or solve the other. This is quite a natural process, a way of learning from experience. Put to more deliberate use, it can help to obtain new insights and perspectives. For example, the techniques your favourite chat show hosts use to prise information out of their guests could be used in your own interviews; or analysis of dynamics among a group of people could be compared with that of an extended family or a small business.

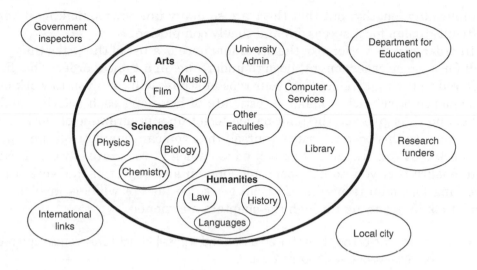

FIGURE 7.2   Systems map of the university (very simplified)

Immersion in the problem This takes time, and is a good reason for defining a problem at an early stage. Once you are aware of the problem, be it of a practical or a theoretical nature, think about it for a bit, and then just 'forget' it for a few days and allow your subconscious to work on it. You might just jump out of the bath shouting 'eureka' as a solution presents itself out of the blue.

Discussion A problem shared is a problem halved, so they say. It is best if you talk with people who share similar problems, and especially those who have found good solutions!

Systems thinking There is a range of ways of looking at systems, i.e. a complex of interrelated things or events such as machines, organizations, social groups or natural phenomena. You can draw a diagram to explore the sequences of cause and effect, or of the influence that factors have on one another. Other types of diagram are organization diagrams, cognitive maps, flowcharts and decision trees. A simple example of a systems map is illustrated in Figure 7.2. See Chapter 16 for examples of other diagrams.

You will probably find it necessary to spend plenty of time by yourself in order to get yourself going. Having the TV on in the background is a real concentration killer. I find even having music on is a distraction – I keep wanting to listen.

7.4 All the things you need to do

A dissertation is probably the biggest academic project that you have ever undertaken. The worst aspect of this is not that the task seems impossibly complex and lengthy, but that there are so many unknowns, making it very difficult to plan for a successful and timely completion.

In order to remove some of the mystique, here is a list of the tasks that you will (or in some cases, might) need to undertake, in a typical order. This list, tailored to the requirements of your type of study, will help you to work out a sequence of activities, make an estimate of how long each activity might take, and thus give you the information to set up a programme of work. You can then use this both to assure yourself that you can complete on time, and to check that you are not falling behind too much in your rate of work. It will also ensure that you do not spend too long on any aspect of the work, thus avoiding last minute panics. You can get some idea of what is involved in each task by scanning through the chapters mentioned.

- Decide on a subject and type of investigation and, if possible, get it provisionally approved by your supervisor (see Chapters 2 and 3).
- Investigate the subject so that you have enough information to write the proposal (see Chapter 4).
- Write a proposal explaining the subject of your research and giving some indication of how you will do it (see Chapter 6). It is a good idea to discuss your proposal with your supervisor, as it represents the foundation of your efforts over the next months.
- Organize your note taking and your archiving system (see Chapter 9).
- Carry out background research through study of the literature to determine what has been done already in the subject (see Chapter 8) in order to see where your study fits into current and past work.
- Investigate methods of data collection and analysis which have been used to do similar studies to your own, and the practical aspects of doing them, e.g. experiments, observations, surveys, reviews, etc. (see Chapters 2, 12, 13 and 14). This will help you to decide just how you do your investigation and enable you to make estimates of what will be involved in time, expense, organization and perhaps getting permissions and access to sources of information.
- Work out a structure for the dissertation (i.e. chapter headings and short lists of contents for each) and write a draft of your preliminary chapter(s) (see Chapters 9 and 16).
- Start writing. It is a good idea to start writing the introductory chapter(s) quite early on while you are immersed in the literature review. Do not try to perfect it – even blocks of notes will be a useful start.
- Plan your project work, i.e. the part of the research that will generate new information (e.g. fieldwork, experiments, trials, archive searches, textual analyses, etc.). This might entail getting permissions for access to institutions, selecting case studies, obtaining documents for analysis, setting up questionnaires, etc. (see Chapters 10 and 11).
- Carry out the project work as planned above. Take into account time required for travel, waiting for responses to questionnaires, getting appointments with people, etc. (see Chapters 11 and 12).
- Sort and analyse the collected information. In some cases, you may need to take some time to learn computer programs to help with the analysis (see Chapters 13 and 14).

- Write up the results of your analysis, devising graphs, diagrams and illustrations to help explain the data.
- Write up how you did the research (it is easier to do this after you have completed it, though it should appear earlier in the dissertation), and write conclusions based on what you have found out (see Chapter 16).
- Prepare a final draft. This is the time to pull all the written work together in a structured form. Check that the length complies with the requirements, ensure that chapters or sections follow a logical sequence, and assess the need for illustrations, graphs and diagrams, etc. You can experiment with layout designs at this stage (see Chapters 17 and 18).
- Write up the final version based on the final draft. This will also involve inserting illustrations, graphs and diagrams, lists of references, contents and finally setting out the layout and page numberings.

7.5 Setting up a programme

At the beginning of a project, when there seems to be loads of time to complete it, it is easy to sit back and believe that planning can be done later, when time starts to run out. After all, there is no need to be all organized when time is not an issue, is there? The trouble is, until you actually assess how much work is involved in writing your dissertation, it is quite difficult to judge whether there actually is loads of time. For this reason, it is a good idea to devise a simple programme early on so that you can reassure yourself that you will not get into a desperate panic later.

In order to be of any real use, a programme should be realistic in its aims. It is easy to plan out a timetable of work that *should* be done, ignoring all the obstacles that might get in the way. For this reason it is important to include in your timing any other commitments you may have, e.g. holidays, sport, other assignments and exam dates. If the objectives are realistic, then you may actually keep referring to the programme that you have spent time devising in order to check on your progress and to plan your next moves.

It helps to break up your project into stages. Give yourself deadlines to complete aspects of the work. This is a common requirement of professional research projects, where intermediate reports are required to check up on the

FIGURE 7.3   Ignoring all the obstacles that might get in the way

progress of the work. You are unlikely to have to submit your work in stages like this, but the satisfaction and comfort of consciously getting parts of the project out of the way are worth the effort. The other advantage of splitting the work into sections is that you set limited goals, ones that you can see that you can achieve without being daunted. In addition, having some intermediate deadlines will stop you getting carried away or dithering on any one aspect of the work and spending far too much time on it.

The easiest way to devise a programme is to set up a table, with a list of tasks on the left-hand side, and the time in weeks along the top (see Figure 7.4). It is best to use the table facility in your word processor or a spreadsheet program for ease of adjustment and neat presentation. If you like, you can include your other activities to make sure that there are no clashes in timing. Try to be realistic, or the programme will become obsolete within a few weeks. If you cannot fit the necessary work into the time available, then reduce the scope of the work.

Your programme will help to motivate you, as you will easily be able to see that whatever you are doing in your list of tasks, the job is useful and a necessary part of the sequence. And the task will also have a defined and meaningful end. You will also be able to check that you are not drifting by spending too much time on particular aspects of the work, and that you allow enough time for the latter stages. Seeing that you will manage to complete on time is a great comfort. If the work does slip in relation to the programme, you will be able to adjust it so that you still find time (even if it is somewhat reduced) for all the essential tasks.

7.6 Starting to write

Even professional writers state what a pain it is to write, and how they need to be a bit insane in order to do it. However, you can take comfort in the fact that you are not writing a novel or some poetry – totally dependent on your own resources. The content of your writing will be based on other people's publications and your own collection of information and observations. You will have plenty of raw materials, so the page will not need to be blank for long!

Perhaps the most difficult step is to start writing. You might feel that you have nothing to write about until you have done all the reading and research. In fact, through just thinking about what you want to do for your dissertation you already know quite a lot. At the start of any project, there has to be some writing done to explain to other people what you intend to do. So this is a good time to start.

At this early stage, you can afford to be uncertain about matters; raise them anyway as points for further investigation. For example, you can start with describing what area of study you want to pursue (e.g. primary education, building management, magazine publishing), and exploring some of the situations

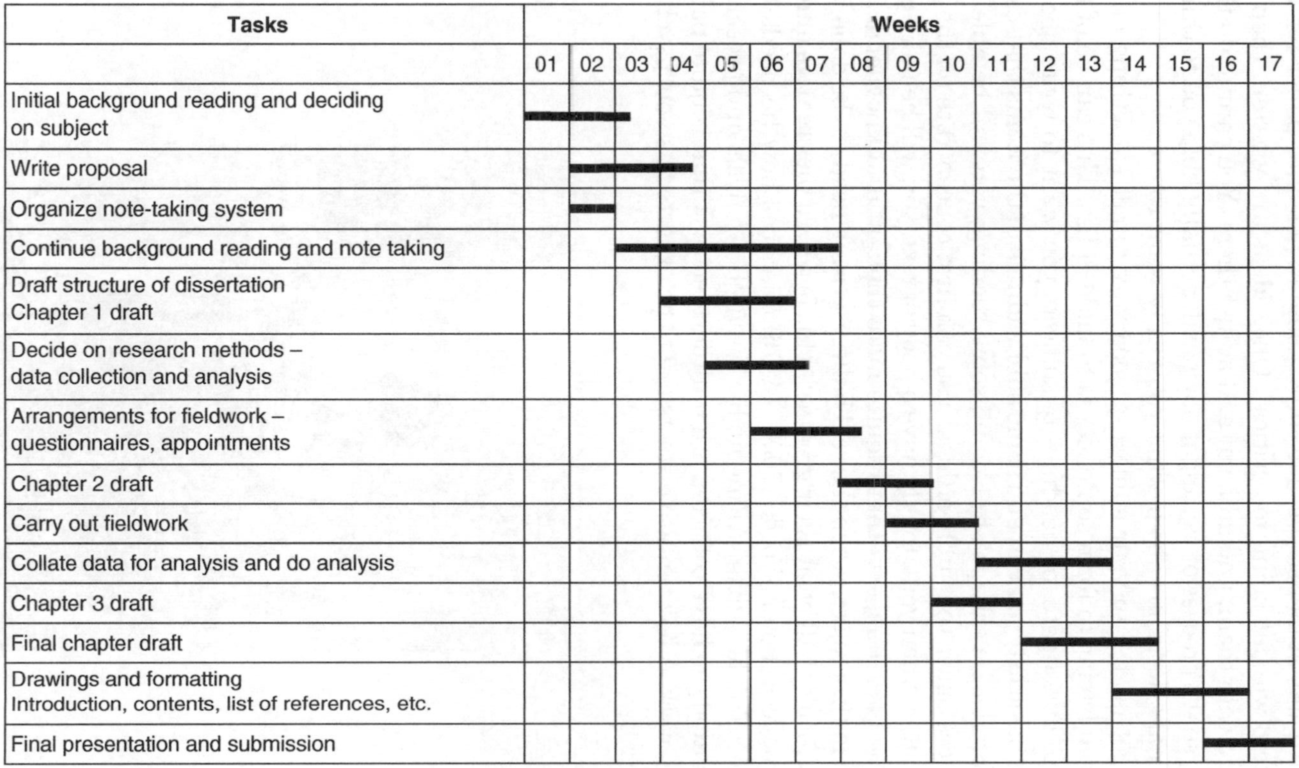

Tasks — Weeks

Tasks	01	02	03	04	05	06	07	08	09	10	11	12	13	14	15	16	17
Initial background reading and deciding on subject	▮																
Write proposal		▮															
Organize note-taking system		▮															
Continue background reading and note taking				▮			▮										
Draft structure of dissertation Chapter 1 draft				▮	▮												
Decide on research methods – data collection and analysis					▮	▮											
Arrangements for fieldwork – questionnaires, appointments						▮	▮										
Chapter 2 draft								▮	▮								
Carry out fieldwork								▮		▮							
Collate data for analysis and do analysis										▮		▮					
Chapter 3 draft										▮	▮						
Final chapter draft													▮	▮			
Drawings and formatting Introduction, contents, list of references, etc.														▮		▮	
Final presentation and submission																▮	▮

FIGURE 7.4 Programme of work

where you could concentrate your investigation (e.g. in relation to the above, first days at school, deep excavations, trends in layout style). What you write is not chiselled into stone, so just let your thoughts get onto paper (or the computer screen) without being too critical. Once ideas are written, then you can play around with them, and add, cut and adjust them. You cannot do this all in your head, so the process of writing it down will actually help you to think about it, and to make decisions about what you really want to do.

As you get more into your subject, a good way to get something onto paper without even having to form sentences is to make a list. This can be of things to do, topics to investigate, or headings of subjects you want to write about. Once you have a basic list, you can add some subheadings to the items that expand on these. Before long, perhaps after doing some reading, you will be able to add a few sentences under the subheadings. You can first concentrate on the bits that are easy. Later, when you already have a body of text, you will be more confident to tackle the harder aspects that require more thought and knowledge.

Later on in the project, when the real bulk of writing needs to be done, the pressure and difficulty will be at their greatest. This is where the creative and original work is produced. Peter Woods (2006: 14–16) describes how he needs to 'crank himself up' before he starts writing up his research. Analysis and presentation of the information you have collected is a multifaceted task that is quite painful and demanding work. A few tentative starts are to be expected as you 'psych yourself

FIGURE 7.5   Things you want to write about

88

up'. People often remark on how they become unsociable when they are involved in creative work: you need to be concentrated on yourself and your own thinking in quite a selfish way. However, do switch off in between your working sessions. If you are quite strict with your timing and set yourself realistic goals (e.g. so many words per day), then you can feel you have really earned your time off. Most professional writers work regular office hours – whether they are inspired or not.

This is a good place to remind you that you must save and back up your work regularly. Computers are notoriously fickle and can ruin your day if your work gets lost or deleted by accident or failure. Keep all your writing recorded in at least two, better three, different formats – data stick, hard drive on your laptop or desktop, your home directory on the university intranet. Make a habit of saving your work manually every 10–15 minutes, and set the program to make auto-recover files every few minutes. I have heard some tragic true stories of work getting 'lost' – perhaps one of the most infuriating and disappointing things that can happen to one's hard-won writing efforts.

7.7 Chapter summary

Self-motivation and self-discipline are needed to write a dissertation, which is perhaps the first substantial piece of work that you have had to devise and carry out completely on your own. Choosing a subject that really interests you is the best motivation to complete the work. Be aware that you are not like a machine, so look after yourself and make the best of your dynamic phases and find ways to provide relief when you get stressed.

There are several techniques that help you to be creative and find solutions to the problems that you are bound to face. Brainstorming, making checklists, devising analogies, immersing yourself in the problem, and a spot of systems thinking might get you out of your habitual ways of thinking and offer some new perspectives on your subject.

Good planning will help to keep you on track and avoid a final panic as the deadline draws near. You will need to decide on a subject and type of investigation and investigate it so that you can write a proposal. Organizing your note taking will ensure that you do not loose any of that carefully researched information. This will set you up for doing the background research and deciding on what methods of data collection and analysis will be appropriate to answer your research questions. Planning your programme of work based on what you need to do and the time available will provide a reality check on your project. To help you do this it is good to draw up a structure for your dissertation with chapter headings and subheadings.

The actual research activities should follow your programme as closely as possible. Of course, there will be some unexpected events along the way that need to be accommodated, but you can adjust your programme to take these into account.

7.8 What should I do now?

Whatever stage you are at in your project, if you have not done so yet, set up a programme of work. You can use the example in Figure 7.4 as a model and adjust it to your own particular needs. I produced this one using Microsoft Word 6 table function, though the Excel spreadsheet program could also be used. Use the line drawing function on the drawing toolbar for the horizontal time bars. Try to be realistic and take into account your preferred method of working and also your other commitments. It is usually difficult to judge just how long each task will take (usually longer than you think). However, as time will always be a limiting factor you will often have to cut the work to fit the time – a reasonable justification for limiting the scope of your work. The main thing is to get the proportions between the various stages of the work to be reasonable.

Start writing something. If you are still at the beginning, outline the area of your study, bringing in any information or quotations from things you have read. Try to define a focus for your project in the form of questions or aims. If you are further on, you could make a start on your background chapter, using the notes you have made from your reading in order to set the scene for your individual work. You could also write out a structure for your dissertation in the form of a list of headings and subheadings.

FIGURE 7.6   You may be faced with a combination of problems

If you are unclear of what you want to do, or of how to progress, define the problem as you see it, and try out one or more of the ideas-generating techniques above. You may be faced with a combination of problems that make you feel helpless and lost. Try to break them down into different aspects and tackle each one in turn. Once you have found solutions, start by putting them down in writing and listing what actions you want to take. Even if you don't start working on them straight away, at least you have a record to fall back on.

7.9 References to more information

Davies, P. (2002) *Get Up and Grow: How to Motivate Yourself and Everybody Else Too.* London: Hodder Mobius. This book is good on motivation, and referred to in this chapter. Read this to get the full story.

There are many books on creative thinking. De Bono became a creative thinking guru in the 1970s and 1980s with a string of books and public appearances. Here are some of his most popular – and easy to read – books.

De Bono, E. (1997) *Lateral Thinking: A Textbook of Creativity.* Harmondsworth: Penguin.
De Bono, E. (1996) *Teach Yourself to Think.* Harmondsworth: Penguin.
De Bono, E. (1993) *Serious Creativity: Using the Power of Lateral Thinking to Create New Ideas.* London: Harper Collins.

I found a few more books on thinking creatively and problem solving – worth delving into:

Bransford, J.D. (1993) *The Ideal Problem Solver: A Guide for Improving Thinking, Learning, and Creativity*, 2nd edition. New York: Freeman.
Smith, F. (1992) *To Think: In Language, Learning and Education.* London: Routledge.
Gilhooly, K.J. (1996) *Thinking: Directed, Undirected and Creative*, 3rd edition. London: Academic.

The following books offer lots of advice on writing. I have put them in order of accessibility and the level of academic stage that they are aimed at.

Smith, P. (2011) *How to Write an Assignment: Improving Your Research and Presentation Skills*, 8th edition. Plymouth: How To Books.
Pirie, D.B. (1985) *How to Write Critical Essays: A Guide for Students of Literature.* London: Routledge.
Hall, G.M. (ed.) (2013) *How to Write a Paper*, 5th edition. London: Wiley-Blackwell.
Bowden, J. (1991) *Writing a Report: How to Prepare, Write & Present Really Effective Reports*, 9th edition. Plymouth: How To Books.
Murray, R. (2011) *How to Write a Thesis*, 3rd edition. Buckingham: Open University Press.
Berry, R. (2000) *The Research Project: How to Write It*, 4th edition. London: Routledge.
Woods, P. (2006) *Successful Writing for Qualitative Researchers*, 2nd edition. London: Routledge.

8

How Can I Find and Review the Literature?

Chapter contents

8.1 Information overload?

It is well known that this is an information age; we are drowning in the stuff. There can be no excuse that there is a lack of information on your subject. The problem is in knowing where to look for suitable literature and to be able to sort it and select what is relevant and of sufficiently good quality. Any trawl through the Internet will demonstrate what a lot of rubbish there is on every subject under the sun. Even a visit to the library or a good bookshop can be a daunting experience: 'Goodness! Do I really have to read all this stuff!' is a typical reaction. No, you don't. But you will have to read some of it, and the skill is in finding what is the essential information.

Luckily, there are easy-to-learn, sophisticated methods of trawling for information. No need to spend hours in dusty archives (unless that is central to your project), no need to buy lots of expensive books, but there is a need to get skilled in search and find techniques.

Where you look will depend on the subject you have chosen. Some sources cover most subjects; others are specialized in a narrow range, and will hence provide more detail.

Here are lists of places you can search:

LIBRARIES

- Your university or college library – this should be your first choice. Here, not only will you find a huge amount of information, but you will also be able to find out about all the other information sources listed below.
- Specialist libraries – subject libraries in university departments, professional libraries in professional institutions, technical libraries in technical (research) establishments.
- Private libraries – in stately homes, institutes, organizations.
- Local libraries – sometimes have special collections of local interest.

INFORMATION SERVICES

- Government departments such as standards institutes, records offices, statistical offices.
- Pressure groups and voluntary organizations in such areas as heritage, conservation, historic preservation, sustainability and just about every other subject.
- Research establishments, e.g. space, buildings, medical, social, etc.
- Professional organizations and trade bodies.

THE INTERNET AND INTRANETS

- The full gamut of the World Wide Web.
- Your own organization's intranet. Often providing lecture notes and course material as well as other specialist information, e.g. research papers, professorial lectures.

MUSEUMS AND GALLERIES

- Apart from the exhibits, these usually produce a range of printed and electronic information.
- Private collections of historical records and artefacts might be found.

PEOPLE

- There are experts in every field. Some will be willing to advise you. Try the members of your own university staff at first, many of whom will be involved in research. Ask a

FIGURE 8.1   There are experts in every field

professor in your subject area to suggest who might have the specialist knowledge that you are seeking.
- Your library will contain guides to professionals and experts.
- In some cases, local knowledge will be needed: search out the relevant local experts (e.g. local historians, social workers, ornithologists, etc.),

8.2 Library searches

The library will normally be your first access point for information. Your library will contain information in a wide variety of formats:

- Printed (books, journals and newspapers).
- Electronic (Internet databases, electronic journals, e-books).
- Audio-visual (DVDs, CDs).

I am sure that you have used the library many times before, but have you really used all the sophisticated search facilities available? It is not sufficient at this level of study just to visit the shelves to see what is there, even if you have consulted the online catalogue first. There will be a wide range of resources and search facilities provided, together with a series of training sessions and leaflets in the use of these. Find out what is available and attend the training sessions so that you can use the full services of the library with confidence. Being adept at making searches will save you lots of time and frustration, as well as ensuring that you get hold of all the latest information you need.

Try to get the latest publications (unless you have special reasons not to) for two reasons. First, information becomes quickly outdated and new findings are constantly being made; and second, the reference lists at the end of the books which will guide you to further sources will not be too out of date. The information in fast-moving subjects, such as management and business, will become rapidly obsolete, but in the humanities, older publications can have lasting value.

Here are some of the facilities you should investigate.

Library catalogues

All libraries now have an electronic catalogue accessed through their computer terminals. You will probably be able to access this online from elsewhere too via the intranet and/or Internet. This means that you can do searches from home or from elsewhere in the university. If the book you want is not on the shelves, reserve it so that you can receive it when it is returned. Do keep track of renewal dates: forgetting can turn out to be very expensive!

FIGURE 8.2   Library

To widen your search or to locate a book or other publication not available in your library, catalogues of other libraries (national and worldwide) can easily be consulted via the web. The books or publications can be borrowed through inter-library loans, although a fee is usually charged for this kind of loan.

Useful web addresses are:

- The British Library Public Catalogue (BLPC), with details of over 10 million books, journals, reports, conferences and music scores: http://blpc.bl.uk.
- European national libraries: www.theeuropeanlibrary.org.

- The Library of Congress of the USA, with over 17 million books: www.loc.gov/index.html.
- Looking worldwide, try: www.libdex.com.
- Newspapers, including UK national, many provincial and various international papers, can be found at the British Library Newspaper's Catalogue: www.britishnewspaperarchive.co.uk.

FIGURE 8.3   Don't forget journals and newspapers

Don't forget the journals and newspapers. These are often catalogued and stored separately from the books in the library. As they appear regularly, they tend to be very up to date. They are based on defined subject areas, and vary in content from newspaper type articles to the most erudite research papers. To track down articles and papers in past issues, see the next two points.

If you are at home on vacation, or on an industrial placement, or if you live some distance away from your university or college, you can probably arrange to use your local university or college library, certainly for reference and possibly for lending (various schemes are in operation: consult your librarian).

Databases

There are online databases of publications on the university network, or on the web. Access to these is, depending on the licensing arrangements, from library terminals, university computers or your own computer over the Internet. Databases contain huge amounts of sources, usually searched by using key words. Some provide only citations and abstracts. Citations are the basic author and publication details; abstracts are short summaries of the contents of the article. In these cases, you will have to get hold of the book or journal article for the full information. Some databases provide the full text of the publication as plain text or even in facsimile, i.e. looking as originally printed. Citation indexes list the publications in which certain books and articles have been used as a reference.

Previous postgraduate dissertations produced in your university should be listed on a database. Copies of undergraduate dissertations might also be listed, though you might have to consult your own department collection. It is helpful to see what other students have done before you.

As there are many databases to choose from, and many are subject-specific, it is best to consult the information provided by your library to identify the best ones for you to search. You may need to obtain a password to get access (e.g. Athens authentication); again, consult library information. Your library will also provide training sessions in using electronic databases, which will save you much time in the long run.

A useful hint when using computer-based searches: instead of printing out your search results on paper, copy them to disk, so that you can easily view and edit them at a later time. The useful references can then be transferred to your bibliography without having to type them out again (ideally using a bibliographic database program such as Endnote: see Chapter 9).

Librarians

They are there to help you. Ask at the help desk if you get stuck. There are often subject librarians who have specialist knowledge in specific subject areas; they will be able to help you explore more elusive sources. Libraries usually run free training sessions on all aspects of searching for information, often with specialist advice in the various subject areas. Find out when these take place so that you can make the best use of the services offered.

8.3 The Internet

The first reaction with most people when asked a question they don't know the answer to is to 'Google it', usually consulting Wikipedia for a quick answer. With thousands of pages being added every day, the World Wide Web (WWW) is the biggest single source of information in the world – according to one estimate there are over 50 billion pages on the WWW. However, the content is of extremely variable quality, and the biggest challenge when using it is to track down good quality material. You can easily waste hours trawling through rubbish in search of the goodies. Careful use of search terms helps to eliminate the trash. Usually, the more precise your search parameters, the more manageable the search results will be. Not all information on the web is free.

A useful search engine for academic publications is Google Scholar, which will bring up journal articles related to the key words you enter. A good trick is to log on to Athens on your library website before you make the search. The results should then provide links to the publications that you can access and download free of charge.

8.4 Evaluating web sources

Anyone can add pages to the World Wide Web, so how can you judge if the information you have found is reliable? Here are seven different tests you can make to judge the quality of the contents.

- Is it accurate? Does it say what sources the data are based on? Compare the data with other sources. If they diverge greatly, is there some explanation for this?
- What authority is it based on? Find out who authored the pages, and whether they are recognized experts or a reputable organization. Check if other publications are cited or if they provide a bibliography of other articles, reports or books. You may need to track down the 'home page' to get to the details. Also see if there is a postal address and phone number to indicate the 'reality' of the organization. Web addresses that end in 'ac' (meaning academic) are likely to be university or college addresses and therefore point to some intellectual credibility – no guarantee of quality but nevertheless a useful indicator.
- Is it biased? Many pressure groups and commercial organizations use the web to promote their ideas and products, and present information in a one-sided way. Can you detect a vested interest in the subject on the part of the author? Find out more about the authors – e.g. does the information about animal experiments come from an antivivisection league, a cosmetics company, or an independent research institute?
- How detailed is the information? Is the information so general that it is of little use, or so detailed and specialized that it is difficult to understand? Investigate whether it is only fragmentary and misses out important issues in the subject, and whether the evidence is backed up by relevant data. There may be useful links to further information, other websites or printed publications.
- Is it out of date? Pages stay on the web until they are removed. Some have obviously been forgotten about and are hopelessly out of date. Try to find a date on the page, or the date when the page was updated (perhaps on the View/Page Info option on your web browser). Note that some updates might not update all the contents. Check any links provided to see if they work.
- Have you cross-checked? Compare the contents with other sources of information such as books, articles, official statistics and other websites. Does the information tally with or contradict these? If the latter, can you see why?
- Have you tried pre-evaluated 'subject gateways'? The information on these sites has been vetted by experts in the relevant subjects, so can be relied upon to be of high quality. Try www.hw.ac.uk/libwww/irn/pinakes/pinakes.html for a selection of gateways.

8.5 Search techniques for online catalogues, databases and the net

Here are a few basic hints on how to make effective searches for relevant literature. In order to find what you want, it must first be clear what you are looking for. Searches rely on single words or a combination of several words. Every subject will contain several crucial terms that distinguish it from other subjects, so the trick is to select these. If you are unfamiliar with the subject, look it up in a specialist dictionary or an encyclopaedia to see what terms are used so that you can build up your own list of key words. Remember also the use of different words and spellings in parts of the world, e.g. car/automobile, lift/elevator, pavement/sidewalk, organisation/organization.

FIGURE 8.4   In order to find out what you want, you must first be clear what you are looking for

Databases usually provide the option of a free text search, or a key word, subject or index search. The former looks for your chosen word(s) in all the text contained in the database, while the latter only searches the key words, subject lists or index lists provided by the authors with their books or papers. These lists focus on the subject matter of the publication, so give a more reliable guide to the contents. Many databases include a thesaurus – a list of indexing terms that will help you to use the standard terms. Sometimes the number of articles to which the term is assigned is given.

It is usually possible to narrow your search by indicating place and time, where these are relevant. The publication date is a basic piece of bibliographic data.

Adding an asterisk (*) to words or parts of words automatically widens the search parameters in the form of wildcards. For example, 'automa*' will find all the words starting with that stem, e.g. 'automation', 'automatic', 'automaton', etc. Inserting the * symbol into a word takes care of different spelling versions, e.g. 'labo*r' will find 'labour' and 'labor'. Boolean logic is a fancy word for the technique of using connecting words such as 'and', 'or' and 'not'. These refine the search by defining more closely what you want to include or not. For example:

- Schools and finance: this narrows down your search by only selecting records that contain both terms.
- (Lifts or elevators): this widens your search by selecting records that contain either or both terms. Note that 'or' statements must be in brackets.
- Nurseries and playschools not schools: this eliminates the terms that you do not want to consider. However, be careful that you do not eliminate useful records.

It is best if you keep the search terms simple and search several times using different variations and terms.

8.6 Doing a literature review

The background of your research is normally based on a review of the literature. You need to know what other people have written on your chosen subject so that first, you do not duplicate work already done, and second, to find out what aspects of the subject are worth exploring further. This will provide you with a good argument about why you should investigate your chosen research topic and help you to formulate your research questions and, subsequently, to plan your research project.

The literature review should form a distinctive section near the beginning of your dissertation, acting as an introduction to the subject, a review of the state of the art of relevant knowledge, and an identification of the gaps worth exploring. As indicated by the title, it requires you to read and comment on a wide range of publications focusing on your chosen subject. To find these publications, you need to perform library and other searches based on the key works central to your topic of interest.

These are the sort of issues that you should be looking for and make notes on when you study the publications:

Theory From what viewpoint has the writing been written? Is it a factual report based on scientific evidence or is it opinion from a person with a particular interest to promote? Are there some basic assumptions that form the foundation of the arguments – e.g. the necessity of state aid, or conversely, the necessary dynamics of the free market? Sometimes, the writing is based on the perspective of an 'ism', such as modernism, anarchism, traditionalism, etc. It is good to compare literature on your subject based on different theoretical positions.

History Every subject has a past. It may help to understand the present situation if you know how it developed over time. Sometimes there are problems due to inflexibility in reacting to changing conditions, or in the inability to cope with new situations.

State of the art What are the latest developments in thinking and action in your chosen subject? What are the current problems that are being addressed? What issues are suggested for further research? What conflicts in argument are there within the subject?

Research methods What techniques were used in the various research projects to investigate the issues, how was data collected and analysed, and what sort of presentation methods were used to explain the outcomes? These will provide you with useful guidance for how to carry out your own research.

In order to structure your review, you need to set up a framework taking into account the above issues and forming them into an argument. Argument about what, you might ask. Well, the point of the literature review is to convince the reader that you are basing your research on an identified problem within your chosen subject. So you need to demonstrate that you are familiar with the work done by others and have identified a gap in knowledge that is worth investigating or an issue worth exploring further. So you need to make a case for your choice of research topic. Therefore, it is useful to sketch out the main steps in your argument before you start writing, and then to fit the notes from what you have read into the relevant steps. Let us take an example of a subject that most students will be familiar with – financial support for undergraduate students:

Steps in the argument:

1. The government, for many years, has aimed to make university education affordable for everyone of the required ability, whatever their means.
2. Recent spending cuts and policies promoting privatization have made it impossible to fund needy students with money from the public purse.
3. A system of student loans has been introduced to support the costs of undergraduate education.
4. However, according to the literature, the present scheme is unfair, as well-off students can repay their loans quickly to avoid mounting interest payments, while poorer students will spend many years paying interest, and as a result have to repay more than their richer colleagues.
5. A more equitable system should be introduced to eliminate this unfairness.

So, notes about the history of student grants and other government schemes can be reviewed and explained and arranged under point 1. Use your knowledge gained from reading to discuss the trends towards privatization and its effects on the grant system under point 2. You can then investigate the latest system of student loans, and how it responds to current thinking under point 3. The arguments for and against this can be evaluated under point 4 and the problem of unfairness revealed. In addition, how these arguments have been supported by evidence and the research methods used should be examined. Then, under point 5, you can make it the aim of your research to explore the different solutions to this problem suggested in the literature, and come up with your own conclusions on the matter. This will then lead on naturally to your statement of the research questions that you want to tackle in your dissertation, which should form the next section of your dissertation.

An important part of the literature review is to get the citation and referencing correctly formulated. For details of how to do this, refer to Chapter 17.

8.7 Chapter summary

There are numerous sources of information, in fact, more than ever before. The choice includes traditional published material in the form of printed books and journals and information presented in electronic form. There are often overlaps between these – some publications are available in many formats.

Your university or college library is the best place to start, despite the temptation to 'Google' whatever you are wanting to find out. The library collection has been built up by experts in the subjects you are studying and specialist informationalists (librarians), so the resources offered will be aimed at academic objectives. Once you have mastered the various techniques of literature searching, you can apply these to your own Internet searches.

The library will provide you with a wide range of resources in the form of books, journals, CDs, films, recordings, databases, etc., and your subject librarian will be at hand to provide you with advice if necessary. Courses in doing searches and dealing with the information found will also be offered. Libraries throughout the world are linked by an inter-library loan system, so you are not limited to the offerings of your local one.

The Internet provides access to the greatest collection of information ever, but as anyone can post up just about anything, it is essential that you evaluate carefully the accuracy and currency of the data you collect. This can be done by checking the credentials of the authors, comparing with other sources and by gauging the level of detail provided. Using pre-evaluated subject gateways will provide some independent monitoring of the quality of the information.

The use of key words is the basis for most searches for information. You can derive the relevant key words for your searches from your dissertation title and chapter headings, as well as important concepts that appear in the literature.

8.8 What should I do now?

If you have not been to a library training session for some time, now is the time to book yourself in. There are always new sources of information being introduced, especially access to electronic databases, so make sure that you are up to date with all the facilities. You may need a password to access some, so you will not be able to sit at a terminal and work it out yourself. Also look for the latest information bulletins in the library, particularly in your subject.

It is much easier to find information if you know what you are looking for. This might sound obvious, but it does require some careful thought before making searches. Make a list of the all the main concepts and other terms that appear in your title, aims, background, research problem and methods sections of your proposal. This should give you a list of key words on which you can base your searches. Look up the most important ones first.

Once you have found some useful publications, use the reference lists and bibliographies in them to lead you on to other sources. Unfortunately this only goes backwards in time. If you want to look the other way, consult a citation database and look up the title of the book, article, etc. you are currently reading. This will list the publications that have cited that one as a reference.

Despite what I said above about knowing exactly what you are looking for, do let chance play some part in your quest. Keep your eyes and ears

open for possible leads to information. Discussions on the TV or radio, informal conversations, and chance meetings are all possible sources. In the library, instead of tracking down a particular book, try exploring a section of the shelves containing books with the relevant class number, i.e. the number given according to the subject. For a start, you will immediately see what is actually available, and you may come across authors you are not familiar with.

Do read the next chapter before you return the publications you have borrowed. It is essential that you are systematic in taking notes and making records of the publications, and the next chapter explains how you can do this.

FIGURE 8.5   Keep your eyes and ears open for possible leads to information

8.9 References to more information

I have given a short description of what you may find useful in the following books, starting with searching and reviewing the literature.

Further reading

Hart, C. (2001) *Doing a Literature Search*. London: Sage. A whole book providing a guide on how to search the literature in the social sciences.
Hart, C. (1998) *Doing a Literature Review*. London: Sage. A guide through the multidimensional sea of academic literature with techniques on how to deal with the information when you have found it.
Ridley, D. (2012) *The Literature Review: A Step-by-Step Guide for Students*, 2nd edition. London: Sage. Does what it says on the cover!

On the Oxford Brookes University library catalogue there were 2350 references to information guides! Many of these were bibliographies devoted to a particular subject; you could search on your university or college catalogue for one relevant to your topic. Here are some that you may find useful, depending on your subject interest.

Herron, N. (2002) *The Social Sciences: A Cross-Disciplinary Guide to Selected Sources*, 3rd edition. Greenwood Village. CO: Libraries Unlimited.

Stebbins, L. (2005) *Student Guide to Research in the Digital Age: How to Locate and Evaluate Information Sources*. Greenwood Village, CO: Libraries Unlimited.

Allen, M. (2005) *Sports, Exercise, and Fitness: A Guide to Reference and Information Source*. Greenwood Village, CO: Libraries Unlimited.

Aby, S., Nalen, J. and Fielding, L. (2005) *Sociology: A Guide to Reference and Information Sources*. Greenwood Village, CO: Libraries Unlimited.

Jacoby, J. and Kibbee, J. (2007) *Cultural Anthropology: A Guide to Reference and Information Sources*. Greenwood Village, CO: Libraries Unlimited.

Kahl, C. (2007) *International Relations, International Security, and Comparative Politics: A Guide to Reference and Information Sources*. Greenwood Village, CO: Libraries Unlimited.

And there are a multitude of books to help you navigate the Internet. Always try to get the latest edition; they get out of date fast! The first one is specifically aimed at students and I think is really useful.

O'Dochartaigh, N. (2012) *Internet Research Skills*, 3rd edition. London: Sage.

Dolowitz, D., Buckler, S. and Sweeney F. (2008) *Researching Online*. Basingstoke: Palgrave Macmillan.

Shaw, M. (2007) *Mastering Online Research: A Comprehensive Guide to Effective and Efficient Search Strategies*. Cincinnati: F+W Publications.

9

How Can I Manage All the Notes?

9.1 Introduction

A good dissertation will be based on wide reading, and contain references to all the important literature in the chosen subject. This means that you will have to spend considerable time trawling through the library and other sources of information, collecting a whole range of relevant information and views on your subject. All this collected material will have to be recorded somehow and stored for further use in such a way that you can find what you want when you need it for your writing. This requires considerable organization on your part at the outset, to get your system up and running for when you start. Trying to change your system of recording, storage and retrieval of information halfway through will be an enormous task, and well worth avoiding! So you do need to have a sound system to start with, and to be very disciplined in following it through. This will ensure that you will not have to waste time searching for that oh-so-important but dimly remembered quotation, on a page you cannot

FIGURE 9.1   This is an information age

remember in a book you borrowed from the library three months ago, by an author whose name you have forgotten.

The following tips will give you a range of methods to choose from, which you can adapt to your own preferred working methods and the scale of your dissertation. You will find that the skills you develop in this activity will be of invaluable use in many other fields of endeavour. Remember, this is an information age, so acquiring a sound method of avoiding information overload by good management will be well worth the effort.

9.2 Reading techniques

Faced with a line of books on the library shelf that all seem to have some relevance to your subject, it is easy to become overwhelmed by the sheer amount of reading and recording that needs to be done. At this point you need to be aware of methods of 'filleting' a book in order to see quickly how much of it is relevant and what you need to record for later use, and different reading techniques relevant to different stages in the searching process. There is no need to read whole books in order to find the material you require. There are actually several ways of reading that can be used to good effect in the appropriate situations. Freeman and Mead (1999: 31–41) suggest the following levels of reading:

- *Scanning* – a focused approach, looking for one particular piece of information, as one would look in a dictionary or an encyclopaedia. Here the importance of the index is obvious. The essential thing is that you deliberately ignore everything except the one item for which you are scanning.
- *Skimming* – a quick review of the contents, introduction, review and abstract in order to get an idea of the content of the book to judge its relevance for your own area of study. A closer look would entail looking at the chapter headings, their introductions and conclusions, and even reading the first and last sentences of paragraphs to get a gist of the main arguments. A review of the diagrams, tables and illustrations also gives valuable clues to the content and approach.
- *Reading to understand* – involves detailed study of a passage, chapter or paper, in order to really absorb all the facts, ideas and arguments. It might be necessary to read it more than once, and to take notes to record and comment on the contents.

- *Word-by-word reading* – used when following detailed instructions when you need to understand every word. This will be needed when reading assignment and exam questions, and instructions on the use of research methods, such as surveys or experiments.
- *Reading for pleasure* – used when you read for relaxation and enjoyment, for example, when reading a novel or a comic book.

Another reading technique is called 'speed reading'. This involves a technique of using the eyes to scan pages of text very quickly, getting the brain to absorb the meaning without reading along the lines as you do normally. A ruler is used to guide the eyes' progress down the lines of the pages. This is a skill that undoubtedly needs a lot of practice, and is probably suitable only for the type of reading where you need to find out the outline of a story or argument, rather than particular details. In case you are interested, and have plenty of time to practise, I have added a few references to books on this in the last section of this chapter.

FIGURE 9.2 Word-by-word reading

9.3 Identifying useful material

First, you really do need to know what you are looking for. The easiest way to limit a search is to select a series of key words that are relevant to your subject. You may not know all of these at the outset, but you will develop a list as you become more familiar with the terminology used and the important concepts and issues involved. These will help you to track down the publications that might be relevant in the library.

Book titles generally contain the most important words used in the text, so this is the obvious place to start. Select the books that mention one or some of your key words in the title, then look at the list of contents at the beginning. Do your key words occur here? Are whole chapters dedicated to them? If so, it is worth investigating more closely. If not, look in the alphabetical index at the back. Are your key words mentioned, and if so, how many pages do they appear on? Look up some of the mentioned pages and read what is written about the word. Do this for several of your key words, and you will be able to decide whether there is enough of interest for you to use the book for further study. If your key words do not appear, or not in the sense or context that interests you, you can reject the book.

This technique can be used on any published information, though the convenient list of contents and index might not be present. Other useful places to look in a book or other publication are the introduction, the reviews on the book jacket, and perhaps the conclusions section. Academic papers normally have an abstract at the beginning that summarizes the contents very succinctly. They also often identify a list of key words. The use of key words when surfing the Internet is obviously a crucial part of the search process, as you read in Chapter 8.

If you find a nugget of information in the text that seems relevant, but you need more, look to see if there is a reference cited in that passage. Then, look up the reference details at the back of the chapter or book, and there you will have another publication to track down – hopefully with more of the information you need.

Getting to the required information on websites requires similar techniques. Look at the contents list for guidance. More sophisticated sites have a search function where you can insert your key words.

9.4 Organizing your system

So now you have a pile of books or other publications in front of you, all containing what is probably valuable information. You cannot be sure if you will use all of this, because you will only discover what is really essential when you get into the writing stage, but you need to record anything that might be useful. This is why it is important to compile your own 'library' of notes that you can draw on at later stages in your dissertation.

Before considering what notes to take and how to take them, let us first look at the formats you could use for recording and storing these notes.

There are two basic formats for notes:

Take note

- Paper-based
- Computer-based

Paper-based notes

The paper-based format needs no electronic equipment, though a few accessories make life easier. The principle behind this system is to write your notes on sheets of paper and then order the sheets in such a way that you can find the notes when you need them later.

You can use A4 sheets of paper and store them in ring binders. The idea is to store your notes under certain headings so that you can find what you have collected on that subject. The headings can be various, depending on your subject and how you will be approaching it. You will have to work out the best method yourself. The kinds of headings commonly used are:

- key words
- author names
- publication titles
- dates (particularly useful in historical studies)
- subjects – or aspects of the main subject.

Some academics advise you to make several copies of your notes so that you can file them under several headings. This way you can find the material whether, for example, you are looking for the writings of a particular author, or information about a particular subject or about a particular date. It is best to keep the notes short, that is, concentrated on one topic or aspect of the subject. Start another page when the topic or your notes change. This is because you may want to search out all your notes on one topic, so you can pull out all the pages under that topic heading. Several ring binders will be needed for storing your A4 sheets.

FIGURE 9.3   You can make and take your notes anywhere

The greatest advantage of this format is that you can make and take your notes anywhere without needing any equipment apart from paper and a pen. The main disadvantage is that you will need to rewrite the material from your handwritten notes on the computer when you use them.

Reference management software

The computer-based alternatives to writing notes and references on paper are quickly superseding the old methods because of their labour-saving features and ability to link with bibliographic databases. The current main ones are Endnote, Procite and Citation. Check if they are available on your university or college network, and which is the favoured program. Also get some training in how to use it to make use of all the features – it will save you time and frustration. There are also free programs available on the Internet (see http://en.wikipedia. org/wiki/Comparison_of_reference_management_software for comparisons).

The basic requirements of the system using a computer format are similar to those of a paper-based one. Notes should be short and on a single topic, they should be thoroughly referenced, and they should be stored under allotted key words. The major advantages of a computer-based system are that you have much more powerful search facilities; your notes are easily retrieved, copied, revised and edited; and you do not need to rewrite your reference information (lots of complicated formatting and punctuation), you can just copy it for lists etc. You can also store all your notes on a compact data stick or remotely on a server. You can easily produce lists of references based on the citations in your text, and adjust the referencing system to any format required. Some programs (such as Endnote) are linked to bibliographic databases, so you can download bibliographic data without typing anything.

The main disadvantage is that, in order to avoid copying out, you need to have your own computer with you wherever you need to make the notes – not such a problem if you own a laptop or tablet. Whichever program you decide to use, you need to work out exactly how you will do it, and test it before putting it into general use.

Notes content

There are several bits of information that you must record for each and every one of the notes that you take:

- The author(s) of the text – surname and first names. Perhaps the name on the book is the editor of the book, who has compiled a series of chapters or papers by various authors. In this case you will also need all the name(s) of the author(s) of the relevant text.
- The title of the book – including any subtitle. If it is a journal or a newspaper, you will have to record the full name of the journal or newspaper.
- If it is an article or a paper in an edited book, journal or newspaper with different authors for different chapters or papers, then the title of the relevant chapter or paper is also required.
- If it is a website, take note of the URL (web address) and the date accessed (in case it is later removed).
- The date of the publication (in a book, look on the reverse of the title page for this).

- The place it was published (ditto).
- The name of the publisher (ditto).
- The number(s) of the page(s) containing the information you have made notes from.
- Also useful is a reference to where you found the information, e.g. the library and the book code number, so that you can easily track it down again.
- You might also use material from lectures or conferences. In this case, give full details including speaker, title of talk, conference title, venue and date.

This information, attached to every note, will enable you to fully reference it, and to find the original information again if you need to.

So how will you set about recording the information that you want to collect?

9.5 Taking notes

The purposes of note taking are to make:

1. A record – when you develop your ideas and start writing you will need to have your collected information and ideas to hand. Your notes will be your own 'library' of relevant material. This will include direct quotations as well as transcripts.
2. A précis – to make the information manageable, it is usually necessary to distil the valuable essences relevant to your subject of study.
3. An interpretation – your own view of the value and quality of the information and opinions found in the literature is an important component of the dissertation. Recording these in your notes helps to invoke an analytical approach to reading.
4. A commentary – notes need not always be directly related to the pieces of text that you are reading. Often it is worth recording your thoughts in relation to your study as they occur. Often, flashes of inspiration or insight occur at unexpected moments, and are quickly forgotten if not written down immediately.

Making notes also helps you to concentrate on what you are reading, and to listen carefully at lectures and conferences.

Notes are really useful when you come to writing the first drafts of your dissertation. You can use them as a prompt to start; after all, you have already begun writing as soon as you have started taking notes. They can be used to help you structure your writing, perhaps by physically laying out the notes in sequence on a table.

FIGURE 9.4   Flashes of inspiration

Reviewing and reordering the sequence is simple and fast. The requirement that notes are single subject, short and well defined is obviously of
great value in this context.

There are many recommendations made by lecturers about how to actually
do note taking. Here are some dos and don'ts:

- Do ensure that you have a supply of your chosen medium for recording notes always to hand, or at least a notebook of some kind. Notes made on the back of an envelope *always* get lost!
- Don't make notes on the book or publication that you are reading: it spoils your reading and anyone else's later reading of the text, and loses the point of extracting information for your own 'library' of notes.
- Do use your own words. This demands not only that you have understood the text, but that you will understand what it means when you come to read it again. It is best to read the passage in question carefully, then put it aside as you make the notes from memory. This will also avoid any danger of plagiarism.
- Don't mix up direct quotations, your own notes summarizing the text, and your own com-mentary on the text (opinions, prompted ideas, comparisons, etc.). Make a separate note 'card' for each. Quotations should be short and make a significant point, or explain an important concept.
- Do keep notes to one subject or key word. This will help you greatly when you want to find everything you have noted on one subject or key word.
- Don't forget to insert all the reference information on each note, including page number where it can be found.
- Do sort your notes into your system as soon as possible, especially if you have made them in a non-standard format that needs transferring to your system (e.g. card system or computer database).
- Do make a list of all the publications you have referred to, using a standard format. You can generate this list automatically when using a bibliographic database program.

9.6 Chapter summary

Large parts of your dissertation will be based on notes that you make, most of which
come from the readings you have made. Using appropriate reading techniques – such
as scanning, reading to understand, word-by-word reading – will save you a lot of time
and enable you to review a large amount of literature. You can identify useful material
initially by selecting appropriate titles, and then checking the contents lists and indexes to
locate what you are looking for. Academic papers always have an abstract that summarizes the contents of the paper – a really time-saving feature. Tracking down references
found at the end of publications often leads to additional useful literature.

The purposes of note taking are to provide a record of what you have read or heard, to précis the material, to enable you to provide a commentary or interpretation of the matter. Note taking can be done either on paper or using a computer. Both share the same requirement for carefully noting all the information about the source and for allocating key words to each note. Notes are an invaluable resource when you start writing your chapters. They provide you with the raw material to forge into a finished work.

9.7 What should I do now?

You should, before you start reviewing the literature and taking notes, devise your personal system for recording, storing and retrieving them. The average dissertation might use 100–150 notes based on 40–50 references, so it is definitely worth getting a well-organized system in place. On the basis of what you have read above, explore the options for what format and medium to write your notes, how you will sort them into categories, and how you will store them and retrieve them as you need them.

Here is a set of questions that you should answer. It will provide a checklist to develop and test your system.

1. Will you use a paper-based system or a computer-based reference management system? This is a pretty fundamental decision as it is difficult to change formats once established. With the latter, although you do not necessarily need your own laptop, it does simplify the process and eliminate copying out notes. It also enables you to easily generate lists of references in any format at the touch of a button, and to simply access your notes for other writing tasks.

2. If you decide to use a paper-based system, will you print out standard forms on your sheets of paper? If you do so, you will be prompted to fill in the important reference details every time you start a new note.

3. If you decide to use a computer-based system, which reference management software will you use? You will have to find out which ones are readily available to you (check on your university or college intranet), and ideally choose one that you can install on your laptop if you have one.

4. How will you store your notes? This is not a problem with computer-based systems, apart from the issue of keeping backups in various formats (e.g. hard disk, data stick, server file). Paper-based formats need more thought. Keep in mind that you may want to search in different ways, e.g. by subject or by author. Consider colour coding and separate folders. You might even want to go to the extent of duplicating notes and filing under different headings.

5. How will you retrieve your notes? This is where the use of key words or subject categories becomes essential. In any system, if you can easily find all the notes you made on the particular aspect of your subject that you want to write about, you are halfway to producing your first draft.

FIGURE 9.5   How will you retrieve your notes?

Try out your system with a set of about 10–15 notes. Make real notes that will be useful to you anyway, and make them as diverse as possible, so as to test your storage and retrieval system thoroughly. You could even explain your system to a colleague and ask him or her to try to extract some specific piece of information: unfamiliarity with the notes will create a sterner test.

9.8 References to more information

First, some books about note taking and organizing your information. Most books about how to do research will have a section on this, but you may want to compare advice and approaches with those given in this chapter. The first two are examples of these; there are plenty more mentioned at the end of earlier chapters in this book.

Further reading

Blaxter, L., Hughes, C. and Tight, M. (2010) *How to Research*, 4th edition. Buckingham: Open University Press.
Leedy, P. and Ormrod, J. (2010) *Practical Research: Planning and Design*, 9th edition. New York: Pearson.

Here are some books more narrowly dedicated to taking notes and getting organized. The two books by Fry complement each other well.

McWhorter, K. (2009) *College Reading and Study Skill*, 11th edition. New York: Longman.
Fry, Ronald W. (1997) *Take Notes*. London: Kogan Page.
Fry, Ronald W. (2000) *Get Organized*, 2nd edition. Franklin Lakes, NJ: Career Press.
Open University (2007) *Reading and Taking Notes*. Buckingham: Open University Press.

Below is information about bibliographic database programs. Check what is available on your college/university network before you make an expensive decision to buy a program yourself.

Endnote. Institute for Scientific Information. www.endnote.com.
Procite. ISI Research Software. www.procite.com/pchome.html.
Citation. Oberon Development Ltd. www.citationline.net. Nice website with free download demo version.

Agrawal, A. (2009) *Endnote 1 -2 -3 Easy! Reference Manual for the Professional*, 2nd edition. Heidelberg: Springer.
Edhlund, B. (2007) *Manuscript Writing Using Endnote and Word*. Stallardlholmen: Form & Kunskap.

If you are interested in speed reading, here are some books. But beware, these skills take time and practice to perfect. Have you really got the time now?

Buzan, T. (2010) *The Speed Reading Book*. London: Pearson Education.
Smith, A. (2010) *Speed Reading Book: How to Master the Art of Speed Reading*. London: Smith Kindle Publishing.

10

What's All This About Ethics?

Chapter contents

10.1 Introduction

Ethics is about moral principles and rules of conduct. What have these got to do with writing a dissertation? Quite a lot actually; they focus on your behaviour towards other people and their work. You are not producing your dissertation in a vacuum. You definitely will be basing your information and ideas on work done by other people, and you may well be interacting with other people in a more personal way during your study. It is therefore important to avoid unfairly usurping other people's work and knowledge, invading their privacy or hurting their feelings.

Unless otherwise stated, what you write will be regarded as your own work; the ideas will be considered your own unless you say to the contrary. The worst offence against honesty in this respect is called plagiarism: directly copying someone else's work into your report, dissertation, etc. and letting it be assumed that it is your own. Equally serious is claiming sole authorship of work that is in fact the result of collaboration.

10.2 Honesty – acknowledging other people's work and avoiding plagiarism

An important part of a dissertation study is to find out what has already been written by other people on the chosen subject. You will be expected to collect and report on facts and ideas from a wide range of sources, so there is no need to feel that everything you write has to be 'original'. Even the greatest thinkers have 'stood on the shoulders of giants' in order to make their discoveries. Jean Renoir (1952), the French film producer, expressed his views on this very strongly when he talked in a filmed interview about his 1930s film *Une Partie de Campagne*, which he based on a story by Guy de Maupassant:

> Maupassant's story offered me an ideal framework on which to embroider. This notion of using a framework begs the question of plagiarism – something I whole-heartedly approve of. To achieve a new Renaissance, the State should encourage plagiarism. Anyone guilty of plagiarism should be awarded the Legion of Honour! I'm not joking: plagiarism served the world's great writers as well. Shakespeare reworked stories from Italian authors, amongst others, Corneille took Le Cid from Guillén de Castro, Molière ransacked the classics; and all were right to do so.

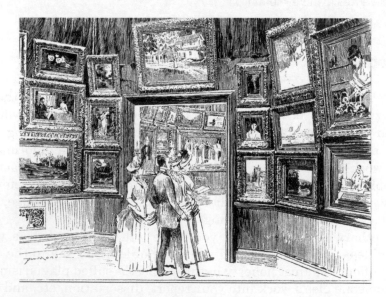

FIGURE 10.1   Other people's work can be an inspiration

This obviously has to be taken with a pinch of salt! There is, however, real truth in the view that other people's work can be an inspiration and guide to ones' own. The point is that the sources of work on which you base your writing must be acknowledged. Renoir made sure of this in the title of his film: *Une Partie de Campagne – de Guy de Maupassant*. In order to maintain an honest approach, there must therefore be a clear distinction between your ideas and writings and other people's.

Your university or college will have strict regulations covering the issues of plagiarism and collaboration, and you should make yourself familiar with these. These extracts from the Oxford Brookes University Student Conduct Regulations provide a typical example:

> Candidates must ensure that coursework submitted for assessment in fulfilment of course requirements is genuinely their own and is not plagiarized (borrowed, without specific acknowledgement, or stolen from other published or unpublished work).
>
> Quotations should be clearly identified and attributed, preferably by the use of one of the standard conventions for referencing. Assessed work should not be produced jointly unless the written instructions specify this. Such co-operation is cheating and any commonality of text is plagiarism.

The penalties which a module/subject leader may impose for plagiarism are:

1. a formal written warning; or
2. a reduction of marks for the piece of work; or
3. no marks for the piece of work; or
4. a 'fail' grade for the module concerned.

You may think that you could easily get away with copying some chunks of text from the Internet; after all, there are millions of pages to choose from. However, the source can easily be tracked down by your supervisor or marker using Turnitin, a web-based text-matching tool that allows academic staff to check students' work for improper use of sources or potential plagiarism by comparing it against enormous and continuously up-dated databases (including web pages and student work). Turnitin produces an 'Originality Report' for each submitted piece of work which indicates all the matches in the student assignment to the web-based sources on its database. Turnitin may be used as part of an investigation into an alleged case of plagiarism but its primary use is to support students' academic development and enhance good academic practice.

The penalties for transgressing college regulations, even inadvertently, are heavy; so how can problems be avoided? The solution lies in a good system of referencing and acknowledgement. Credit will be given for evidence of wide reading of relevant texts, so there is no need to be shy of quoting your sources. There are two ways of incorporating the work of others into your text: the first is by direct quotation, and the second by paraphrase. These can be referenced in several widely recognized systems, for example the Harvard system.

Generally, all systems identify the sources in an abbreviated form within the text to pinpoint the relevant sections, and cross-reference these to a full description in a list at the end of the chapter or dissertation, or in some cases in a footnote at the bottom of the page. You should decide on one system and then use it consistently. There might be advice given in your course description as to which system is preferred. For a full account of the practical aspects of how to do your referencing, refer to Chapter 17.

How much referenced material should you use? This depends on the nature of your dissertation. Obviously, if you are making a commentary on someone's writings, or comparing the published works of several people, it will be appropriate to have numerous references. In other cases, say a report on a fieldwork project, only a few may be sufficient to set out the background to the study. You may be able to get advice on this issue from your tutor.

Where does the boundary lie between paraphrasing (which requires referencing) and your own writing based on the ideas of others (which does not)? This is a matter of judgement. Substitution of a few words, reordering sentences, or cutting out a sentence here and there, are not enough to make it your own work. A sound method of avoiding accusations of plagiarism is to carefully read the source material, and then put it away out of sight. Rely on your memory and own words to describe and interpret the ideas.

Here is a brief example in two parts to demonstrate skills in paraphrasing, using a quotation from Leedy and Ormrod's book, *Practical Research* (2010).

First the quotation – a word-for-word copy of a section of their text. Note the citation at the end.

> Any research study involving human beings should respect participants' rights to privacy. Under no circumstances should a research report, either oral or written, be presented in such a way that others become aware of how a particular participant has responded or behaved (unless, of course, the participant has specifically granted permission, in writing, for this to happen). (Leedy and Ormrod, 2010: 102)

In the first example that follows, I have made a summary in my own words of the main points, which are attributed to the author. I kept the text in front of me so that I could make an accurate account. The length was reduced to just one sentence, and again there is the citation.

> Leedy and Ormrod (2010: 102) states that the privacy of human subjects must be maintained by making it impossible to attribute particular responses (unless written permission is given by the participants).

For my second example I put the text aside and wrote a commentary in my own words on the content, i.e. my interpretation of the issues raised. The source does not need to be cited in this case.

> Do anonymize the responses from your participants, unless you have written permission to make attributions.

If your dissertation were to be published, there are strict limitations as to how much direct quotation or illustrative material you are allowed to use without asking permission from the original author or copyright holder. For example, all poetry or song lyrics, as well as illustrations and figures, need permission, as does the quotation of more than about 400 words from a single prose work. However, for an unpublished student academic work like yours, these limits do not apply. Even more reason, then, to acknowledge your sources, in gratitude that you do not need to go through the process of gaining permissions!

10.3 Respect for other people

Many dissertation subjects require the getting of information from people, whether they are experts or members of the general public. This data collection may be in the form of interviews or questionnaires, but could also be types of experiments. Whenever dealing with other people, you must be sensitive to issues of privacy, fairness, consent, safety, confidentiality of information, impartiality, etc. This is actually quite a complex subject, and it requires real thought about how your plans for getting information or opinions from people can be carried out in a way that complies with all these ethical issues.

Below are some of the main aspects to check.

FIGURE 10.2   Getting information from other people

Inform people

Participants have a right to know why you are asking them questions and to what use you will put the information that they give you. Explain briefly before interviewing and add an explanatory introduction to questionnaires. If you will be conducting some kind of test or experiment, you should explain what methods you will use.

> *Example* – You are stopping people in the street to ask them where they have walked from and where they are going. Explain that you are conducting a college study to assess the pattern of pedestrian movements in the town centre.

Ask permission and allow refusal to participate

Do not assume that everyone is willing to help you in your research. Once they are informed about the project they should be clearly given the choice to take part or not. A more formal agreement like the one suggested in the previous section will be appropriate for extended projects or those of a sensitive or intimate nature.

Example – You want to test people's skills in balancing on a tightrope, depending on the tension of the rope. You will need to explain exactly what you wish them to do, safety measures taken, clothing and footwear required, time and place of the experiment, who will be observing, and other data required (e.g. age, weight, size, etc.). This will enable the possible participants to judge whether they want to take part or not.

Respect privacy through anonymity

Most surveys rely on the collection of data, the sources of which do not need to be personally identified. In fact, people are far more likely to give honest replies to questions if they remain anonymous. You should check that the way data are collected and stored ensures anonymity – omit names and addresses etc. Treat data as numbers wherever possible.

Example – You are distributing a questionnaire to households about vandalism and intimidation on a housing estate, asking questions about the levels and sources of the problems. To ensure anonymity, the questionnaires must not contain anything that may identify the respondent, e.g. even a family profile might do this. Delivery and collection of the questionnaires should also be considered to ensure that the information cannot get into the wrong hands.

Attribution

If anonymity is not desired or even possible, e.g. when obtaining particular views of named influential people, the information collected must be accurately attributed to the source. Agreement must be obtained that the opinions/ information given can be used in your dissertation.

Example – You are interviewing a leader of a trade union organization and the manager of a firm about an industrial dispute relating to a pension scheme. There must be no confusion in your account of the interviews about who said what. Ask before the interviews if you will be allowed to quote them in your dissertation.

Obtain authorization

It is good practice to send a draft of the parts of your work containing the views or information given by named sources to those concerned, asking them to check that your statements are accurate and that they are allowed to be included in your dissertation.

Example – In the above example, if the interviews are lengthy, and the opinions are contentious in what is probably a sensitive situation, you will gain respect and cover yourself against problems if you get a signed copy of the drafts of your accounts of the individual interviews from the respective people. This is absolutely necessary if you quote people directly. If you say you will do this in advance, you will be likely to get a less cautious response during the interview, as there is an opportunity for the interviewee to check for accuracy.

Fairness

In any tests or experiments, thought should be given to ensure that they are fair, and can be seen to be so. Participants will feel cheated if they perceive that they are not treated equally or are put at some kind of disadvantage.

Example – You have devised a simple test to gauge people's manual dexterity on equipment that can only be used by the right hand. Left-handed people will feel justifiably disadvantaged.

Avoid sexism

The way language is used can often lead to sexism, particularly the use of masculine labels when the text should actually refer to both men and women. Bias, usually towards the male, is also to be avoided in your research.

Example – Avoid the use of words such as 'manpower' rather than 'labour power', 'one-man show' rather than 'one-person show', and the generic 'he' or 'his' when you are referring to a person of either sex. Research bias can occur when you devise a study that assumes the 'boss' is a man, or that all primary school teachers are women.

Be punctual, convenient and brief

Punctuality, brevity and courteousness are essential qualities to help your efforts to gain information. Appointments should be made and kept. Time is a valuable commodity for almost everybody, so it will be appreciated if you regard it as such.

Example – You need to get expert information on the intricacies of management procedure in a hotel reception. You turn up three-quarters of an hour late, just at a time when a large crowd of business people (note – not businessmen) normally arrive to check in. You have missed your 'slot' and will cause real inconvenience if you start asking questions now.

Be diplomatic and avoid offence

On the whole, people are willing to help students in their studies. However, do not abuse this willingness by being arrogant and insensitive. You might be dealing with delicate issues, so try and get informed about the sensitivities and feelings of the participants. Above all, do not make people appear ridiculous or stupid!

Example – Don't regard yourself as the host of a chat show when, say, interviewing a group of elderly people in a residential home about their past lives. They may have very different views on what is proper to talk about, so avoid the pressure tactics and 'clever' questions used to prise out information not willingly given.

FIGURE 10.3   Avoid causing offence

Give thanks

Any help should be acknowledged with thanks, whether verbal or, in the case of questionnaires or letters asking for information, written.

> *Example* – Adding a short paragraph at the end of the questionnaire thanking the person for answering the questions is easily done, as is a simple expression of thanks before leaving after an interview.

10.4 Scientific honesty and subjectivity

This refers back to some of the issues raised in Chapter 5 about philosophy. The main point I want to make here is that of being scrupulously honest about the nature of your findings, even (and especially) if they tend to contradict the main thrust of your argument. Good quality research is not achieved by using the techniques of a spin doctor. Politicians might want to put the right kind of gloss on data collected for them in order to bolster their arguments, but this is not tolerated in academic work. Data should speak for themselves. Your analysis should reveal the message behind the data, and not be used to select only the results that are convenient for you.

As with most things, this kind of honesty can be more complicated than at first glance. Consider the following scenario.

> A study is being carried out of the use of animals in experiments to develop new products, in this case, an anti-ageing pill that may have useful properties for combating Alzheimer's disease. The data on the level of discomfort that the animals suffer, based on medical measurements and observations, are contradictory and difficult to quantify. The researcher carrying out the study feels that an anti-ageing pill is not really a medicine, so testing on animals is not justified. However, the experimenters argue that if many human lives can be prolonged by fighting off the horrible effects of Alzheimer's, then the slight suffering of some animals is justified.

How will the researcher present the data in an honest and balanced way?

It would be easy to present one side of the argument and stress the amount of suffering caused to animals in the search for an elixir of youth. That the animals suffer can be derived from the data. By interpreting the data on the animals' discomfort level as demonstrating cruelty, and by ignoring the likely medical benefits of the pill, a strong case could be made for discontinuing the experiments.

However, such certainty is not inherent in this situation. Much better, i.e. more honest, would be if the researcher discussed the issues driving the research, and the difficulty of gauging the level of suffering of the animals, and concentrated on assessing the strengths of the opposing arguments, taking into account the uncertainties of the data and of the eventual properties of the product.

If you can achieve a balanced view, it is probably not necessary to specifically state your personal attitude to the issues. However, there are situations where it is impossible to rise above the events and be a detached observer. For example, if you are a committed and active supporter of a ban on hunting with dogs, and make a study of this sport, you should declare your interest. Your arguments may well be valid and based on good evidence, but you are unlikely to seek supporting evidence for the other side!

Another way to ensure that you will avoid being accused of spin or false interpretation of the evidence is to present all the data you have collected as fully and clearly as possible. This may be the results of a questionnaire, measurements of activities or any other records relevant to your study. You can then base your analysis on these data, and it is open to the reader to judge whether your analysis is correct and whether your conclusions are valid. All arguments are open to challenge, but if you present the raw materials on which your arguments are based then at least the discussion has a firm foundation.

I can't help getting emotionally involved in issues that I am researching!

I don't, I keep a balanced view

How do you do that?

It's easy. I just stay sitting on the fence!

FIGURE 10.4

10.5   Chapter summary

The ethics of research fall into two categories, the first focused on one's honesty in writing and presenting the work, and the second on how one treats people who are the subject of your research.

The way to use the work of others in your report while avoiding plagiarism is to conform to a strict method of citation and referencing. There are several established systems for doing this, and you will have to find out from your course-specific instructions which one will be acceptable. The basic principle of all of these systems is to identify the parts of your text that use someone else's ideas or writings, and to attribute them to the original author, giving precise information of the source. Honesty in your writing is also achieved if you avoid bias, present a balanced argument and ensure that even data that is contrary to what you expect is presented.

Respect for other people is the basis for relations with the subjects of your research. They should be fully informed about the nature and purpose of the research in which they will be taking part, and must be guaranteed their confidentiality and anonymity. If names and opinions of the participant are to be attributable, then their permission must be sought. All necessary permissions must be obtained before the fieldwork is carried out, and you should deal with everyone fairly and courteously. This all requires careful forethought and planning.

10.6 What should I do now?

The issues of ethics pervade almost all aspects of academic work. Some of these issues are based on simple common sense and civilized behaviour, such as one's relationships with colleagues and other people. Others are more formal in character and require real organizational effort in order to fulfil the requirements, such as systematically employing a sound referencing system, and gaining permissions for use of information and activities. You should therefore:

- Check out your university or college regulations on plagiarism and advice offered on how to avoid it. You may be able to use Turnitin yourself to test the quality of your referencing.
- Consider carefully how you will use the written work and ideas of other people in your dissertation. Will you be discussing and comparing their ideas, or will you be developing ideas of your own based on those of others? You will probably do some of both.
- Consciously devise a method to differentiate between quotation, summary, paraphrase and commentary so that you will be aware of which mode you are writing in at any time.

- Examine your plans for getting information from other people. Systematically organize them to take account of all the relevant ethical issues. This will entail matters of procedure as well as content in written and verbal form. You can use the bullet points of aspects above as a checklist.

10.7 References to more information

Although ethical behaviour should underlie all academic work, it is in the social sciences (as well as medicine etc.) that the really difficult issues arise. Researching people and society raises many ethical questions that are discussed in the books below. The first book has a chapter that is short and useful. The second is a comprehensive guide for students. The other books on this list are far more detailed and really aimed at professional researchers – though the issues remain the same for whoever is doing it.

Further reading

Robson, C. (2011) *Real World Research: A Resource for Social Scientists and Practitioner-Researchers*, 3rd edition. Chichester: Wiley. See Chapter 9.

Oliver, P. (2010) *The Student's Guide to Research Ethics*. Maidenhead: Open University Press. This covers a wide range of ethical issues that you might face.

Laine, M. de (2000) *Fieldwork, Participation and Practice: Ethics and Dilemmas in Qualitative Research*. London: Sage. The main purposes of this book are to promote an understanding of the harmful possibilities of fieldwork, and to provide ways of dealing with ethical problems and dilemmas. Examples of actual fieldwork are provided that address ethical problems and dilemmas, and show ways of dealing with them.

Mauthner, M. (ed.) (2002) *Ethics in Qualitative Research*. London: Sage. This book explores ethical issues in research from a range of angles, including: access and informed consent, negotiating participation, rapport, the intentions of feminist research, epistemology and data analysis, tensions between being a professional researcher and a 'caring' professional. The book includes practical guidelines to aid ethical decision-making rooted in feminist ethics of care.

Geraldi, O. (ed.) (2000) *Danger in the Field: Ethics and Risk in Social Research*. London: Routledge. Read this if you are going into situations that might be hazardous.

There are also books about ethics that specialize in certain fields. Here are some examples. You could search out some in your subject perhaps.

Whitbeck, C. (2011) *Ethics in Engineering Practice and Research*. Cambridge: Cambridge University Press.

Farrell, A. (2005) *Ethical Research with Children*. Maidenhead: Open University Press.

Alderson, P. and Morrow, V. (2011) *The Ethics of Research with Children and Young People*. London: Sage.

McNamee, M. and Bridges, D. (eds) (2002) *The Ethics of Educational Research*. Oxford: Blackwell Publishers.

For nurses, the best resource is probably the online document from the Royal College of Nursing on Research Ethics: www.rcn.org.uk/__data/assets/pdf_file/0007/388591/003138.pdf (accessed 11 April 2013).

11

What Sorts of Data Will I Find?

11.1 The nature of data

'Data' means information, or according to the *Oxford English Dictionary*, 'known facts or things used as basis for inference or reckoning'. Strictly speaking, 'data' is the plural of 'datum', and so is always treated as plural. When you do any sort of enquiry or research, you will collect data of different kinds. In fact, data can be seen as the essential raw material of any kind of research. They are the means by which we can understand events and conditions in the world around us. This chapter discusses the nature of data and their different characteristics.

Data, when seen as facts, acquire an air of solidity and permanence, representing the truth. This is, unfortunately, misleading. Data are not only elusive, but also ephemeral. They may be a true representation of a situation in one place, at a particular time, under specific circumstances, as seen by a particular observer. The next day, all might be different. For example, a daily survey of people's voting intentions in a forthcoming general election will

FIGURE 11.1 How can you tell whether they are telling the truth about their intentions?

produce different results daily, even if exactly the same people are asked – because some change their minds according to what they have heard or seen in the interim period. If the same number of people is asked in a similar sample, a different result can also be expected. Anyway, how can you tell whether they are even telling the truth about their intentions? Data can therefore only provide a fleeting and partial glimpse of events, opinions, beliefs or conditions.

Not only are data ephemeral, but they are also corruptible. Inappropriate claims are often made on the basis of data that are not sufficient or close enough to the event. Hearsay is stated to be fact, second-hand reports are regarded as being totally reliable, and biased views are seized on as evidence. The further away you get from the event, the more likely it is that inconsistencies and inaccuracies creep in. Memory fades, details are lost, recording methods do not allow a full picture to be given, and distortions of interpretations occur. Harold Pinter, the English playwright, described the situation like this:

> Apart from any other consideration, we are faced with the immense difficulty, if not impossibility, of verifying the past. I don't mean merely years ago, but yesterday, this morning. What took place, what was the nature of what took place, what happened? If one can speak of the difficulty of knowing what in fact took place yesterday, one can I think treat the present in the same way. What's happening now? We won't know until tomorrow or in six months' time, and we won't know then, we'll have forgotten, or our imagination will have attributed quite false characteristics to today. A moment is sucked away and distorted, often even at the time of its birth. We will all interpret a common experience quiet differently, though we prefer to subscribe to the view that there's a shared common ground all right, but that it's more like a quicksand. Because 'reality' is quite a strong firm word we tend to think, or to hope, that the state to which it refers is equally firm, settled and unequivocal. It doesn't seem to be, and in my opinion, it's not worse or better for that. (Pinter, 1998: 21)

It is therefore a rash researcher who insists on the infallibility of his or her data, and of the findings derived from them. A measure of humility in one's belief in the accuracy of knowledge, and also practical considerations which surround the research process, dictate that the outcomes of research tend to be couched in 'soft' statements, such as 'it seems that', 'it is likely that', 'one is led to believe that', etc. This does not mean, however, that progress towards useful 'truths' cannot be achieved.

It is important to be able to distinguish between different kinds of data, because their nature has important implications for their reliability and for the sort of analysis to which they can be subjected. Data that have been observed, experienced or recorded close to the event are the nearest one can get to the truth, and are called *primary data*. Written sources that interpret or record primary data are called *secondary sources*. For example, you have a more approximate and less complete knowledge of a political demonstration if you read the newspaper report the following day than if you were at the demonstration and had seen it yourself. Not only is the information less abundant, but it is coloured by the commentator's interpretation of the facts.

Another distinct pair can be made between types of data. Much information about science and society is recorded in the form of numbers, e.g. temperatures, bending forces, population densities, cost indices, etc. The nature of numbers allows them to be manipulated by the techniques of statistical analysis. This type of data is called *quantitative data*. In contrast, there is a lot of useful information that cannot be reduced to numbers. People's opinions, feelings, ideas and traditions need to be described in words. Words cannot be reduced to averages, maximum and minimum values or percentages. They record not quantities, but qualities. Hence they are called *qualitative data*. Given their distinct characteristics, it is evident that when it comes to analysing these two forms of data, quite different techniques are required.

Let us examine the nature of these two pairs of characteristics of data.

FIGURE 11.2 Population densities

135

11.2 Primary and secondary data

Primary data

Primary data are present all around us. Our senses deal with them all our waking lives – sounds, visual stimuli, tastes, tactile stimuli, etc. Instruments also help us to keep track of factors that we cannot so accurately judge through our senses: thermometers record the exact temperature, clocks tell us the exact time, and our bank statements tell us how much money we have. Primary data are as near to the truth as we can get about things and events. Seeing a football match with your own eyes will certainly get you nearer to what happened than reading a newspaper report about it later. Even so, the truth is still somewhat elusive – 'Was the referee really right to award that penalty? It didn't look like a handball to me!'

There are many ways of collecting and recording primary data. Some are more reliable than others. It can be argued that as soon as data are recorded, they become secondary data owing to the fact that someone or something had to observe and interpret the situation or event and set it down in the form of a record, i.e. the data have become second-hand. But this is not the case. The primary data are not the actual situation or event, but a record of it, from as close to it as possible – that is, the first and most immediate recording. 'A researcher assumes a personal responsibility for the reliability and authenticity of his or her information and must be prepared to answer for it' (Preece, 2000: 80). Without this kind of recorded data it would be difficult to make sense of anything but the simplest phenomenon and be able to communicate the facts to others.

FIGURE 11.3 First and most immediate recording

So, what sorts of primary data are there? I can think of four basic types:

- Observation – records, usually of events, situations or things, of what you have experienced with your own senses, your eyes, ears, etc., perhaps with the help of an instrument, e.g. camera, tape recorder, microscope, etc.
- Participation – data gained by experiences can perhaps be seen as an intensified form of observation, e.g. the experience of learning to drive a car tells you different things about cars and traffic than just watching.

- Measurement – records of amounts or numbers, e.g. population statistics, instrumental measurements of distance, temperature, mass, etc.
- Interrogation – data gained by asking and probing. For example, information about people's beliefs, motivations, etc.

These can be collected, singly or together, to provide information about virtually any facet of our life and surroundings. So, why do we not rely on primary data for all our research? After all, they get as close as possible to the truth. There are several reasons, the main ones being time, cost and access. Collecting primary data is a time-consuming business. As more data usually means more reliability, the efforts of just one person will be of limited value. Organizing a huge survey undertaken by large teams would overcome this limitation, but at what cost? Also, it is not always possible to get direct access to the subject of research: for example, many historical events have left no direct evidence.

Secondary data

Secondary data are data that have been interpreted and recorded. We could drown under the flood of secondary data that assails us every day. News broadcasts, magazines, newspapers, documentaries, advertising, the Internet, etc. all bombard us with information wrapped, packed and spun into digestible soundbites or pithy articles. We are so used to this that we have learned to swim, to float above it all and only really pay attention to the bits that interest us. This technique, learned through sheer necessity and quite automatically put into practice every day, is a useful skill that can be applied to speed up your data collection for your dissertation.

Chapter 8 discusses the sources of secondary information; here we will look at the different types of secondary data that you might want to uncover. Depending on the subject of your choice, particular types of data will probably be more important to you than others. The descriptions given below will help you to decide where to focus your search efforts.

Books, journal papers, magazine articles, newspapers present information in published written form. The quality of the data depends on the source and the methods of presentation. For detailed and authoritative information on almost any subject, go to refereed journals: all the papers will have been vetted by leading experts in the subject. Other serious journals, such as some professional and trade journals, will also have authoritative articles by leading figures, despite the tendency of some to put emphasis on one side of the issues, e.g. a steel federation journal will support arguments for the use of steel rather than other building materials. There are magazines for every taste, some entirely flippant, others with useful and reliable information. The same goes for books – millions of them! They range from the most erudite and deeply researched volumes, e.g. specialist encyclopaedia and academic tomes, to ranting polemics and commercial pap.

FIGURE 11.4   So gullible as to believe everything we read

It is therefore always important to make an assessment of the quality of the information or opinions provided. You actually do this all the time even without noticing it. We have all learned not to be so gullible as to believe everything that we read. A more conscious approach entails reviewing the evidence that has been presented in the arguments. When no evidence is provided, on what authority does the writer base his or her statements? It is best to find out who are the leading exponents of the subject you are concentrating on. Apart from getting marks for recognizing these and referring to them, you will be able to rely on the quality of their writings. At this stage of your studies, you are not expected to challenge the experts – leave this for when you do a PhD!

Television broadcasts, films, radio programmes, recordings of all sorts provide information in an audio-visual non-written form. The assertion that the camera cannot lie is now totally discredited, so the same precautions need to be taken in assessing the quality of the data presented. There is a tendency, especially in programmes aimed at a wide public, to over-simplify issues. Also, the powerful nature of these media can easily seduce one into a less critical mood. Emotions can be aroused that cloud one's better judgement. Repeated viewings help to counter this.

The Internet and DVDs combine written and audio-visual techniques to impart information. Remember the issues raised in Chapter 8 about assessing the accuracy of any data presented on the World Wide Web.

You cannot always be present at an event, but other people might have experienced it. Their accounts may be the nearest you can get to an event. Getting information from several witnesses will help to pin down the actual facts of the event.

It is good practice, and especially necessary with secondary data, to compare the data from different sources. This will help to identify bias, inaccuracies and pure imagination. It will also show up different interpretations that have been made of the event or phenomenon. Far from being an annoyance, this could provide a rich subject of debate in your dissertation. Academic writing thrives on controversy. You will thus have the opportunity to weigh up the evidence, to set up your argument, and to come to your own conclusions on the matter.

11.3 Quantitative and qualitative data and levels of measurement

The other main dual categories applied to data refer, not to their source, but to their nature. Can the data be reduced to numbers or can they be presented only in words? It is important to make a distinction between these two types of data because it affects the way that they are collected, recorded and analysed. Numbers can provide a very useful way of compressing large amounts of data, but if used inappropriately they lead to spurious results. So how can these two categories be distinguished?

Quantitative data

Quantitative data have features that can be measured, more or less exactly. Measurement implies some form of magnitude, usually expressed in numbers. As soon as you can deal with numbers, then you can apply mathematical procedures to analyse the data. These might be extremely simple, such as counts or percentages, or more sophisticated, such as statistical tests or mathematical models.

Some forms of quantitative data are obviously based on numbers: population counts, economic data, scientific measurements, to mention just a few. There are, however, other types of data that initially seem remote from quantitative measures but can be converted to numbers. For example, people's opinions about fox hunting might be difficult to quantify. But if, in a questionnaire, you give a set choice of answers to the questions on this subject, then you can count the various responses. The data can then be treated as quantitative.

FIGURE 11.5   People's opinion about fox hunting

Typical examples of quantitative data are census figures (population, income, living density, etc.), economic data (share prices, gross national product, tax regimes, etc.), performance data (sport statistics, medical measurements, engineering calculations, etc.) and all measurements in scientific endeavour.

There are different ways of measuring data, depending on the nature of the data. These are commonly referred to as *levels of measurement* – nominal, ordinal, interval and ratio.

Nominal If you have a diverse collection of different animals, you could sort them into groups of the same type, e.g. lion, tiger, elephant, giraffe, etc. This most basic level of measurement is called nominal (i.e. referring to names). You might think that there is not much mathematical analysis you can apply to a list of names – counting the number of names and the number of cases in each category is about it! However, you can represent this information on a bar graph to compare the different sizes of the groups. You can also compare percentages of each group to the total, or one to another, and find the mode (the value that occurs most frequently in the groups). If you have two types of nominal measurement of a group, e.g. types of front teeth (sharp and pointy or flat and blunt) and eating habits (carnivore, herbivore, mixed), you can use the chi-squared statistical test to show up the differences between the expected and the observed values (read more about straightforward statistical tests in Chapter 14). Common uses of the nominal level of measurement in research are male/female, religious affiliations, racial types, occupations, naming of chemicals, plant species, building types, etc.

Ordinal If the animals were well behaved, you could perhaps stand them in a row in order of height. Now you have measured them in an ordinal fashion, i.e. put them into an order – big to small – by comparing bigger and smaller rather than actually measuring their size. They

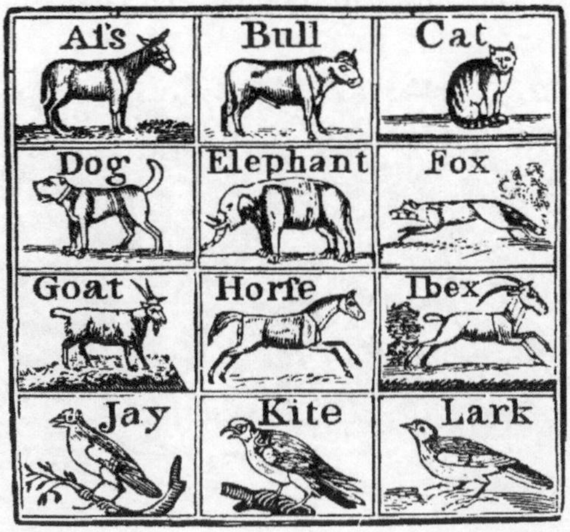

FIGURE 11.6   Nominal

probably will not be in equal steps of size; there may be a few very big or very small animals, and a lot somewhere near the middle. Now you can analyse data measured at this level by finding the mode and the median (in this case the middle size). You can also determine the percentage or percentile rank, and again, if you have two types of measurement (e.g. size and fierceness), you can use the chi-squared test. You can also show relationships by means of rank correlation. Examples of the ordinal level of measurement are levels of education (none, primary, secondary, college or university), skills (unskilled, semi-skilled, skilled), clothes sizes (S, M, L, XL, XXL, and nowadays even XXXL), and many devised especially for multiple-choice answers to questionnaires (like very much, like, neutral, dislike, dislike very much).

Interval If you ask some people how much they like the different animals in your collection, scoring them in a range from 1–10 (the higher the more liked), then you will be getting them to measure on an interval scale. Unlike the uneven steps in animal sizes, the equal steps in this measurement scale give an accurate gauge of the distance between levels of liking, e.g. you can work out an average score for each animal and get an accurate comparison of their popularity. However, as there is no meaningful nought, you cannot say that a score of 4 indicates half the popularity of a score of 8. This would be like saying that a room with a temperature of 45 °F is half as hot as one measured at 90 °F. Actually, temperature is a good example of an interval scale: in neither Fahrenheit nor Celsius measures does 0° mean a total absence of warmth. You can, however, truthfully say that the difference between scores of 4 and 8 and between 2 and 6 is the same, just as you can say that the difference between 45 °F and 90 °F and between 65 °F and 110 °F is the same. You can use additional quite sophisticated statistical tests on this level of measurement (e.g. standard deviation, *t*-test, *F*-test and the product moment correlation).

Ratio If you counted how many lions, tigers, elephants, giraffes, etc. you had in your collection, then you would be using the ratio level of measurement. Here the nought will mean no animals. Any kind of measurement that has a meaningful nought falls into this category, e.g. distances in miles, light measurement in lux, age in years – you will be able to think of many more yourself. The distinctive quality of the ratio level of measurement is that you can express values in terms of multiple and fractional parts, e.g. half as big, three times as expensive, etc. This is the most versatile level of measurement, open to a wide range of statistical tests, but I will not bore you with the names of them all!

Qualitative data

Qualitative data cannot be accurately measured and counted, and are generally expressed in words rather than numbers. The study of human beings and their societies and cultures requires many observations to be made that are to do with identifying, understanding and interpreting ideas, customs, mores, beliefs and other essentially human activities and attributes. These cannot be pinned down and measured in any exact way. These kinds of data are therefore descriptive in character, and rarely go beyond the nominal and ordinal levels of measurement.

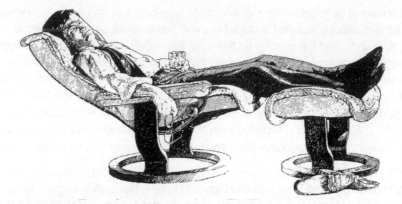

FIGURE 11.7   Concepts such as comfort, while elusive, are nonetheless detectable

This does not mean that they are any less valuable than quantitative data; in fact their richness and subtlety lead to great insights into human society.

Words, and the relationships between them, are far less precise than numbers. This makes qualitative research more dependent on careful definition of the meaning of words, the development of concepts and the plotting of inter-relationships between variables. Concepts such as poverty, comfort, friendship, etc., while elusive to measure, are nonetheless real and detectable.

Typical examples of qualitative data are literary texts, minutes of meetings, observation notes, interview transcripts, documentary films, historical records, memos and recollections, etc. Some of these are records taken very close to the events or phenomena, while others may be remote and highly edited interpretations. As with any data, judgements must be made about their reliability. Qualitative data, because they cannot be dispassionately measured in a standard way, are more susceptible to varied interpretations and valuation. In some cases even, it is more interesting to see what has been omitted from a report than what has been included. You can best check the reliability and completeness of qualitative data about an event by obtaining a variety of sources of data relating to the same event; this is called triangulation.

The distinction between qualitative and quantitative data is one of a continuum between extremes. You do not have to choose to collect only one or the other. In fact, there are many types of data that can be seen from both perspectives. For example, a questionnaire exploring people's political attitudes may provide a rich source of qualitative data about their aspirations and beliefs, but might also provide useful quantitative data about levels of support for different political parties. What is important is that you are aware of the types of data that you are dealing with, during collection or analysis, and that you use the appropriate levels of measurement.

11.4   Chapter summary

Data are the raw material of research, though they are often ephemeral, difficult to understand and ambiguous. Data come from two basic sources, primary and secondary.

Primary data are those that are collected directly from the field, usually through observation, participation, measurement or interrogation. You gain direct experience through your senses of sight, hearing, feeling, smelling and even perhaps tasting. The nearer to the event or phenomena you can get, the more accurate the data tend to be.

Secondary data are those that have been recorded and interpreted by others. This is usually in the form of printed information or based on other media such as film, broadcasts and recordings of all sorts. It is important to verify the source of the data to judge their accuracy and freedom from bias. The different interpretation made by people is often a fruitful subject of discussion.

Data are of two major types, quantitative and qualitative.

Quantitative data are those that can be counted or mathematically manipulated, usually with statistical methods. The method of measurement – nominal, ordinal, interval and ratio – is an important feature of these data, as it determines the extent to which they can be statistically analysed.

Qualitative data cannot be accurately measured, and words rather than numbers are used in their analyses. This form of data is related to the ideas, opinions, habits, customs and beliefs of people, so it depends on individual interpretation and reasoned argument in order to make sense of them.

11.5 What should I do now?

You will soon have to begin collecting information about your topic of research. When doing your background reading, you have probably already seen what information has been collected and analysed by other people. This could give a good indication of what kind of data you will be searching for. Consider the types of data that you might, or are planning to, collect and first ask yourself the questions in Figure 11.8 overleaf:

These might be surprisingly difficult questions to answer, as it is not always obvious what data will be required and from where they can be obtained. You might well have to spend some time thinking about this. It is a good idea to make some lists of data you will need to collect, and then try to sort them into categories: primary and secondary; quantitative and qualitative. These pairs are not connected, so do the same exercise with each pair.

If, for example, you are interested in the types and quality of nursing care in old people's homes, the data might be already available in statistics collected by

- Has the information you want already been recorded somewhere by someone else?

- Or do you have to go out to collect the information yourself directly from people or by observing phenomena?

- Are the data you will collect easily quantifiable and measureable?

- Or are they difficult to describe and pin down exactly?

FIGURE 11.8

the government or other organizations (secondary data). On the other hand, you may want to pinpoint particular homes to see how these compare (primary data). How you measure the type and quality of nursing care is not easy to do in a general way. What does 'type of nursing care' mean? Can you break it down into several categories (nominal measurement) or into degrees of care (ordinal measurement)? Both of these will be quantitative data in the sense that you are putting some kind of measurement to them, though you will have to make a qualitative assessment in order to fit them into these orders. How do you measure quality? Can you do it by counting the number of nurses and the hours they are in attendance (quantitative data) or will you assess the attitudes of the nurses to the patients by observing their behaviour (qualitative data)?

Very often, unmeasurable, abstract concepts such as effectiveness, efficiency, etc. have to be broken down into components in order to apply them in a meaningful way to your investigation. Some of these components will be measurable and dealt with quantitatively; others will be qualitative and rely on descriptions and comparisons. So if you are using general abstract terms like this in your dissertation title, and in the questions you are posing, ask what they mean in the context you are using them. Try to see how they can be broken down into less abstract components that can be studied and measured more easily.

You are likely to end up with a variety of data types you need to collect. This is altogether normal, and actually an advantage, as you can then demonstrate to the examiner of your dissertation how well you can deal with the collection and analysis of a range of different kinds of data.

11.6 References to more information

What counts as data, and what to do with them, are a big subject in research and get dealt with exhaustively in most books about academic writing, which can be overwhelming at this stage of your studies. Below are some useful other ways of looking at this aspect, without getting too deeply into technicalities. If you have other books about research to hand, look up the index to see what they have to say about data.

Further reading

Leedy, P. and Ormrod, J. (2010) *Practical Research: Planning and Design*, 9th edition. New York: Pearson. Chapter 5 provides a rather nice philosophical approach to the nature of data.

Blaxter, L., Hughes, C. and Tight, M. (2010) *How to Research*, 4th edition. Buckingham: Open University Press. The first part of Chapter 8 provides another angle on data and its forms.

12

How Do I Collect Data?

12.1 Where are the necessary data?

Data (the plural form of 'datum') are the raw materials of research. You need to mine your subject in order to dig out the ore in the form of data, which you can then interpret and refine into the gold of conclusions. So, how can you, as a prospector for data, find the relevant sources in your subject?

Although we are surrounded by data, in fact bombarded with them every day from TV, posters, radio, newspapers, magazines and books, it is not so straightforward to collect the correct data for our purposes. It needs a plan of action that identifies and uses the most effective and appropriate methods of data collection. This chapter briefly explains the most common methods. You should read this with your research problem in mind, so that you can select the most promising approaches for further investigation. As data collection must be quite rigorous to ensure that you have enough of the right data, you will probably need to follow up the details of the chosen methods in books providing more comprehensive guidance. A list is provided at the end of this chapter. Whatever subject you are doing, collecting secondary data will be a must. You will inevitably need to ascertain the background to your research question/problem, and also get an idea of the current theories and ideas. No type of project is done in a vacuum, not even a pure work of art. Collecting primary information is much more subject-specific, so you will have to judge what is appropriate here. Consider whether you need to get information from people, in single or large numbers, or whether you will need to observe and/ or measure things or phenomena. You may need to do several of these: for example, in healthcare you may be examining both the people and their treatments, or in education you may be looking at both the education system and the building and its effects on the pupils.

You are probably wasting your time if you amass data that you are unable to analyse, either because you have too much, or because you have insufficient or inappropriate analytical skills or methods to make the analysis. I say probably, because research is not a linear process, so it is not easy to predict exactly how many data will be 'enough'. What will help you to judge the type

FIGURE 12.1 Wasting your time if you amass data that you are unable to analyse

of and amount of data required is to decide on the methods that you will use to analyse them (see Chapters 14 and 15 for this). In turn, the decision on the appropriateness of analytical methods must be made in relation to the nature of the research problem and the specific aims of the research project. This should be evident in your overall argument that links the research question/problem with the necessary data to be collected and the type of analysis that needs to be carried out in order to reach valid conclusions.

12.2 Collecting secondary data

You have already been doing this to some extent when preparing the ground-work for your dissertation. All subjects require secondary data for the back-ground to the study. Others rely greatly on them for the whole project, for example, when doing a historical study (i.e. of any past events, ideas or objects, even the very recent past). Numerous other subjects might rely heav-ily on secondary data such as economics, politics, geography and many others.

There are numerous types of secondary data, the main being documentary sources in the form of written and non-written materials, and survey data in the form of statistical information. They can be quantitative or qualitative in nature.

- Written materials – reports, production records, minutes of meetings, accounts, letters, books, journals, magazines, government publications, etc.
- Non-written materials – television and radio programmes, videos, films, music, works of art, etc.
- Survey data – statistical data from government census on, for example, unemployment, education, economics, market surveys, sales figures, employment attitudes, etc.

The advantages of using sets of secondary data are that they have been pro-duced by expert researchers, often with large budgets and extensive resources, way beyond the means of a single student, so they cut out the need for time-consuming fieldwork. If collected over a long period, they enable longitudinal studies (tracing developments over time). Secondary data can be used to compare with primary data you have collected in order to triangulate the findings and put your data into a larger context. The disadvantage is that you miss out on the experience and skills gained by having to generate your own primary data from real-life situations.

One of the main problems faced by the researcher seeking historical and recorded data is that of locating and accessing them. Another is often that of authenticating these sources, and another is the question of interpretation. Locating historical data can be an enormous topic. Activities can involve any-thing from unearthing city ruins in the desert to rummaging through dusty archives in an obscure library or downloading the latest government statistical data from the Internet. Even current data might be difficult to get hold of. For instance, many current economic data are restricted and expensive to buy. It is impossible to give a full description of sources that might be relevant to undergraduate student research, as the detailed nature of the subject of research determines the appropriate source, and, of course, the possible range of subjects is enormous. However, here are some of the principal sources.

Libraries and archives These are generally equipped with sophisticated catalogue systems which facilitate the tracking down of particular pieces of data or enable a trawl to be made to identify anything which may be relevant. International computer networks can make remote searching possible. See your own library specialists for the latest techniques. Apart from these modernized libraries and archives, much valuable historical material is contained in more obscure and less organized collections, in remote areas and old houses and institutions. The attributes of a detective are often required to track down relevant material, and that of a diplomat to gain access to private or restricted collections.

Museums and collections These often have efficient cataloguing systems that will help your search. However, problems may be encountered with searching and access in less organized and restricted and private collections. Larger museums often have their own research departments that can be of help.

Government departments and commercial/professional bodies These often hold much statistical information, both current and historic.

The Internet This is a constantly expanding source of information of all types, used by most official and professional bodies to disseminate data and statistics of every kind.

The field Not all historical artefacts are contained in museums. Ancient cities, buildings, archaeological digs, etc. are available for study *in situ*. Here, various types of observation will be necessary to record the required data.

Two issues will be important when you collect secondary information, particularly of a historical nature. The first is the issue of authenticity. Authentication of historical data can be a complex process, and is usually carried out by experts (one of which you might have to become!). A wide range of techniques are used, for example, textual analysis, carbon dating, paper analysis, locational checks, cross-referencing and many others. The second is the issue of interpretation. Although interpretation is an integral part of the analysis of the data, a correct interpretation of the historical evidence should be made before any real analysis is done. For example, a detailed historical analysis of an event will be worthless if the historical data have not been correctly interpreted, for example, if you did not detect that the evidence was highly biased.

The wealth of purely statistical data, especially those of more recent date, provides a powerful resource for research into many subjects. You will often

FIGURE 12.2   Not all historical artefacts are contained in museums

find, however, that the data recorded are not exactly in the form that you require (for example, when making international comparisons on housing provision, the data might be compiled in different ways in the different countries under consideration). In order to extract the exact data you require, you will have to extrapolate from the existing data.

12.3 Collecting primary data

This entails going out and collecting information by observing, recording and measuring the activities and ideas of real people, or perhaps watching animals, or inspecting objects and experiencing events. This process of collecting primary data is often called survey research.

You should only be interested in collecting data that are required in order to investigate your research problem. Even so, the amount of relevant information you *could* collect is likely to be enormous, so you must find a way to limit the amount of data you collect to achieve your aims. The main technique for reducing the scope of your data collection is to study a sample, i.e. a small section of the subjects of your study. There are several things you must consider in selecting a sample, so before discussing the different methods of data collection, let us first deal with the issue of sampling.

12.4 Sampling

When you organize any kind of limited survey to collect information, or when you choose some particular cases to study in detail, the question that inevitably arises is: how representative will the collected information be of the whole population? In other words, will the relatively few people you ask, or situations you study, be typical of all the others?

When we talk about 'population' in research, it does not necessarily mean a number of people. Population is a collective term used to describe the total quantity of cases of the type that are the subject of your study. So a population can consist of cases that are objects, people, organizations or even events, e.g. school buildings, miners, police forces, revolutions.

Where the objects of study are big and complex, for example, towns or businesses, it might only be possible to study one or very few cases. Here, a case study approach is applicable, which enables a detailed investigation into the selected case or cases. You will have to judge which cases you choose on the basis of how typical they are of their type (population).

If you wish to survey the opinions of the members of a small club, there might be no difficulty in getting information from each member, so the results of the survey will represent the opinions of the whole club membership. However, if you wish to assess the opinions of the members of a large trade union, apart from organizing a national ballot, you will have to devise some way of selecting a sample of the members who you are able to question,

FIGURE 12.3   No difficulty in getting information from each member

and who are a fair representation of all the members of the union. Sampling must be done whenever you can gather information from only a fraction of the population of a group or a phenomenon that you want to study. Ideally, you should try to select a sample that is free from bias. You will see that the type of sample you select will greatly affect the reliability of your subsequent generalizations.

There are basically two types of sampling procedure – random and non-random. Random sampling techniques give the most reliable representation of the whole population, while non-random techniques, relying on the judgement of the researcher or on accident, cannot generally be used to make accurate generalizations about the whole population.

Random sampling

Random sampling at its simplest is like a competition draw. Represent all the cases in your population on slips of paper, put them into a hat and draw out the slips in a random fashion. As with all samples, the larger the sample, the better. However, the issues are not always as simple as this. Here are a few basic guidelines.

First, a question should be asked about the nature of the population: is it homogeneous or are there distinctly different classes of cases within it? Different sampling techniques are appropriate for each. The next question to ask is which process of randomization will be used? The following gives a guide to which technique is suited to the different population characteristics.

Simple random sampling This is used when the population is uniform or has similar characteristics in all cases, e.g. a production of chocolate bars from which random samples are selected to test their quality.

Simple stratified sampling This should be used when cases in the population fall into distinctly different categories (strata), e.g. a business whose employees are of three different categories – sales, production and administration. An equally sized randomized sample is obtained from each stratum separately to ensure that each is equally represented. The samples are then combined to form the complete sample from the whole population.

Proportional stratified sampling Used when the cases in a population fall into distinctly different categories (strata) of a known proportion of that population, e.g. a university in which 40 per cent of students study arts and 60 per cent study sciences. A randomized sample is obtained from each stratum separately, sized according to the proportion of each stratum to the whole population, and then combined as previously to form the complete sample from the population.

153

Cluster sampling or area sampling Here, cases in the population form clusters by sharing one or some characteristics but are otherwise as heterogeneous as possible, e.g. shoppers at supermarkets. They are all shoppers, each cluster experiencing a distinct supermarket, but individuals vary as to age, sex, nationality, wealth, social status, etc.

Systematic sampling This is used when the population is very large and of no known characteristics, e.g. the population of a town. Systematic sampling procedures involve the selection of units in a series (for example, on a list) according to a system. Perhaps the simplest is to choose every *n*th case on a list, for example, every 50th person in a telephone directory or list of rate-payers. It is important to pick the first case randomly, i.e. don't necessarily start counting from the first name on the list. The type of list is also significant – not everyone in the town owns a telephone or is a rate-payer.

Non-random sampling

Non-random sampling can be useful for certain studies, but it provides only a weak basis for generalization.

Accidental sampling or convenience sampling This involves using what is immediately available, e.g. studying the building you happen to be in, examining the work practices in your firm, etc. There are no ways of checking to see if this kind of sample is in any way representative of others of its kind, so the results of the study can be applied only to that sample.

Quota sampling Used regularly by reporters interviewing on the streets, quota sampling is an attempt to balance the sample interviewed by selecting responses from equal numbers of different respondents, e.g. equal numbers from different political parties. This is an unregulated form of sampling, as there is no knowledge whether the respondents are typical of their parties. For example, Labour respondents might just have come from an extreme left-wing rally.

Theoretical sampling A useful method of getting information from a sample of the population that you think knows most about a subject. A study on homelessness could concentrate on questioning people living in the street. This approach is common in qualitative research where statistical inference is not required.

Another three methods can be briefly mentioned. *Purposive sampling* is where the researcher selects what he or she thinks is a 'typical' sample. *Systematic matching sampling* is when two groups of very different size are compared by selecting a number from the larger group to match the number and characteristics of the smaller one. Finally, the *snowball technique* is when you contact a small number of members of the target population and get them to introduce you to others, e.g. of a secret society.

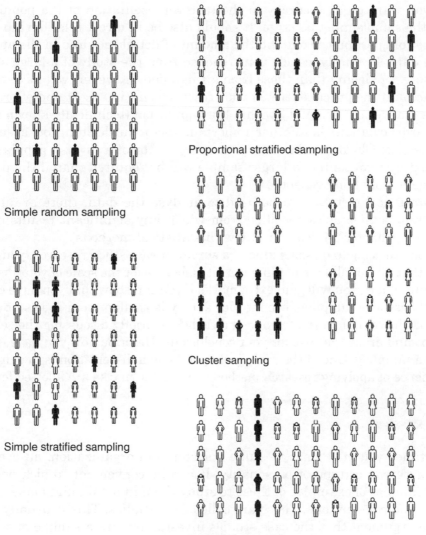

Simple random sampling

Proportional stratified sampling

Simple stratified sampling

Cluster sampling

Systematic sampling

FIGURE 12.4 Random sampling diagrams

Sample size

Once you have selected a suitable sampling method, the remaining problem is to determine the sample size. There is no easy answer to this problem. If the population is very homogeneous, and the study is not very detailed, than a small sample will give a fairly representative view of the whole. In other cases, you should consider the following.

If you want great accuracy in the true representation of the population, then the sample must be large. It should also be in direct relationship to the number of questions asked and the amount of detail required in the analysis of the data. Normally, conclusions reached from the study of a large sample are more convincing than those from a small one. However, you have to take into account the practicalities of your resources in time, cost and effort.

The amount of variability within the population (technically known as the standard deviation) is another important factor in deciding on a suitable sample size. Obviously, in order that every sector of a diverse population is adequately represented, a larger sample will be required than if the population were more homogeneous.

If statistical tests are to be used to analyse the data, there are usually minimum sample sizes specified from which any significant results can be obtained. Chapter 14 deals briefly with statistical methods.

If you are going to do some kind of a survey or case study research, you might think that all this about sampling is a bit elaborate for the scale of your dissertation. But in fact, you will gain extra marks if you can show that you have considered the issue of sampling, even if your survey is small or your case study is an obvious choice. Demonstrate your knowledge by briefly discussing the relevant options and argue the case for your conclusions. Describe how you have carried out the sampling. One of the main points of doing a dissertation is to gain some experience of applying research methods – valuable marks are allotted for this.

Case studies

Sometimes you may want to study a system, an organization, an event, or even a person or type of personality. It can be convenient to pick one or a small number of examples of these to study them in detail, and make assessments and comparisons. These are called case studies. This is usually based on the argument that the case studies investigated are a sample of some or many such systems, organizations, etc., and so what you can find out in the particular cases could be applicable to all of them. You need to make the same kind of sampling choice as described above in order to reassure yourself, and the reader, that this in fact holds good.

Alternatively, if there is a large variation between such systems, organizations, etc. it may not be possible to find 'average' or representative cases. What you can do here is to take several very different ones, e.g. those showing extreme characteristics, those at each end of the spectrum, and perhaps one that is somewhere in the middle. Take, for example, exercise regimes for increasing fitness. You could compare the results of one that is based purely on weight training, one based purely on aerobic exercises, and one that combines both approaches. Other examples could be discipline regimes in education, density of housing accommodation, top–bottom and bottom–top management structures, different perspectives of stakeholders, etc. You can probably think of some more relevant to your subject.

12.5 Questionnaires

Asking questions is an obvious method of collecting both quantitative and qualitative information from people. Using a questionnaire enables you to organize the questions and receive replies without actually having to talk to every respondent. As a method of data collection, the questionnaire is a very flexible tool, but you must use it carefully in order to fulfil the requirements of your research. While there are whole books on the art of questioning and questionnaires, it is possible to isolate a number of important factors to consider before deciding to use a questionnaire.

Before examining the form and content of a questionnaire, let's briefly consider why you might choose this form of data collection, and the ways in which you could deliver the questionnaire.

One of the main features of a questionnaire is its impersonality. The questions are fixed, i.e. do not change according to how the replies develop, and they are the same for each respondent, and the person posing the questions is remote. The responses can be completely anonymous, allowing potentially embarrassing questions to be asked with a fair chance of getting a true reply. Another feature is that there are no geographical limitations: the respondents can be anywhere in the world as long as they can be reached by post or online using email or other web-based communications. Questionnaires can be a relatively economic method, in cost and time, of soliciting data from a large number of people. Time for checking facts and for pondering on the questions can also be taken by the respondents, which tends to lead to more accurate information.

There are three basic methods of delivering questionnaires: personally, by post and online. The advantages of personal delivery are that you can help respondents to overcome difficulties with the questions, and that you can use personal persuasion and reminders to ensure a high response rate. You can also find out the reasons why some people refuse to answer the questionnaire, and you can check on responses if they seem odd or incomplete. This personal involvement enables you to devise more complicated questionnaires. Obviously, there are problems both in time and in geographical location that limit the scope and extent to which you can use this method of delivery.

Postal questionnaires do not suffer from these two limitations. However, the most serious problem is that the rate of response is difficult to predict or control, particularly if there is no system of follow-up. The pattern of non-response

- You must establish exactly which variables you wish to gather data about, and how these variables can be assessed. This will enable you to list the questions you need to ask (and those that you don't) and to formulate the questions precisely in order to get the required responses.

- The language must be unmistakably clear and unambiguous and make no inappropriate assumptions. This requires some clear analytical effort.

- In order to get a good response rate, keep questions simple and the questionnaire as short as possible.

- Clear and professional presentation is another essential factor in encouraging a good response.

- Consider how you will process the information from the completed forms. This may influence the layout of the questionnaire, e.g. by including spaces for codes and scoring.

can have a serious effect on the validity of your sample by introducing bias into the data collected. Consider the cost in choosing postal distribution. It might be your only method of questioning people spread over a large area or situated in relatively inaccessible regions.

Online email and other web-based formats are quick to set up and cost nothing to distribute. But, the same as with postal surveys, getting a good response rate may be difficult if you do not target your respondents sufficiently precisely. There is more about online options below.

Here are some simple rules to devising a questionnaire. It is not always easy to carry them out perfectly.

It is a good idea to pre-test the questionnaire on a small number of people before you use it in earnest. This is called a pilot study. If you can, test it on people of a type similar to that of the intended sample to anticipate any problems of comprehension or other sources of confusion. You will get some good marks for this.

It is good practice, when sending out or issuing the questionnaire, to courteously invite the recipients to complete it, and encourage them by explaining the purpose of the survey, how the results could be of benefit to them, and how little time it will take to complete. Include simple instructions on how to complete the responses. Some form of thanks and appreciation of their efforts should be included at the end. If you need to be sure of a response from a particular person, send a preliminary letter, with a reply-paid response card, to ask if he or she is willing to complete the questionnaire before you send it.

For the actual design of the questionnaire, you should consult books that deal with this in detail. This will speed up the process and help you to avoid common pitfalls. If you get it right you have a good foundation for your data collection. See the end of this chapter for useful references.

Doing a questionnaire survey online is becoming ever more popular and easy. Contacting people online is so much quicker and cheaper than any other way. The only problem is getting to the people you want to question if you have not got their email addresses or other way of identifying them. Social networks can help here. A useful and simple-to-use, free program for compiling and analysing online questionnaires is called Survey Monkey. You can download it from the Internet at www.surveymonkey.com. You will need to register in order to use it. It will help you to design your survey and customize how it looks. It even provides standard questions from its own question bank. For collecting your responses, you can send your survey with a weblink by email, or post on Facebook or Twitter, or embed your survey on your blog or website. In order to analyse your results, it enables you to filter, crosstab and make graphs of results. It allows you to export your responses in multiple formats in case you want to use more sophisticated forms of analysis.

12.6 Interviews: structured, semi-structured and open

While questionnaire surveys are relatively easy to organize, and prevent the personality of the interviewer having effects on the results, they do have certain limitations. They are not suitable for questions that require probing to obtain adequate information, as they should only contain simple, one-stage questions. It is often difficult to get responses from the complete sample; questionnaires tend to be returned by the more literate sections of the population.

The use of interviews to question samples of people is a very flexible tool with a wide range of applications. Because of their flexibility, interviews are a useful method of obtaining information and opinions from experts during the early stages of your research project. Though suitable for quantitative data collection, they are particularly useful when qualitative data are required. There are two main methods of conducting interviews: face-to-face and telephone.

Face-to-face interviews can be carried out in a variety of situations: in the home, at work, outdoors, on the move (e.g. while travelling). They can be used to question members of the general public, experts or leaders, specific segments of society, e.g. elderly or disabled people, ethnic minorities, both singly and in groups. Interviews can be used for subjects both general or specific in nature, and even, with the correct preparation, for very sensitive topics. They can be one-off or repeated several times over a period to track developments. As the interviewer, you are in a good position to judge the quality of the responses, to notice if a question has not been properly understood and to encourage the respondent to be full in his or her answers. Using visual signs, such as nods, smiles, etc., helps to get good responses.

Telephone interviews avoid the necessity of travelling to the respondents, and all the time and problems associated with contacting people personally. Telephone surveys can be carried out more quickly than face-to-face, especially if the questionnaire is short (20–30 minutes at the most). However, you cannot use visual aids to explain questions, and there are no visual clues such as eye contact, smiling, puzzled looks between you and the interviewee. Voice quality is an important factor in successful phone interviews. You should speak clearly and loudly, using standard pronunciation and sounding competent and confident. For interviewing very busy people, you can pre-arrange a suitable time to ring – but do be punctual.

FIGURE 12.5   A suitable time to ring

The structuring of the interview depends on the type of information you wish to collect. If you want very precise answers to very precise questions, perhaps for statistical analysis, then use a tightly structured interview with closed questions similar to a questionnaire. At the other extreme, if you want to explore a situation and get information that you cannot foresee, then an open and unstructured form of interview is best. A semi-structured interview falls between the two, achieving defined answers to defined questions, while including more open-ended questions for issues to be explored.

The most important point when you set up an interview is to know exactly what you want to achieve by it, how you are going to record the information, and what you intend to do with it. Although there is a great difference in technique for conducting interviews 'cold' with the general public and interviewing officials or experts by appointment, in both cases the personality and bearing of the interviewer are of great importance. You should be well prepared in the groundwork (i.e. writing letters for appointments, explaining the purpose of the interview), in presenting the interview with confidence, friendliness, good appearance, etc., and in the method of recording the responses (tape recording, writing notes, completing forms, etc.).

12.7 Standardized scales and tests

A wide range of standardized scales and tests have been devised by social scientists and psychologists to establish people's abilities, attitudes, aptitudes, opinions, etc. A well-known example of one of these is the IQ or intelligence test. The objective of the tests is usually to measure in some way the abilities of the subjects according to a standardized scale, so that easy comparisons can be made. One of the main problems is to select or devise a suitable scale for measuring the often rather abstract concepts under investigation, such as attitude (e.g. to school meals, military service, capital punishment, etc.).

It is safer to use tried and tested standard scales, of which there are several, each taking different approaches according to the results aimed at. One of the most commonly used is the Lickert scale which has a summated rating approach. There is also, among others, the Thurlstone scale, which aims to produce an equal appearing interval scale; and the Guttman scale, which is a unidimensional scale where items have a cumulative property.

Here is an example of a Lickert scale so that you get the idea of what it is like:

Strongly agree 1	2	3	4	5 Strongly disagree

The 'questions' are expressed as statements (e.g. the Labour Party still represents the workers) and the respondent is asked to ring one of the numbers in the scale 1–5. Another way of expressing the same thing is just to use words:

Strongly agree	Tend to agree	Neither agree nor disagree	Tend to disagree	Strongly disagree

Place these responses at the head of five columns situated to the right of the column of statements, and ask the respondent to tick the chosen column next to each statement.

You can use any dichotomous combination you like, e.g. like/dislike, want/ not want, probable/improbable. You just have to be careful that there are gradations of the opinion or feelings, unlike accept/reject, which is either one or the other. As an alternative to five, you can have three or seven stages (best to keep to odd numbers so that you get a middle value).

You can see that a score is automatically given by the response, so you can easily count the number of different scores to analyse the results. A useful precaution to prevent over-simplification of responses is to ask many questions about the same topic, all from different angles. This form of triangulation helps to build up a more complete picture of complex issues. You can then also weight the results from the different questions: that is, give more importance to those that are particularly crucial by multiplying them by a chosen factor.

12.8 Accounts

This is a method of qualitative data collection used mainly in sociological research. It is used to find information on people's actions and feelings by asking them to give their own interpretation, or account, of what they experience. Accounts can consist of a variety of data sources: people's spoken explanations, behaviour (such as gestures), personal records of experiences and conversations, letters and diaries. As long as the accounts are authentic, there should be no reason why they cannot be used as an argued explanation of people's actions.

Since the information must come directly from the respondents, you must take care to avoid leading questions, excessive guidance and other factors which may cause distortion. You can check the authenticity of the accounts by cross-checking with other people involved in the events, examining the physical records of the events (e.g. papers, documents, etc.) and checking with the respondents during the account-gathering process. You will need to transform the collected accounts into working documents that can be coded and analysed. Read more about this in Chapter 15.

12.9 Observation

This is a method of recording conditions, events and activities through looking, not asking. The aim is to take a detached view of the phenomena, and be 'invisible', either in fact or in effect (i.e. by being ignored). Observation can also be used for recording the nature or conditions of objects, for example, buildings. This type of observation is often referred to as a survey, and can range from a preliminary visual survey to a detailed survey using a range of instruments for measurement.

As an activity, as opposed to a method, observation is of course required in many research situations, for example, observing the results of experiments, the behaviour of models, and even the reactions of people to questions in an interview. Observation can be used to record both quantitative and qualitative data.

Observation can record whether people act differently from what they say or intend. They can sometimes demonstrate their understanding of a process better by their actions than by verbally explaining their knowledge. For example, a machine operator will probably demonstrate more clearly his or her understanding of the techniques of operating the machine by working with it than by verbal explanation.

Observation is not limited to the visual sense. Any sense, e.g. smell, touch, hearing, can be involved, and these need not be restricted to the range perceptible by the human senses. A microscope or telescope can be used to extend the

FIGURE 12.6 Observation can record whether people act differently from what they say

capacity of the eye, just as a moisture meter can increase sensitivity to the feeling of dampness. You can probably think of instruments that have been developed in every discipline to extend the observational limits of the human senses.

On the one hand, observations of objects can be a quick and efficient method of gaining preliminary knowledge or making a preliminary assessment of their state or condition. For example, after an earthquake, a quick visual assessment of the amount and type of damage to buildings can be made before a detailed survey is undertaken.

On the other hand, observation can be very time-consuming and difficult when the activity observed is not constant (i.e. much time can be wasted waiting for things to happen, or so much happens at once that it is impossible to observe it all and record it). Instrumentation can sometimes be devised to overcome the problem of infrequent or spasmodic activity, e.g. automatic cameras and other sensors.

Here are a few basic hints on how to carry out observations:

- Make sure you know what you are looking for. Events and objects are usually complicated and much might seem to be relevant to your study. Identify the variables that you need to study and concentrate on these.
- Devise a simple and efficient method of recording the information accurately. Rely as much as possible on ticking boxes or circling numbers, particularly if you need to record fast-moving events. Obviously, you can leave yourself more time when observing static

163

objects to notate or draw the data required. Record the observations as they happen. Memories of detailed observations fade quickly.

- Use instrumentation when appropriate or necessary. Instruments that make an automatic record of their measurements are to be preferred in many situations.
- If possible, process the information as the observations progress. This can help to identify critical matters that need study in greater detail, and others that prove to be unnecessary.
- If you are doing covert observations, plan in advance what to do if your presence is discovered, to avoid potentially embarrassing or even dangerous situations!

12.10 Experiments and models

The world around us is so complicated that it is often difficult to observe a particular phenomenon without being disturbed by all the other events happening around us. Wouldn't it be useful to be able to extract that part of the world out of its surroundings and study it in isolation? You can often do this by setting up an experiment or by creating a model in which only the important factors (variables) that you want to consider are selected for study. This enables you to manipulate the variables in order to see what happens if you make certain changes. The results can then be used to collect data on the observed phenomenon, which in turn can be analysed, often providing information to form the basis of further testing. Experiments and models are used in many subject areas, but particularly those that are based on things or the interaction between things and people ('things' include systems or techniques as well as objects or substances).

There are many locations where experiments can be carried out, but the laboratory situation is the one that provides the greatest possibilities for control. Use of models is the other method of obtaining information about the real world in a controlled situation. In these methods, the collection and analysis of data are inextricably linked. The preliminary data on which the experiments and models are based are used to create new data, which, in their turn, can be used for further analysis.

The difference between an experiment and a model is that:

- An experiment is used to examine actual phenomena, which are controlled in scope and size.
- A model provides an artificial version of the phenomenon for study, either by mimicking it at a reduced scale or by abstracting it diagrammatically or mathematically (often using computer techniques).

Checks should be carried out on both models and experiments to test whether the assumptions made are valid. In models, comparisons are made with the real phenomenon. In experiments, a control group is used to provide a 'baseline' against which the effects of the experimental treatment may be evaluated. The

FIGURE 12.7   Provides an artificial version of the phenomenon

control group is one that is identical (as near as possible) to the experimental group, but does not receive experimental treatment (for example, in a medical experiment, the control group will be given placebo pills instead of the medicated pills). As you see in this example, experiments are not only a matter of bubbling bottles in a laboratory. They can involve people as well as things – only it is more difficult to control the people! Models, on the other hand, are normally based on materials or mathematics, but can involve people such as in simulations or prototypes (e.g. flight deck simulators or prototype car seats). Often, the human aspect comes with the manipulation of the model to see what happens.

Experimental designs

Generally, experiments are designed and carried out in order generate data in order to examine causes and effects (studying dependent and independent variables), and are used to find explanations for them – e.g. what happens if, and why? The design of the experiments depends on the type of data required, the level of reliability of the data required, and practical matters associated with the problem under investigation. In order for the experiment to be of any use, it must be possible to generalize the results beyond the confines of the experiment itself.

There is plenty of scope for setting up experiments that so simplify, and even falsify, the phenomenon extracted from the real world that completely wrong conclusions can be arrived at. This is why it is important to briefly explain the different kinds of experiment that can be set up, and the strength

165

FIGURE 12.8   When a pre-test is not possible

of the conclusions that can be drawn from the observations. Experiments are commonly divided into three general types:

- Pre-experimental designs – simple experiments that do not contain the full checking procedures found in true experimental designs.
- True experimental designs – contain the following essential ingredients: random sampling to choose materials/subjects to be experimented on (experimental group), a control group for comparison of results, and a pre-test to check that the experimental group and control group have identical properties.
- Quasi-experimental designs – miss out on random sampling, or compare the results of separate experiments made over time.

Models

You can use models to mimic a phenomenon (rather than isolating it as in an experiment) in a form that can be manipulated, in order to obtain data about the effects of the manipulations. According to Broadbent (1988: 91), models can have three basic functions:

- Descriptive – two types being isomorphic, i.e. a true representation in all detail of the object (e.g. a wiring diagram), and homomorphic, i.e. a simplified representation

166

showing a selection of features (e.g. a tourist road map).

- Concept structuring – for defining, collecting, ordering and predicting data.
- Exploratory – in order to test or generate hypotheses.

The essential qualities of any model are that it should be constructed for a particular purpose and that it should, in some way, reduce the complexity of the real situation. In order to make a model, you must understand the system that lies behind the phenomena in reality, in order to gauge what are the important variables and how they interact. The actual form of the model can be diagrammatic, physical or mathematical. Qualitative models emphasize the relationships between entities without try-

FIGURE 12.9   It should be constructed for a particular purpose

ing to quantify them, while quantitative models not only describe the relationships but also accurately measure their magnitude.

You should carry out checks on your model to test whether the assumptions you have made in order to set it up are valid. You should also check the results you obtain by using a model against data collected from the actual case that it is modelling, to assess whether the data correspond to it.

Diagrammatic models

A simple method of representing systems is the creation of diagrams. A wide range of techniques can be used to portray various aspects of a system; most of them are qualitative. They can be used to map causes and effects, lines of influence, to illustrate the components of a system or an organization, or to track a sequence of events, either planned or recorded after the event.

Diagramming is commonly used to explore a real-life situation in order to investigate what the important variables in the system are and the manner in which they influence each other. It promotes understanding of complicated situations and interrelationships. The understanding gained can often then be used in the construction of a physical or mathematical model.

Physical models

These are three-dimensional representations of an object or a building at a reduced scale. The lavish architectural display model is a familiar spectacle in the developer's boardroom, but is not usually the type of model that is useful for research purposes. Models devised for the purpose of research must be specifically designed to produce data that can be used to test the variables that are central to the problem being investigated. Thus, a model you would make to test the acoustics of a concert hall would be very different from one you would make to test mechanical methods of steering a car. Physical models can be qualitative or quantitative in nature.

One of the main problems you will face when designing a spatial physical model for producing quantitative data is the problem of scaling. It raises the question: do materials and forms of energy behave identically at any scale? Usually, the answer is no. In a model made to test the acoustics of a concert hall, the frequency and amplitude of the sound source may have to be scaled down, as may the texture and density of the materials used to line the hall. In mechanical models, the different behaviour of materials at small scale must be compensated for. To overcome the scaling problem, full-scale prototypes are used where possible.

Mathematical models

These are invariably quantitative models and are divided into two major categories, *deterministic* and *stochastic* models. These categories relate to the predictability of the input: deterministic models deal only with predetermined inputs, e.g. loads and material strengths of a structural system, whereas stochastic models are designed to deal with unpredictable inputs, e.g. traffic flows in a road system.

The computer is an invaluable tool in the construction of mathematical models. Spreadsheet programs provide a systematic two-dimensional framework for devising models, and furnish facilities for cross-calculations, random number generation, setting of variable values and the build-up of series of formulae.

12.11   Chapter summary

It is a waste of time to collect unnecessary data, so you will have to decide before you start what data you will need. Actually, it is sometimes difficult not to stray away from the focus of your research, as there is so much interesting stuff out there!

For collecting secondary data, use your own and other libraries, museums and collections, government and professional data collections, and of course the Internet. In some subjects, the data are outside in historic sites or even underground.

For collecting primary data, you need to set up a system of questioning, observing, recording, measuring, etc. – whatever is appropriate. Questionnaires provide a structured way of collecting data, both qualitative and quantitative, from a large number of cases, especially if you use the post or the Internet. Compiling the questionnaire requires care and attention to detail in order to get the information you need. Interviews are generally more flexible than questionnaires, and so provide opportunities to explore issues not considered before. However, they are time-consuming, so limit the number of cases that you can manage.

You can use standardized scales and tests to make analysing the collected data easier with quantitative methods, while the data from accounts and observations are generally qualitative, and require more laborious methods for analysis. Investigating case studies is a good way of finding out the workings of particular organizations or situations in detail.

If you are selecting a few cases from a larger group (population) then you will have to consider what sampling method you should use. The choice in random sampling is: simple random, simple stratified, proportional stratified, cluster or area, and systematic sampling – all dependent on the characteristics of your population. Avoid non-random sampling if possible, as you cannot rely on getting a representative sample, but sometimes there is no other way. Options are: accidental or convenience, quota and theoretical. The bigger the sample size the better, assuming you can cope with the numbers.

Experiments and models provide a way to select a particular phenomenon and reproduce it in a controlled form so that you can manipulate the variables to see what effects they produce. You can make them as simple or as complicated as you wish, the important thing is to ensure that they reflect the situation in reality so that results gained are relevant to real-life situations.

12.12 What should I do now?

Having waded through this rather long chapter, you will have got a good idea of what kinds of data there are and what your options are for getting hold of the necessary data required for your dissertation research. What you really need to decide now is just what data you will have to gather, and then to choose suitable collection methods. You will probably find that your project is not so simple as to require only one data collection method. In all cases, secondary data will be required, if only to provide some background information on which to base the research. You might need to use two or three different methods for data collection, one for each aspect of your investigations, or to triangulate the information on just one subject.

For example, if you were studying the effect of particular television programmes on children's play habits, you might want to make observations and set up questionnaires to get the children's and their parents' views; consult statistics about publicity and toy and video sales to get data about the promotion of the programmes; interview the programme makers; read previous research on the subject to find methodological approaches to studying this subject and so on.

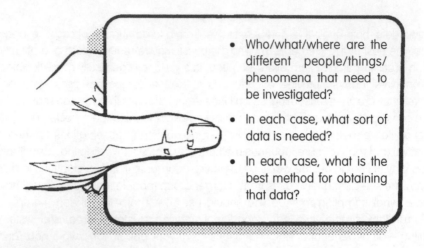

- Who/what/where are the different people/things/phenomena that need to be investigated?

- In each case, what sort of data is needed?

- In each case, what is the best method for obtaining that data?

As usual, a good way to approach this is to ask yourself a series of questions, the answers to which should form a simple argument.

You should make a list of the answers to the questions above, and then see how you could organize the data collection in a manageable way. You will quickly see whether it is practicable to do everything on the list. Consider not only the amount of data you need to collect (e.g. how many questions you need to ask of how many people, how sophisticated the model should be) but also the issues of where you have to go, when and how you can get access to the information, how much equipment do you need. Don't attempt too much – you will stress yourself out! Rather, narrow the scope of the research to ensure that it can be reasonably completed on time and within your resources. For example, in the television programme project above, you could restrict your investigations to the children's perspective, and avoid the commercial and production aspects.

The results of your deliberations can now be fed into your project plan, with allotted timing for each data collection task.

12.13 References to more information

There are hundreds of books about data collection methods and sampling techniques. On top of these, there are the examples in the previous dissertations done on your course, which you can consult for the nature of data collected and their use of methods. Apart from perhaps looking at a few of the books below, consult your library catalogue for books that deal specifically with how to do dissertations in your own subject, e.g. management, health-care, social studies, architecture, etc.

These books look in more detail at the different aspects of sampling and data collection. For more choice, look up key words such as sampling, questionnaires, survey research, etc. in your library catalogue.

Here are some books on research in general. I have pointed out the sections on data, data collection, sampling, etc. which are useful because of their brevity.

Further reading

Seale, C. (ed.) (2012) *Researching Society and Culture*, 3rd edition. London: Sage. See the first six papers in Part Two.

Holliday, A. (2007) *Doing and Writing Qualitative Research*, 2nd edition. London: Sage. Consult chapters on what counts as data and writing about data.

Fowler, F.J. (2008) *Survey Research Methods*, 4th edition. London: Sage. This book goes into great detail about all aspects of the subject of doing surveys. Good on sampling, response rates, methods of data collection – particularly questionnaires and interviews. Use it selectively to find out more about the particular methods you want to use. This book will also be useful later for analysis, and has a section on ethics too.

Robson, C. (2011) *Real World Research: A Resource for Social Scientists and Practitioner-Researchers*, 3rd edition. Chichester: Wiley. Part III gives valuable information and advice on the tactics of data collection using a wide range of methods. See Chapter 12 for an explanation of standard scales and Part V, dealing with data.

Aldridge, A. and Levine K. (2001) *Surveying the Social World: Principles and Practice in Survey Research*. Buckingham: Open University Press. Another comprehensive book: find what you need by using the contents list and index.

Fink, A. (2002) *The Survey Kit*, 2nd edition. London: Sage. Ten volumes covering all aspects of survey research! This must be the ultimate.

Some books specifically on questionnaires, in order of usefulness:

Peterson, R.A. (2000) *Constructing Effective Questionnaires*. London: Sage.

Gillham, W. (2007) *Developing a Questionnaire*, 2nd edition. London: Continuum.

Dillman, D.A. (2000) *Mail and Internet Surveys: The Tailored Design Method*, 2nd edition. Chichester: Wiley.

Frazer, L. (2000) *Questionnaire Design and Administration: A Practical Guide*. Chichester: Wiley.

And a few on interviewing, again in order of usefulness at your stage of work:

Keats, D.M. (2000) *Interviewing: A Practical Guide for Students and Professionals*. Buckingham: Open University Press.
Jaber, F. (ed.) (2002) *Handbook of Interview Research: Context and Method*. London: Sage.
Wengraf, T. (2001) *Qualitative Research Interviewing: Biographic, Narrative and Semi-Structured*. London: Sage.

And a couple on sampling:

Scheaffer, R.L. (2010) *Elementary Survey Sampling*, 7th edition. Belmont, CA: Duxbury.
Fink, A. (2003) *How to Sample in Surveys*, 2nd edition. Volume 6 of The Survey Kit. London: Sage.

And a couple on case studies, simplest first:

Nisbet, J.D. and Watt, J. (1982) *Case Study*. Rediguide No. 26. Oxford: TRC Rediguides.
Yin, R.K. (2009) *Case Study Research: Design and Methods*, 4th edition. Thousand Oaks, CA: Sage.

Here are some books on modelling, a subject that soon gets immersed in mathematical formulae, though there are computer packages that take much of the sweat out of calculations. I have ordered them in levels of increasing detail and complexity. Look in your library catalogue to see if there are any devoted to your own subject.

Meadows, D. (2009*) Thinking in Systems: A Primer*. London: Earthscan.
Edwards, D. (2007) *Guide to Mathematical Modelling*, 2nd edition. New York: Industrial Press.

Some books dedicated to experimental methods. Again, check out under your own subject headings.

Cohen, L., Manion, L. and Morrison, K. (2007) *Research Methods in Education*. London: Routledge. Chapter 13 gives a comprehensive explanation about experiments. Most books on research methods have a chapter devoted to experimental design.
Field, A. and Hole, G. (2003) *How to Design and Report Experiments*. London: Sage.
Ruxton, G. and Colegrave, N. (2011) *Experimental Design for the Life Sciences*. Oxford: Oxford University Press.
Montgomery, D.C. (2012) *Design and Analysis of Experiments*, 8th edition. New York: Wiley.

13

How Do I Analyse Quantitative Data?

Chapter contents

13.1 Raw data

The results of your survey, experiments, archival studies, or whatever methods you used to collect data about your chosen subject, are of little use to anyone if they are merely presented as raw data. It should not be the duty of the reader to try to make sense of them, and to relate them to your research questions or problems. It is up to you to use the information that you have collected to make a case for arriving at some conclusions. How exactly you do this depends on what kind of questions you raised at the beginning of the dissertation, and the directions you have taken in order to answer them.

The data you have collected might be recorded in different ways that are not easy to read or to summarize. Perhaps they are contained in numerous questionnaire responses, in handwritten laboratory reports, recorded speech, as a series of photographs or observations in a diary. It can be difficult for even you, who have done the collecting, to make sense of it all, let alone someone who has not been involved in the project.

The question now is how to grapple with the various forms of data so that you can present them in a clear and concise fashion, and how you can analyse the presented data to support an argument that leads to convincing conclusions. In order to do this you must be clear about what you are trying to achieve.

13.2 Refer to the research questions

This is a very good time to return to your research proposal, and to any revisions you might have made in the interim, to refocus on exactly what you intended to do so many weeks/months ago. What are the burning issues that you wanted to tackle? What were the stated aims of your research? What specific questions or problems were raised? What sort of answers were you aiming at?

Now you can briefly review that information you have collected and assess whether you really have kept to the issues raised in the proposal. Are the data likely to produce the answers you were seeking? If you have not strayed from the intended route, then it is likely that you will be able to go on to analyse the data successfully as intended. But, what if you feel that as time went by you got diverted from your original intentions, that unexpected events occurred that led you to consider different, perhaps more important issues, or that your interests were drawn to aspects about which you were not aware before? Now is the time to consider the best way ahead in the light of changed circumstances.

FIGURE 13.1   If you have not strayed from your intended route

Your original proposal was not written in stone! You based it on the knowledge and understanding you had at the time. The process of collecting data about your subject has put you in a much stronger position to understand better the important issues in your chosen field. In order to produce a good dissertation, you must now reconsider the main aims of the research and revise them on the basis of your new direction. I presume that the changes will not be huge, more a realignment than a new beginning. But what is important is that you redefine questions or problems so that you will be able to produce some answers or solutions based on the data that you have collected. It is best to actually formulate these questions or problems in writing; you will need to discuss them anyway at the beginning of your dissertation. If you have already written the first chapters, review these in the light of your most recent thoughts.

13.3 Analysis according to types of data

There are several reasons why you may want to analyse data. Some of these are the same as the reasons why you wanted to do the study in the first place. The reasons I can think of why you will want to use analytical methods are in order to enable you to:

- measure
- make comparisons
- examine relationships
- make forecasts
- test hypotheses
- construct concepts and theories
- explore
- control
- explain.

This book is much too short to be able to describe all the analytical methods possible. I can just review some of the main methods, and refer you to more specialized publications where you can get detailed instructions on how to do the analysis.

The common way to categorize data for both collection and analysis is to distinguish between quantitative and qualitative data (see Chapter 11). You must have done this already when you did your data collection. However, life is rarely as tidy as theory. You possibly have some of both types of data – not a bad thing as they can provide different perspectives on a subject. In fact, some of the analytical methods can be used both quantitatively and qualitatively. These are mentioned where appropriate. As the subject of analysis is

175

rather large and of essential importance to your dissertation, I have spread it over two chapters. This one continues with a discussion of quantitative analysis, and the next takes on the techniques of qualitative analysis.

13.4 Quantitative analysis

Quantitative analysis deals with numbers and uses mathematical operations to investigate the properties of data. The levels of measurement used in the collection of the data, i.e. nominal, ordinal, interval and ratio (see Chapter 11), are an important factor in choosing the type of analysis that is applicable, as is the numbers of cases involved. Statistics is the name given to this type of analysis, and is defined in this sense as:

> The science of collecting and analysing numerical data, especially in, or for, large quantities, and usually inferring proportions in a whole from proportions in a representative sample. (Oxford Encyclopaedic Dictionary)

Most surveys result in quantitative data, e.g. numbers of people who believed this or that, how many children of what age do which sports, levels of family income, etc. However, not all quantitative data originate from surveys. For example, content analysis is a specific method of examining records of all kinds (e.g. radio and TV programmes, films, etc.), documents or publications. A checklist is made to count how frequently certain ideas, words, phrases, images or scenes appear in order to be able to draw some conclusions from the frequency of their appearance (e.g. the perception of modern architecture in the media).

One of the primary purposes of doing research is to describe the data and to discover relationships among events in order to describe, explain, predict and possibly control their occurrence. Statistical methods are a valuable tool to enable you to present and describe the data and, if necessary, to discover and quantify relationships. And you do not even have to be a mathematician to use these techniques, as user-friendly computer packages (such as Excel and Statistical Package for the Social Sciences (IBM SPSS)) will do all the presentation and calculations for you. However, you must be able to understand the relevance and function of the various displays and tests in relationship to your own sets of data and the kind of analysis required.

The most straightforward process is to describe the data in the form of tables, graphs and diagrams. For this, a spreadsheet program such as Excel is quite sufficient. This will order and display the data in a compact form so that you can make comparisons, detect trends and measure amounts and combinations of amounts. If you do not know how to use a spreadsheet for this, attend a course of instruction or find a handbook to guide you.

If you need to do more sophisticated analysis, then there is a wide range of statistical techniques that you can employ using IBM SPSS. Many tests bear exotic names like Kruskal's gamma, Kendall's coefficient of concordance, Guttman's lambda, and chi-squared and Kolmogorov–Smirnov tests. However, don't be put off by these, as you will only be required to use the most common ones and there are simple rules as to when and how they should be applied. Even so, it is always advisable to consult somebody with specialist statistical knowledge in order to check that you will be doing the right thing before you start. Also, attend a course, usually made available to you by your college or university, in the use of IBM SPSS or any other program that is available to you.

FIGURE 13.2   Consult somebody with statistical knowledge

Another factor to be taken into account when selecting suitable statistical tests is the number of cases about which you have data. Generally, statistical tests are more reliable the greater the number of cases. Usually, more than 20 cases are required to make any sense of the analysis, though some tests are designed to work with less. Always consult the instructions on this issue for the particular tests you want to use. It may affect your choice.

There is not space (or need) in this book to explain in detail the range of tests and their uses. There are many books that specialize in just this. It will, however, help your understanding if I give a general description of statistics and the various branches of the discipline.

13.5 Parametric and non-parametric statistics

The two major classes of statistics are parametric and non-parametric statistics. You need to understand the meaning of a parameter in order to appreciate the difference between these two types. A parameter of a population (i.e. the things or people you are surveying) is a constant feature that it shares with other populations. The most common one is the 'bell' or 'Gaussian' curve of a normal frequency distribution.

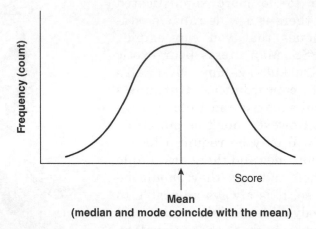

FIGURE 13.3   A Gaussian curve

This parameter reveals that most populations display a large number of more or less 'average' cases with extreme cases tailing off at each end. For example, most people are of about average height, with those who are extremely tall or small being in a distinct minority. The distribution of people's heights shown on a graph would take the form of the normal or Gaussian curve.

Although the shape of this curve varies from case to case (e.g. flatter or steeper, lopsided to the left or right), this feature is so common among populations that statisticians take it as a constant – a basic parameter. Calculations of parametric statistics are based on this feature.

Not all data are parametric, i.e. populations sometimes do not behave in the form of a Gaussian curve. Data measured by nominal and ordinal methods will not be organized in a curve form. Nominal data tend to be in the dichotomous form of either/or (e.g. this is a cow or a sheep or neither), while ordinal data can be displayed in the form of a set of steps (e.g. the first, second and third positions on a winners' podium). For those cases where this parameter is absent, non-parametric statistics may be applicable.

Non-parametric statistical tests have been devised to recognize the particular characteristics of non-curve data and to take into account these singular characteristics by specialized methods. In general, these types of test are less sensitive and powerful than parametric tests; they need larger samples in order to generate the same level of significance.

13.6 Statistical tests: parametric

The two classes of parametric statistical tests are descriptive and inferential.

Descriptive statistics

Descriptive statistics provide a method of quantifying the characteristics of the data, where their centre is, how broadly they spread and how one aspect of the data relates to another aspect of the same data. The 'centre of gravity' of the data, their point of central tendency, can be determined by finding the 'mode' or the 'median' and any one of several 'means'. These measures have their own characteristics and applications and should be chosen with regard to the data being analysed. The most familiar is the average value, technically called the arithmetic mean.

The measure of the dispersion (or spread) of the data, how flat or steep the Gaussian curve appears, is an indication of how many of the data closely resemble the mean. The flatter the curve, the greater is the amount of data that deviate from the mean, i.e. the fewer that are close to the average. The horizontal length of the curve also gives an indication of the spread of values and the extent of the extremes represented in the data, while the occurrence of a non-symmetrical curve indicates a skewness in the data values.

Inferential statistics

Inferential statistical tests go beyond describing the characteristics of data and the examination of correlations between variables. As the name implies, they are used to produce predictions through inference, based on the data analysed. This entails making predictions about the qualities of a total population on the basis of the qualities of a sample. This exercise is commonly carried out in quality control in production processes, where a sample of the production is tested in order to estimate the qualities of the total production. Three parameters (qualities) are commonly estimated: central tendency (proportion of products which are close to the norm, e.g. within permitted size tolerance); variability (e.g. range of sizes occurring); and probability (e.g. the proportion of acceptable products produced).

As with all predictions made from samples, the representative quality of the sample is crucial to accuracy, i.e. the sample must be as typical of the whole as possible.

Correlation

Apart from examining the qualities of a single set of data, the main purpose of statistical analysis is to identify and quantify relationships between variables. This is the type of research called *correlation* research. But remember, the mere discovery and measurement of correlations is not sufficient on its own to provide research answers. It is the interpretation of these discoveries that provides the valuable knowledge that will give answers to your research question.

The technical term for the measure of correlation is the coefficient of correlation. There are many types of these, the Pearson r being the most common. It is possible to measure the correlation between more than two variables if you use the appropriate tests. However, be wary about assuming that because a strong statistical correlation between variables can be demonstrated, there is necessarily a causal bond between the variables. It may be purely chance or the influence of other factors that, say, leads to areas of high-density development in cities having high crime rates. You must carefully question the assumptions on which such a causal assertion is made, and review the facts to examine if such a causality is verifiable in other ways.

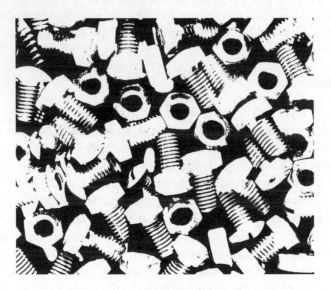

FIGURE 13.4   The sample must be as typical of the whole as possible

13.7 Statistical tests: non-parametric

Statistical tests built around discovering the means, standard deviations, etc. of the typical characteristics of a Gaussian curve are clearly inappropriate for analysing non-parametric data. Hence, non-parametric data cannot be statistically tested in the above ways.

There are tests that can be used to compare the qualities of two or more groups or samples, to analyse the rankings made by different judges, or to compare the data from observed and theoretical sources. Detailed information about which tests to use for particular data sets can be obtained from specialized texts on statistics and your own expert statistical adviser. It is perhaps a good place to warn you that computer statistical packages (e.g. IBM SPSS) will not distinguish between different types of parametric and non-parametric data.

In order to avoid producing reams of impressive looking, but meaningless analytical output, it is up to you to ensure that the tests are appropriate for the type of data you have.

13.8 Discussion of results

Both spreadsheet and statistical programs will produce very attractive results in the form of charts, graphs and tables that you can integrate into your dissertation to back up your argument. The important issue is that you have carried out the appropriate analysis related to what you want to demonstrate or test. Explain what data you have collected, perhaps supplying a sample to show their form (e.g. a questionnaire return), give the reasons for doing the particular tests for each section of the investigation, and then present the results of the tests.

Graphs, tables and other forms of presentation always need to be explained. Do not believe that the reader knows how to read them and that they are self-explanatory in relation to your argument. Spell out in words the main features of the results and explain how these relate to the parts of the sub-problems or subquestions that you are addressing. Now draw conclusions. What implications do the results have? Are they conclusive or is there room for doubt? Mention the limitations that might affect the strength of the result, e.g. limited number of responses, possible bias or time constraints. Each conclusion will only form a small part of the overall argument, so you need to fit everything together like constructing a jigsaw puzzle. The full picture should clearly emerge at the end. It is best to devote one section or chapter to each of the subproblems or subquestions. Leave it to the final chapter to draw all the threads together in order to answer the main issue of the dissertation.

Computer programs provide you with enormous choice when it comes to presenting graphs and charts. It is best to experiment to see which kind of presentation is the clearest. Consider whether you will be printing in mono-chrome or colour, as different coloured graph lines will lose their distinctiveness when reduced to shades of grey. It is also a good idea to set up a style that you maintain throughout the dissertation.

13.9 Chapter summary

Quantitative analysis is based on mathematical techniques called statistics. But before any analysis can begin, the raw data collected must be collated in such a way as to make it relevant to your research questions and amenable to analysis. You may want to do several things to the data, e.g. measure, make comparisons, examine relationships, etc. The best way to sort the data is to use a spreadsheet to put the values against the different variables or questions used. If you are using IBM SPSS, there is an inbuilt spreadsheet, or you can import from Excel.

Parametric statistics are for data that follow a normal distribution curve (also called bell or Gaussian). Descriptive statistics describe the 'shape' of the data, correlation looks for links between variables, and inferential statistics makes predictions on the basis of these correlations. Non-parametric statistics are used to analyse data that do not follow a normal distribution curve.

The results of statistical analysis are displayed using graphs, bar charts, pie charts, etc. for descriptive statistics, and various tables and values are used for the other types of tests.

13.10 What should I do now?

If you are not experienced in doing quantitative analysis and see the need to do it to analyse your findings, now is the time to learn. You will definitely need to go on a short course in using the relevant computer programs, such as spreadsheets and statistics. IBM SPSS is the most commonly used statistical package, and has become very user friendly, so you should experience few practical problems. Find out from your computer centre or library when the course takes place, and book yourself in.

One of your first jobs will be to enter all the data onto a spreadsheet, e.g. all the answers to all the questions from the questionnaires. Before you embark on any actual analysis, first take time to examine the nature of your data and what kind of analysis you want to subject them to. Will you be measuring them, making comparisons, examining relationships, etc.? Are the data parametric or non-parametric? If you are doing some statistical tests, you will have to ensure that you select the right ones. This will require some reading about statistical tests and possibly getting some advice from staff. Do not become too ambitious: keep it simple and within your level of understanding. It is quite easy to get carried away with doing grandiloquent sounding tests as they are carried out just as fast as any other; but could you really explain what they are about?

FIGURE 13.5   Leave yourself plenty of time to discuss the results

Leave yourself plenty of time to discuss the results in writing and to work on the conclusions. This is, of course, the whole point of gathering all the data in the first place and making the effort to test them. One of the commonest faults in undergraduate dissertations is that the impressive displays of graphs, tables, charts, etc. are left for the reader to interpret. So relate the conclusions directly back to the questions asked or problems posed at the beginning of the dissertation, and check that your overall argument is still sound. Then you will have achieved the purpose of all your research work.

13.11 References to more information

For a more detailed, though straightforward, introduction to statistics, see:

Preece, R. (2000) *Starting Research: An Introduction to Academic Research and Dissertation Writing*. London: Continuum. See Chapter 7.

Diamond, I. and Jeffries, J. (2000) *Beginning Statistics: An Introduction for Social Scientists*. London: Sage. This book emphasizes description, examples, graphs and displays rather than statistical formula. A good guide to understanding the basic ideas of statistics.

For a comprehensive review of the subject see below. I have listed these in order of complexity, simplest first. The list could go on for pages with ever increasing abstruseness. You could also have a browse through what is available on your library shelves to see if there are some simple guides there.

Wright, D. and London, K. (2009) *First (and Second) Steps in Statistics*. London: Sage.

Field, A. (2013) *Discovering Statistics with IBM SPSS Statistics*, 4th edition. London: Sage.

Byrne, D. (2002) *Interpreting Quantitative Data*. London: Sage.

Corder, G. and Foreman, D. (2009) *Nonparametric Statistics for Non-Statisticians: A Step by Step Approach*. Hoboken: Wiley.

And for a good guide on how to interpret official statistics, look at the section by Clive Seale in Part 2 of the following book.

Seale, C. (ed.) (2012) *Researching Society and Culture*, 3rd edition. London: Sage.

14

How Do I Analyse Qualitative Data?

Chapter contents

14.1 Qualitative research

Doing research is not always a tidy process where every step is completed before moving on to the next. In fact, especially if you are doing it for the first time, you often need to go back and reconsider previous decisions or adjust and elaborate on work as you gain more knowledge and acquire more skills. But there are also types of research in which there is an essential reciprocal process of data collection and data analysis.

Qualitative research is the main one of these. This does not involve counting and dealing with numbers but is based more on information expressed in words – descriptions, accounts, opinions, feelings, etc. This approach is common whenever people are the focus of the study, particularly small groups or individuals, but can also concentrate on more general beliefs or customs.

Frequently it is not possible to determine precisely what data should be collected as the situation or process is not sufficiently understood. Periodic analysis of collected data provides direction to further data collection. Adjustments to what is further looked at, what questions are asked, and what actions are carried out are based on what has already been seen, answered and done. This emphasis on reiteration and interpretation is the hallmark of qualitative research.

14.2 Qualitative data collection and analysis

The essential difference between quantitative analysis and qualitative analysis is that with the former, you need to have completed your data collection before you can start analysis, while with the latter, analysis is carried out concurrently with data collection. With qualitative studies, there is a constant interplay between collection and analysis that produces a gradual growth of understanding. You collect information, review it, collect more data based on what you have discovered, then analyse again what you have found. This is quite a demanding and difficult process, and is prone to uncertainties and doubts. At the level of an undergraduate dissertation, you will have to be careful not to be too ambitious, as the restricted time you have does not allow for lengthy delving and pondering. Keep the study focused and limited in scope so that you can complete the process. The important criteria for the examiner will be whether you have correctly used the methods and whether your conclusions are based on evidence found in the data collected.

Bromley (1986: 26) provides a list of ten steps in the process of qualitative research, summarized in Figure 14.1.

According to Robson, 'the central requirement in qualitative analysis is clear thinking on the part of the analyst' (2011: 468), where the analyst is put to the test as much as the data! Although it has been the aim of many researchers to make qualitative analysis as systematic and as 'scientific' as possible, there is still an element of 'art' in dealing with qualitative data. However, in order to convince others of your conclusions, there must be a good argument to support them. A good argument requires high-quality evidence and sound logic. In fact, you will be acting rather like a lawyer presenting a case, using a quasi-judicial approach such as used in an enquiry into a disaster or scandal.

Qualitative data, represented in words, pictures and even sounds, cannot be analysed by mathematical means such as statistics. So how is it possible to organize all these data and be able to come to some conclusions about what they reveal? The certainties of mathematical formulae and determinable levels of probability are not applicable to the 'soft' nature of qualitative data,

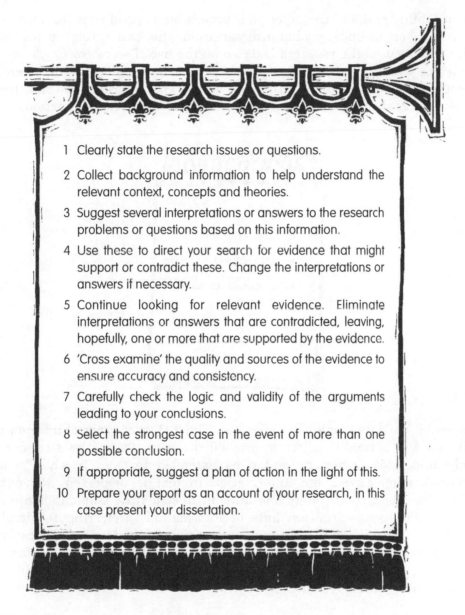

1 Clearly state the research issues or questions.

2 Collect background information to help understand the relevant context, concepts and theories.

3 Suggest several interpretations or answers to the research problems or questions based on this information.

4 Use these to direct your search for evidence that might support or contradict these. Change the interpretations or answers if necessary.

5 Continue looking for relevant evidence. Eliminate interpretations or answers that are contradicted, leaving, hopefully, one or more that are supported by the evidence.

6 'Cross examine' the quality and sources of the evidence to ensure accuracy and consistency.

7 Carefully check the logic and validity of the arguments leading to your conclusions.

8 Select the strongest case in the event of more than one possible conclusion.

9 If appropriate, suggest a plan of action in the light of this.

10 Prepare your report as an account of your research, in this case present your dissertation.

FIGURE 14.1

which are inextricably bound up with human feelings, attitudes and judgements. Despite this, software has been developed that can carry out the essential tasks of systemizing, organizing and analysing qualitative data. Programs such as NVivo, ATLAS.ti, MAXQDA and others are designed to take the sweat out of coding, creating memos, text and code searching, reporting and retrieving information. You will, however, have to weigh up the suitability of the program for your project, and spend time learning how to use it. For an undergraduate dissertation, this can rarely be justified, unless the focus of the research is based on the use of software.

With or without the help of computer programs, there are some essential activities that are necessary in all qualitative data analysis. Miles and Huberman (1994: 10–12) suggested that there are three concurrent flows of action:

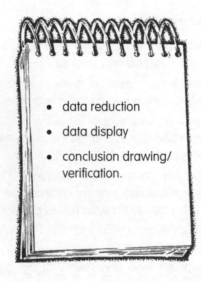

- data reduction
- data display
- conclusion drawing/ verification.

The activity of data display is important. The awkward mass of information that you will normally collect to provide the basis for analysis cannot be easily understood when presented as extended text, even when coded, clustered, summarized, etc. Information in text is dispersed, sequential rather than concurrent, bulky and difficult to structure. Our minds are not good at processing large amounts of information, preferring to simplify complex information into patterns and easily understood configurations. Consequently, if you use suitable methods to display the data in the form of matrices, graphs, charts and networks, you not only reduce and order the data, but also can analyse it.

14.3 Preliminary analysis during data collection

When you conduct field research it is important that you keep a critical attitude to the type and amount of data being collected, and the assumptions and thoughts that brought you to this stage. It is always easier to structure the information while the details are fresh in the mind, to identify gaps, to allow new ideas and hypotheses to develop, and to challenge your assumptions and biases. Raw field notes, often scribbled and full of abbreviations, and tapes of interviews or events need to be processed in order to make them useful. Much information will be lost if this task is left for long.

The process of data reduction and analysis should be a sequential and continuous procedure, simple in the beginning stages of the data collection, and becoming more complex as the project progresses. To begin with, one-page summaries can be made of the results of contacts, e.g. telephone conversations, visits. A standardized set of headings will prompt the ordering of the information: contact details, main issues, summary of information acquired, interesting issues raised, new questions resulting from these. Similar one-page forms can be used to summarize the contents of documents.

14.4 Typologies and taxonomies

As the data accumulate, a valuable step is to organize the shapeless mass of data by building typologies and taxonomies. These are technical words for the nominal level of measurement (remember Chapter 11), i.e. ordering by type or properties, thereby forming subgroups within the general category.

Even the simplest classification can help to organize seemingly shapeless information and to identify differences in, say, behaviour or types of people. For example, children's behaviour in the playground could be divided into 'joiners' and 'loners', or people in the shopping centre could be divided into 'serious

FIGURE 14.2   Noting the differences in terms of behaviour patterns

shoppers', 'window shoppers', 'passers through', 'loiterers', etc. This can help you to organize amorphous material and to identify patterns in the data. Then, noting the differences in terms of behaviour patterns between these categories can help you to generate the kinds of analysis that will form the basis for the development of explanations and conclusions.

This exercise in classification is the start of the development of a coding system, which is an important aspect of forming typologies. Codes are labels or tags used to allocate units of meaning to the collected data. Coding helps you to organize your piles of data (in the form of notes, observations, transcripts, documents, etc.) and to provide a first step in conceptualization, and helps to prevent 'data overload' resulting from mountains of unprocessed data in the form of ambiguous words.

Codes can be used to label different aspects of the subjects of study. Lofland et al. (2004), for example, devised six classes on which you could devise a coding scheme for 'social phenomena':

- acts
- activities
- meanings
- participation
- relationships
- settings.

The process of coding is analytical, and requires you to review, select, interpret and summarize the information without distorting it. Normally, you should compile a set of codes before doing the fieldwork, based on your background study, and then refine it during the data collection.

There are two essentially different types of coding, one that you can use for the retrieval of text sequences, the other devised for theory generation. The former refers to the process of cutting out and pasting sections of text from transcripts or notes under various headings. The latter is a more open coding system used as an index for your interpretive ideas – reflective notes or memos, rather than merely bits of text.

Several computer programs used for analysing qualitative data (such as Ethnograph and NUDIST) also have facilities for filing and retrieving coded information. They allow codes to be attached to the numbered lines of notes or transcripts of interviews, and for the source of the information/opinion to be noted. This enables a rapid retrieval of selected information from the mass of material collected. However, it does take quite some time to master the techniques involved, so take advice before contemplating the use of these programs.

14.5 Pattern coding, memoing and interim summary

The next stage of analysis requires you to begin to look for patterns and themes, and explanations of why and how these occur. This requires a method of pulling together the coded information into more compact and meaningful groupings. Pattern coding can do this by reducing the data into smaller analytical units such as themes, causes/explanations, relationships among people and emerging concepts, to allow you to develop a more integrated understanding of the situation studied and to test the initial explanations or answers to the research issues or questions. This will generally help to focus later fieldwork and lay the foundations for cross-case analysis in multicase studies by identifying common themes and processes.

Miles and Huberman (1994: 70–71) describe three successive ways that pattern codes may be used:

- The newly developed codes are provisionally added to the existing list of codes and checked out in the next set of field notes to see whether they fit.
- Next, the most promising codes are written up in a memo (described below) to clarify and explain the concept so that it can be related to other data and cases.
- Finally, the new pattern codes are tested out in the next round of data collection.

Actually, you will find that generating pattern codes is surprisingly easy, as it is the way by which we habitually process information. However, it is important not to cling uncritically to initially developed patterns, but to test and develop, and if necessary, reject them as your understanding of the data develops, and as new waves of data are produced.

Compiling memos is a good way to explore links between data and to record and develop intuitions and ideas. You can do this at any time – but it is best done when the idea is fresh! Remember that memos are written for yourself, so the length and style are not important, but it is necessary to label a memo so that it can be easily sorted and retrieved. You should continue the activity of memoing throughout the research project. You will find that the ideas become more stable with time until 'saturation' point, i.e. the point where you are satisfied with your understanding and explanation of the data, is achieved.

It is a very good idea, at probably about one-third of the way through the data collection, to take stock and seek to reassure yourself and your supervisors by checking:

- the quantity and quality of what you have found out so far
- your confidence in the reliability of the data
- the presence and nature of any gaps or puzzles that have been revealed
- what still needs to be collected in relation to your time available.

This exercise should result in the production of an interim summary, a provisional report a few pages long. This report will be the first time that everything you know about a case will be summarized, and presents the first opportunity to make cross-case analyses in multicase studies and to review emergent explanatory variables.

Remember, however, that the nature of the summary is provisional. Though it is perhaps sketchy and incomplete, it should be seen as a useful tool for you to reflect on the work done, for discussion with your colleagues and supervisors, and for indicating any changes that might be needed in the coding and in the subsequent data collection work. In order to check on the amount of data collected about each research question, you will find it useful to compile a data accounting sheet. This is a table that sets out the research questions and the amount of data collected from the different informants, settings, situations, etc. With this you will easily be able to identify any shortcomings.

14.6 Main analysis during and after data collection

Traditional text-based reports tend to be lengthy and cumbersome when presenting, analysing, interpreting and communicating the findings of a qualitative research project. Not only do they have to present the evidence and arguments sequentially, they also tend to be bulky and difficult to grasp quickly because information is dispersed over many pages.

This presents a problem for you, the writer, as well as for the final reader, who rarely has time to browse backwards and forwards through masses of text to gain full information. Graphical methods of data display and analysis can largely overcome these problems and are useful for exploring and describing as well as explaining and predicting phenomena. They can be used equally effectively for one case and cross-case analysis.

Graphical displays fall into two categories: matrices and networks.

FIGURE 14.3   Traditional text-based reports tend to be lengthy and cumbersome

Matrices or tables

The two-dimensional arrangement of rows and columns can summarize a substantial amount of information. You can easily produce these informally in a freehand fashion to explore aspects of the data, to any size. You can also use computer programs in the form of databases and spreadsheets to help in their production. You can use matrices to record variables such as time, levels of measurement, roles, clusters, outcomes and effects. If you want to get really sophisticated, latest developments allow you to formulate three-dimensional matrices.

Networks

A network is made up of blocks (nodes) connected by links. You can produce these maps and charts in a wide variety of formats, each with the capability of displaying different types of data:

- *Flowcharts* are useful for studying processes or procedures. Not only helpful for explanation, their development is a good device for creating understanding.
- *Organization charts* display relationships between variables and their nature, e.g. formal and informal hierarchies.
- *Causal networks* are used to examine and display the causal relationships between important independent and dependent variables, causes and effects.

TASKS: INITIATION AND DESIGN PHASE	grade of difficulty	PET	NVT	GLO	DUN	LTM	DCH	HOL	GRW	BAN
investigation of situation, inception	low	R	P	P	P	P	P	P	R	P/R
formulation of brief	med	R	P/R	P	P	P/D	P	P	P/R	P/R
source land	low	R	P	P	P	P	P	P	P/R	P/R
survey site	high	P	P	N	P	P/R	P	P	P	P
design site layout	med	P	P	N	P	D	P	P	P	P
design house plan layout	high	P/R	P/R	P	P	D	P	P	D	P
3D house design	high	P	P	P	P	P	P	P	D	P
construction design	high	P	P	P	P	P	P	P	D/P	P
structural design	high	P	P	N	P	P	P	P	P	P
planning and building regs applications	high	P	P	P	P	P	P	P	P	P
costing, programming	high	R	P	P	P	P	P	P	P	P
find funds	med	R	P	P	P	P	P	P	P	P
find self-builders	low	R	R	P	P	P	P	P	R	P
select self-builders	med	R	R	P	P	P/R	P	P	R	P
select professionals	low	R	P	P	P	P/R	P	P	P/R	P/R

Key: skill requirement

R	required skill of self-builders
D	deskilling of task to reduce skill requirement
T	training provided to instill skill
P	professional person allocated to task
N	no requirement for skill and task within the scope of the project

Key: skill difficulty grade

LOW	no particular skills, though some instruction necessary
MEDIUM	basic skills requiring limited training and practice
HIGH	sophisticated skills requiring extended training and practice

FIGURE 14.4 Example of a matrix: self-build skills in nine case studies

These methods of displaying and analysing qualitative data are particularly useful when you compare the results of several case studies, as they permit a certain standardization of presentation, allowing comparisons to be made more easily across the cases.

You can display the information in the form of text, codes, abbreviated notes, symbols, quotations or any other form that helps to communicate compactly. The detail and sophistication of the display can vary depending on its function and on the amount of information available. Displays are useful at any stage in the research process.

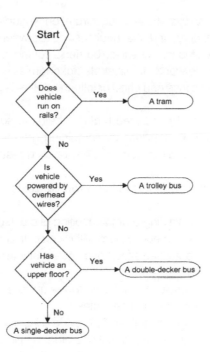

FIGURE 14.5   Example of a network: a flowchart sorting out public transport vehicles

Ordering information in displays

The different types of display can be described by the way that information is ordered in them.

Time ordered displays These record a sequence of events in relation to their chronology. A simple example of this is a project programme giving names, times and locations for tasks of different kinds. The scale and precision of timing can be suited to the subject. Events can be of various types, e.g. tasks, critical events, experiences, stages in a programme, activities, decisions, etc. Some examples of types of time ordered displays are:

Events lists or networks – showing a sequence of events, perhaps highlighting the critical ones, and perhaps including times and dates.

Activity records – showing the sequential steps required to accomplish a task.

Decision models – commonly used to analyse a course of action employing a matrix with yes/no routes from each decision taken.

Conceptually ordered displays These concentrate on variables in the form of abstract concepts related to a theory and the relationships between these. Examples of such variables are motives, attitudes, expertise, barriers, coping strategies, etc. They can be shown as matrices or networks to illustrate taxonomies, content analysis, cognitive structures, relationships of cause and effect or influence. Here is a selection of different types:

- Conceptually or thematically clustered matrix – helps to summarize the mass of data about numerous research questions by combining groups of questions that are connected, either from a theoretical point of view, or as a result of groupings that can be detected in the data.
- Taxonomy tree diagram – useful to break down concepts into their constituent parts or elements.
- Cognitive map – a descriptive diagrammatic plotting of a person's way of thinking about an issue, useful to understand somebody's way of thinking or to compare that of several people.
- Effects matrix – plots the observed effects of an action or intervention, a necessary precursor to explaining or predicting effects.
- Decision tree modelling – helps to make clear a sequence of decisions, by setting up a network of sequential yes/no response routes.
- Causal models – used in theory building to provide a testable set of propositions about a complete network of variables with causal and other relationships between them, based on a multicase situation. A preliminary stage in the development of a causal model is to develop causal chains, linear cause/effect lines.

Role ordered displays These show people's roles and their relationships in formal and informal organizations or groups. A role defines a person's standing and position by assessing their behaviour and expectations within the group or organization. These may be conventionally recognized positions, e.g. judge, mother, machine operator, or more abstract and situation dependent, e.g. motivator, objector. People in different roles tend to see situations from different perspectives: a strike in a factory will be viewed very differently by the management and the workforce. A role ordered matrix will help to systematically display these differences or can be used to investigate whether people in the same roles are unified in their views.

Partially ordered displays These are useful in analysing 'messy' situations without trying to impose too much internal order on them. For example, a context chart can be designed to show, in the form of a network, the influences and pressures that bear on an individual from surrounding organizations and persons when making a decision to act. This will help to understand why a particular action was taken.

Case ordered displays These show the data of cases arranged in some kind of order according to an important variable in the study. This allows you to compare cases and note their different features according to where they appear in the order.

If you are comparing several case studies, you can combine the above displays to make 'meta' displays that amalgamate and contrast the data from each case. For example, a case ordered meta-matrix does this by simply arranging case

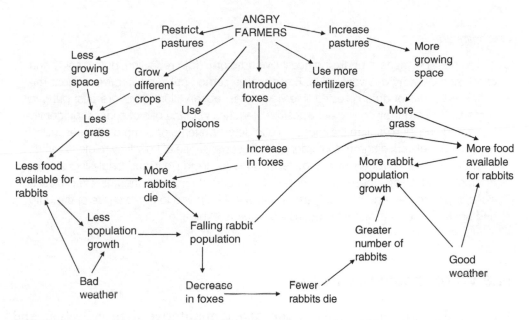

FIGURE 14.6   Example of a network: multiple-cause diagram of a rabbit control system

matrices next to each other in the chosen order to enable you to simply compare the data across the meta-matrix. The meta-matrix can initially be quite large if there are a number of cases. A function of the analysis will be to summarize the data in a smaller matrix, giving a summary of the significant issues discovered. Following this a contrast table can also be devised to display and compare how one or two variables perform in cases as ordered in the meta-matrix.

14.7   Chapter summary

Qualitative research deals with data whose values cannot meaningfully be expressed as numbers. The process of data collecting is often reviewed while in progress and adjusted in the light of the results gained so far. Because the data are generally based on human judgements, feelings, perceptions, beliefs, etc., it is difficult, or indeed impossible, for you as the researcher to completely distance yourself from the results. With some research projects, particularly if there has been little research done in that subject, it will take some time to discover the important variables and to develop a theory.

(Continued)

(Continued)

The principal steps in analysing qualitative data are: data reduction, data display and conclusion drawing and verification. These can be carried out in an iterative fashion. The shapeless mass of data collected (interview notes, observations, etc.) are best put into some kind of order by sorting out types or categories with the use of codes that identify these. You can then explore the coded data to detect patterns or common themes, using matrices or network diagrams, in order to make some sense of how they relate together.

There is a wide variety of display techniques for laying out and analysing events, actions, thoughts, etc. These can be based on, among others, time, themes, effects, decisions, roles, causes and effects. These displays will help you to make sense of the data and draw conclusions about the issues that you are exploring.

14.8 What should I do now?

After reading the above information about qualitative data collection and analysis, how do you think the different techniques could be used in your dissertation? If you are focusing your work on people in society, especially at the level of the individual or small groups, or on people's customs, beliefs, etc., you will not be able to do your research by analysing numbers, you will have to deal with lots of information in the form of written material. As you will probably have gathered, the process can be quite complicated and difficult to do for the first time. It is a great help if you can use a previous research programme as a model, perhaps to test out its methods and findings in a different context. For example, if you are interested in examining the factors that influence work motivation and productivity in an estate agent's office, perhaps a professional research project has already been done on these in a different office setting. This would provide useful guidelines on the main variables to examine, and practical techniques of data collection, display and analysis.

FIGURE 14.7 The project could get horribly out of hand

I suggest that you do the following things to get you on your way. Note how you will be building up an argument for doing your research the way you propose.

- Think carefully about your dissertation topic and ask yourself: what is the nature of what I am going to investigate? Are the variables readily recognizable and easily measurable, and are there more than 20 or 30 cases in my study? If so, a quantitative approach is more suitable. Are the variables open to interpretation, difficult to measure, and are there only a few cases to examine? If yes, then you have to use qualitative research methods to examine these. Note that there may be aspects of your dissertation topic that fall into each of these categories. No problem: you will just have to use whichever type of method is appropriate for each of the aspects.
- If you think that a qualitative approach is appropriate for all or some of your research, examine what are the main factors at play. How are they described, e.g. in inter-personal relationships: jealousy, belief, loyalty, tradition?
- From your background reading, look for writings that specifically describe and explain investigations dealing with these factors, particularly those that were in your area of study. Examine these to see if there are methods used that you could adapt for your own work to get the answers that you are aiming at.
- Set up a plan of work to describe the sequence of data gathering and analysis, the types of activities you will undertake at each step, together with timing. This will help to ensure that you will not bite off more than you can chew. Obviously, there will be some uncertainties: point these out. If there are too many, the project could get horribly out of hand, so alter the setting, eliminate problem areas, find other more familiar ways, or even adjust the research questions to make the work more practicable and less chancy.

If you can, it is really worth talking to your supervisor about your plan to discuss the practical and skill issues. Obviously, the clearer you can draw it up, the more use it will be. The main questions to ask are:

1. Is the plan practically possible given your time, skills and access to your objects of study?
2. Will it produce the answers to the questions posed by your project?
3. Will the project fulfil the requirements of the dissertation assignment?

If the answers are 'yes' to the above questions, then things are looking good. If you managed to get some feedback from your supervisor, make sure that you understood what he or she advised, and reflect how this advice might alter your work. Check again against the questions after you have made any alterations.

14.9 References to more information

As you would expect with this big and complex subject, there is a myriad of books dedicated to explaining all aspects. In the list below, I have tried to explain a bit about each individual book and how it may be of use to you.

I have ordered them in what I think is going from the simplest to the most sophisticated.

Further reading

Robson, C. (2011) *Real World Research: A Resource for Social Scientists and Practitioner-Researchers*, 3rd edition. Chichester: Wiley. This is a resource book and should be used as such. Good for getting more detailed information on most aspects of data collection and analysis. Read the recommendations at the beginning of how to use the book.

Flick, U. (2009) *An Introduction to Qualitative Research*, 4th edition. London: Sage. Part 4 of the book is dedicated to analysing verbal data, with practical advice on documentation, coding, interpretation and analysis. Part 5 is about observation and ethnography, including visual data. Be selective in picking out what is relevant to you, as a lot of it will not be.

Seale, C. (ed.) (2012) *Researching Society and Culture*, 3rd edition. London: Sage. This edited book has chapters by various authors, each on one aspect of research. See the first few chapters in Part 2 for qualitative analysis, choosing whatever is appropriate for your study.

For a really comprehensive though incredibly dense and rather technical guide to qualitative data analysis, refer to:

Miles, M.B., Huberman, A.M. and Saldaña, J. (2013) *Qualitative Data Analysis: A Methods Sourcebook*, 3rd edition. London: Sage. This has a lot of examples of displays that help to explain how they work, but is technically sophisticated so you might find it difficult to understand the terminology in the examples.

And a few more books if you don't find what you want in the above. Your library catalogue will list many more. Try a search using key words, such as 'data analysis', with 'management', 'education' or whatever your particular subject is, to see if there are specific books dedicated to your particular interest.

Silverman, D. (2012) *Interpreting Qualitative Data*, 4th edition. London: Sage. A fantastic range of topics covered here, with interesting sections in Part 2 on why talk matters.

Holliday, A. (2007) *Doing and Writing Qualitative Research*, 2nd edition. London: Sage. A general guide to writing qualitative research aimed at students of sociology, applied linguistics, management and education.

Schwandt, T. (2007) *The Sage Dictionary of Qualitative Enquiry*, 3rd edition. Thousand Oaks, CA: Sage. To help you understand all the technical jargon.

15

Why Do I Need Arguments?

Chapter contents

15.1 Introduction

Your dissertation is probably your first lengthy piece of independent writing. The big question when faced with such a task is how to structure the work so that it forms an integral whole. The structure will provide a guide to the reader, as well as a framework for you to fill as you write. In academic writing, the aim is not to tell a story as one might in a novel, but to set up an argument to support a particular view, analysis or conclusion. In fact, argument will pervade all that you write: you will be trying to persuade the reader that what you have done is worthwhile and based on some kind of intellectual process.

Whatever the subject of the inquiry, there has to be a focus, a central issue that is being considered. You should be able to define this quite clearly when you prepare your proposal, by setting up the main research question and subquestions (or aims, objectives, etc.). The body of the dissertation will then revolve around this focal point, perhaps considering it from different perspectives, or examining causes or finding explanations for the situation. At the end you will have to come to some conclusions, and this is where argument is required. You will need to base these conclusions on evidence, and you should produce some reasoned argument about how this evidence leads to your conclusions. The conclusions should provide answers to the research questions (or attain the objectives etc.). This is where argument is required.

You will also have to argue why you have gone about your investigations in the way you have. Lots of choices will be open to you as to how to carry out your investigations, e.g. which issues to treat as important, which data to collect and which to ignore or reject, who to consult and how to analyse the data, etc. It is up to you to convince the reader that you have good reasons for doing what you have done, and to demonstrate that it needed to be done in order to produce suitable evidence on which to base your conclusions.

No wonder that argument is an important topic to understand. So, as argument will feature as a basic ingredient of your dissertation, what exactly does it consist of and are there different types of argument?

FIGURE 15.1   Argument will feature as a basic ingredient

15.2 The use of language

Let's just start with a quick review of some of the most important aspects of language. Why? Because language is the medium for argument. An argument without language becomes a fight!

We often fail to appreciate the complexity and subtlety of the many uses of language. Here, as in many other situations, there is a danger in our tendency to over-simplify. But here we go with such a simplification. Copi et al. (2010: 64–66) divided the use of language into three very general categories, which have been found useful by many writers on logic and language.

To communicate information, to inform – Normally this is done by devising propositions and then maintaining or refuting them, or presenting an argument about them. This is not to say that the information is true or that the arguments are valid; misinformation is also included in this category. The function of informative discourse is to describe the world and to reason about it.

To express – Poetry, evocative prose, even sales talk and political haranguing, exploit expressive possibilities to the full. Alliteration, analogies, rhythms, rhymes and other devices are often used.

To direct – For the purposes of causing (or preventing) overt action. The most obvious examples of directive discourse are commands and requests. When a soldier is told to fire his gun, there is no informative or emotional content in the command. The form of language is directed at getting results.

FIGURE 15.2   To communicate

FIGURE 15.3   To express

FIGURE 15.4   To direct

In your dissertation you will primarily use the informative function of language, even though you might be studying the use of other forms, e.g. when analysing poetry. In order to inform, it is necessary to assert a statement in such a manner as to get the reader to believe in it. So, what are statements and how are they used?

15.3 Statements

According to Reynolds (1977: 67–76), statements can be classified into two groups: those that state that a concept exists, and those that describe a relationship between two concepts.

Existence statements

These state that a concept exists, and provide a typology or a description. Here are some statements that make existence claims:

That object is a cat.
That house is black and white.
That (event) is a rainstorm.

Each of these statements follows the same basic pattern: it provides a concept, identifies it by a term, and applies it to a thing or an event. The above are examples of existence statements in their simplest form. They can, however, be more complicated without losing their basic form. For example:

If

a)   there are four individuals in a group;
b)   each individual plays a stringed instrument; and
c)   each individual co-operates in the group to perform pieces from the string quartet repertoire;

then the group is a string quartet.

Existence statements can be 'right' or 'wrong' depending on the circumstances. Take, for example, the rather abstract statement, 'It is 5 o'clock in the afternoon here'. This can be seen to be correct anywhere once a day. If, however, we state in a more concrete fashion that, 'It is 5 o'clock in the afternoon on 15 November in London', this can only be correct once and in one place. It can thus be seen that the level of abstraction of a statement has a powerful influence on its potential for correctness, i.e. the more abstract a statement, the more capacity it has for being right, and conversely the more concrete a statement, the more capacity it has for being wrong.

Relational statements

These impart information about a relationship between two concepts. By referring to the instance of one concept, they state that another concept exists and is linked to the first. We rely on relational statements to explain, predict and provide us with a sense of understanding of our surroundings.

There are two broad classifications of relational statements. The first describes an association between two concepts, and the second describes a causal relationship between two concepts.

Here is an associational statement:

If a person is an athlete, then he or she will be physically fit.

By slightly changing the wording of this sentence you can transform it into a *causal statement*:

Becoming an athlete will make a person be more physically fit.

That is, becoming an athlete will cause that person to be more physically fit.

There are three possible types of *correlation* between two concepts:

- Positive – e.g. fast cars have large engines (and vice versa), i.e. high value in one concept associated with high value in a second concept, or low value associated with low value.

- Negative – e.g. grass at low altitudes grows longer, i.e. low value in one concept associated with high value in a second concept.

- None – e.g. men and women have equal rights in a democracy, i.e. no information about associated high or low values in either concept.

The degree of association is often measurable and is usually expressed as +1.0 for maximum positive correlation, 0.0 for no correlation, and −1.0 for maximum negative correlation.

Causal statements describe what is sometimes called a 'cause and effect' relationship. The concept or variable that is the cause is referred to as the 'independent variable' (because it varies independently), and the variable that is affected is referred to as the 'dependent variable' (because it is dependent on the independent variable). For example, in 'running fast makes you out of breath', 'running fast' is the independent variable and 'out of breath' is the dependent variable.

Causal statements can be deterministic, meaning that under certain conditions an event will inevitably follow, e.g. 'if you drop an apple, it will fall'. However, it is not always possible to be so certain of an outcome, so a probabilistic statement might be more suitable, e.g. 'if parents are intelligent, their children are likely to be intelligent too'. A quantification of the order of probability may be possible, e.g. with a probability of 0.7.

Abstraction

Statements of any kind can be made on three levels of abstraction:

- Theoretical statements – abstract statements based on theoretical concepts, e.g. 'bodily comfort depends on environmental conditions'.
- Operational statements – less abstract in that they are based on the definitions of theoretical concepts, which are capable of measurement, e.g. 'the rate of heartbeat relates to the surrounding still air temperature and the level of activity'.
- Concrete statements – based on specific findings, i.e. the measurements themselves, e.g. 'the heart beats at 102 beats per minute at a surrounding air temperature of 32 degrees centigrade at an energy consumption level of 42 kilocalories per hour'.

15.4 Argument

Statements on their own provide information on discrete units. When they are strung together to form a larger structure, they are often referred to as a discourse. Just as with language generally, discourse can be used for information, expression or direction. Again, for your dissertation you will primarily be using the informative type of discourse, sometimes called assertive discourse. This type of discourse consists of, or contains, assertive statements. These are the discourses that invite us to approach them from a logical point of view.

In some assertive discourses, statements are not merely presented for our information (or misinformation, as the case may be); they are connected in a specific, logical way. Some of the statements are offered as reasons for others.

This kind of discourse is termed an argument. It is a discourse that not only makes assertions but also asserts that some of those assertions are reasons for others.

In the case of ordinary speech, the term 'argument' is often used when referring to a dispute, or a situation in which people who hold different views on some controversial subject try to bring the other person around to their way of thinking. But as a technical term in logic, argument is a special kind of discourse, in which a claim is made that one or more particular statements should be accepted as true, or probably true, on the grounds that certain other statements are true. Put another way: by the process of reasoning, using the operation of logic, a conclusion is inferred from the statements given. An argument can be seen as the verbal record of this reasoning.

The minimal ingredients of an argument are:

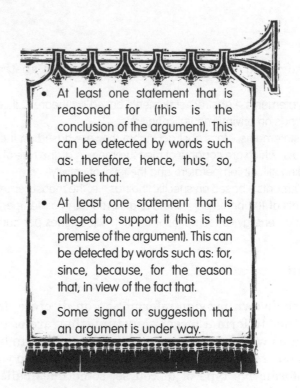

- At least one statement that is reasoned for (this is the conclusion of the argument). This can be detected by words such as: therefore, hence, thus, so, implies that.

- At least one statement that is alleged to support it (this is the premise of the argument). This can be detected by words such as: for, since, because, for the reason that, in view of the fact that.

- Some signal or suggestion that an argument is under way.

It is sometimes difficult to determine whether a discourse is an argument: there are cases, especially in a complex piece of text, when it is impossible to be sure whether the minimal ingredients of an argument are indeed present.

15.5 Different types of argument

In essence, your whole dissertation should be in the form of an argument. Why is this? Because whatever you are writing about, it must be your concern to persuade the reader that you are writing sense, that your conclusions follow from your evidence, and that you are making some valid points about your chosen subject. A dissertation that comes to no conclusions is not worthy of the name; it would be better called a summary or an account.

In the light of what has been discussed above, the nature of your argument will be very much influenced by your philosophical standpoint. It may be based on a purely scientific approach, dealing with facts and looking for verifiable causes and effects, or alternatively it may be based on gaining some kind of understanding of complex social issues where nothing can be stated for certain. You may combine the two approaches where it is relevant. Whatever you do, though, your dissertation should convince the reader that there are good reasons why you come to your conclusions.

So, what are the characteristics of an argument? The most important requirement is the use of logic. This allows us to move from making statements to reaching conclusions. Here are two examples of very basic arguments:

---

1 All cows are animals.

Daisy is a cow.
Therefore Daisy is an animal.

2 Fred is rich and drives a large car.

John is rich and drives a large car.
Mike is rich and drives a large car.
Therefore rich people probably drive large cars.

Compare these two short arguments, and you will doubtless notice that the conclusions differ. The first conclusion is a categorical statement, while the second only asserts a probability. In fact these arguments start from exactly opposite directions.

The first is an example of deductive thinking. It starts by making a general statement and then deducing a particular instance from this. The second is an example of an inductive argument. It makes statements about particular cases and then draws a general conclusion from these.

If the statements (premises) of a deductive argument are true, and if the argument correctly follows the rules of logic (i.e. is valid), then the conclusion must be true. In this way it is like a mathematical calculation, either true or

FIGURE 15.5   Drives a large car

false depending on the correctness of the input and the method. There is nothing you can add to the premises to make the conclusion more true (e.g. that all cows have four legs, they all drink water etc.).

Inductive arguments are more flexible in the sense that, even with correct logic, the conclusion cannot be said to be definitely true or false, only more or less probable. The more supporting evidence you can bring to bear, the greater the probability of the conclusion being correct. For example, if you could name thousands of rich people, all of whom drove large cars, your conclusion would be strengthened. Even if only one or two of them had small cars, the conclusion would not be incorrect.

Just to make things a bit more complicated, inductive arguments do not necessarily only use individual cases to make a general conclusion. They can also be turned round to make a conclusion about a particular case from a general statement, for example:

Most clever students get good exam grades.
Julie is a clever student.
Therefore Julie will probably get a good grade in her finals.

What really marks this out from a deductive argument is that additional statements (premises) can have serious effects on the probability of the conclusion. If Julie also got good grades in her last exams, attends all the lectures, works hard, etc., then the conclusion will be reinforced. If, however, she is bone idle, never reads a book or goes to lectures, and gets paralysed by nerves during examinations, then you might reach just the opposite conclusion.

15.6 Do I need to use logic in my argument?

The simple answer is yes! Whatever argument you follow, even if it is based on qualitative data of the most subjective kind, you need to make a case to support your conclusions. In order to do this, your argument needs to be based on a logical sequence of evidence and conclusions. What does this involve? Well, there are basic rules of logic that can be simply learned, though applying them in a complex argument is a bit more difficult. The aim is to be able to detect a correct logical structure in an argument to determine whether the argument is valid or invalid. So what are the characteristics of logic that govern the structure of argument?

You must remember that logic is concerned not with the truth or falsity of premises (statements) or conclusions, but rather with the correctness of arguments. Therefore we do not say that arguments are true, incorrect or untrue, but we say that they contain valid deductions, correct inductions, or at the other extreme, assorted fallacies. The strict rules below really apply only to deductive arguments as these are limited to reaching firm conclusions solely based on the stated premises: no 'probably', 'might', 'likely to', as is seen in the conclusions of inductive arguments.

Validity of deductive arguments

The validity of deductive arguments is determined only by their logical form, not by the content of the statements which they contain. When the premise or premises of such an argument are related to the conclusion in such a way that the conclusion must be true if the premises are true, then the argument is said to be 'valid'. Any argument where this is not the case is called invalid.

Consider the following examples:

---

1   All diamonds are hard.

Some diamonds are gems.
Therefore some gems are hard.

2   All birds have wings.

All cats are birds.
Therefore all cats have wings.

(Continued)

211

(Continued)

3   All fat cats can fly.

Some pigs are fat.
Therefore some pigs can fly.

4   Some animals eat grass.

Animals that eat grass are herbivores.
Therefore (all) animals are herbivores.

Although some of the premises in arguments 1 and 2 are obviously false, if they were true, the conclusions would have to be true. These arguments are based on valid logical structures. The structure of argument 3 is not valid, even if the premises were true, because it is necessary to be a cat rather then fat in order to fly! In argument 4 both the premises are true but the conclusion is not – invalid logic.

It might be easy in simple sentences like the above to distinguish between valid and invalid arguments, as the premises are short and unambiguous and the construction of the arguments is simple. But arguments are not often stated quite so succinctly in books or research papers, or even undergraduate dissertations, so it is usually necessary to read the text very carefully to distil the argument down to a series of simple statements.

15.7 Fallacies in argument

Logic is the protection against trickery and sloppy thinking. Logic deals with arguments that are based on reason. Mistakes are possible and even frequent in applying forms of logical argument. These mistakes are termed fallacies. However, not all mistakes in argument are genuine mistakes; there are innumerable examples of the calculated use of quasi-reasoning, used in order to convince or convert the unwary.

The recognition of fallacies is not new, many of them having been noted as early as Aristotle. You can probably devise an argument yourself which is entirely logical, whose validity is clearly demonstrated by the conclusion being derived from the premises, and which carefully follows all the rules of syllogism, but which is based on premises that are phoney, tricks and delusions. There are brilliant deceptions for getting people to accept all sorts of false premises as true, and these tricks of argument are so common that even when people realize that they are being hoodwinked they tend to let it pass.

The daily use of argument in normal and academic life is a highly complicated human activity and you cannot successfully study it in a sort of vacuum.

FIGURE 15.6   Valid logical structures

There is no simple connection between the presentation of an argument on one side, and the acceptance of it on the other. Emotional and referential signals often add a significant subtext. For example, even the most abstract and exotic television commercials usually contain some kind of argument, some assertion of reasons and drawing of conclusions, e.g. 'you must buy this because it is so romantic'. Even when you read books on logic you find that the arguments are seldom spelled out fully, except in the examples.

The word 'fallacy' is often used in two ways. Sometimes it is used to describe any kind of attitude that is fraudulent or deceitful, and at other times it is used, in a more narrow sense, to indicate a defective manner of reasoning or a wily or cunning form of persuasion. In the following analysis of fallacies, it is the second meaning that is taken, i.e. when an argument purports to abide by the rules of sound argument but in fact fails to do so. There are two main categories of fallacy – formal and informal.

Formal fallacies have some error in the structure of the logic. Although they often resemble valid forms of argument, the logical route only takes us from A to B by way of disjointed or missing paths. In brief, the fallacy occurs because the chain of reasoning itself is defective.

Informal fallacies, on the other hand, often use valid reasoning in terms that are not of sufficient quality to merit such treatment. They can be linguistic, and allow ambiguities of language to admit error, and leave out something needed to sustain the argument, or permit irrelevant factors to weigh on the conclusion, or allow unwarranted presumptions to alter the conclusions that are reached.

There is not room here to discuss all the different types of fallacy in detail, but I have selected some of those with the greatest relevance to academic research work. Most types of fallacy have been given titles or technical names and are well known to logicians. It is not necessary that you remember the names, though it will impress people if you point out the shortcomings in their arguments by quoting the type of fallacy by its name! The following examples demonstrate a few of these:

1. 'If I run too much I will be tired. Since I have not run at all, I am not tired.'

    Formal fallacy – denying the antecedent. The writer does not recognize that the same result can be produced by different causes.

2. 'The duchess has a fine ship, but she has barnacles on her bottom.'

    Informal fallacy – linguistic. This is a case of careless grammatical construction that causes an ambiguity of meaning.

3. 'The ship of government, like any other ship, works best when there is a strong captain in charge of it. That is why government by dictatorship is more effective.'

    Informal fallacy – relevance presumption. Analogies are often a useful way of describing unfamiliar concepts: in the above, equating government to a ship. The mistake is to assume further similarities that may not exist.

4. 'Talk of the Loch Ness monster is nonsense. We know that it does not exist because every single attempt to find it has failed utterly.'

    Informal fallacy – relevance intrusion. Just because we lack knowledge about something, it is a fallacy to infer that the opposite is the case.

5. 'All musicians are really sensitive people. It happens that some really sensitive people are not properly appreciated. So some musicians are not properly appreciated.'

    Formal fallacy – undistributed middle. The middle term 'really sensitive people' in this example does not refer to all sensitive people – so musicians might not be included.

6. 'If the Americans wanted good trade relations, they would encourage the production of specialist goods in other countries. Since they do support this type of production, we know that they want good trade relations.'

    Formal fallacy – affirming the consequent. In an 'if … then' construction, the 'if' part is the antecedent, and the 'then' part is the consequent. It is alright to affirm the antecedent, but not vice versa. Affirming the consequent is fallacious because an event can be produced by different causes.

FIGURE 15.7   It will impress people if you point out the shortcomings in their arguments

7. 'I don't think we should employ Mr Smith. I am told that he is a poor golf player. Careless people are bad at golf, so I don't think it is a good omen.'

    Informal fallacy – omission. When statements are made about a class, they may be about all or some (or none) of the members. This fallacy occurs when ambiguity of expression permits a misunderstanding of the quantity that is spoken of (i.e. in this example, is it all or some careless people who are bad at golf?).

The above examples will give you an idea of some logical pitfalls. Obviously, in more sophisticated arguments the logic can become very complex, with parts of an argument depending on others, e.g. if not this, then that. To get over this problem, the study of formal logic has developed an almost mathematical system of replacing parts of arguments with symbols – letters (A, B, C, etc.) for premises and conclusions, and signs (e.g. →) for connectives such as 'and', 'if', 'or', 'it is not the case that ...', etc. If you look in a book about formal logic you will see pages of formulae that look like advanced mathematics. (See Figure 15.8.) This is not for the uninitiated!

Obviously, it is important to recognize fallacies when you read or listen to people's arguments. It is just as important to avoid fallacies in your own writing (or to use them to best effect if you intend to deceive!). At this level, you will have to rely on careful reading and analytical thinking and quite a lot of common sense. The above examples are only a small selection of types of fallacy. Whole books are written on the subject, so if you would like to read more about fallacy in all its guises, I can recommend the books by Pirie (1985) as a light-hearted account (from which I adapted some of the above examples), and Fearnside and Holther (1959) for a more serious and technical approach.

(i) $\left|\dfrac{A}{x}\right. \models p_i$ iff $x \in v\,(p_i)$, $i = 1,\,2,\,\ldots$;

(ii) $\left|\dfrac{A}{x}\right. \models \sim B$ iff not $\left|\dfrac{A}{x}\right. \models B$;

(iii) $\left|\dfrac{A}{x}\right. \models B \vee C$ iff $\left|\dfrac{A}{x}\right. \models B$ or $\left|\dfrac{A}{x}\right. \models C$;

(iv) $\left|\dfrac{A}{x}\right. \models \square B$ iff $\left|\dfrac{A}{y}\right. \models B$ for all y in W;

(v) $\left|\dfrac{A}{x}\right. \models (p_i)B$ iff $\left|\dfrac{A'}{x}\right. \models B$ for all structures $A' = (W,\,P,\,v')$

such that
$$v'(p_j) = v(p_j)$$
for all $j \neq i$, $i = 1,\,2,\,\ldots$. (Note: $v'(p_i) \in P$ by the definition of structure.)

The formula A is *valid in* A, $\left|\dfrac{A}{}\right. \models A$, if $\left|\dfrac{A}{v}\right. \models A$ for all y in W.

FIGURE 15.8   Logical language (Fine, 1970: 337)

15.8 Building up your argument: the essential thread

So, what has all this theoretical stuff got to do with your dissertation work? As has been mentioned several times before, the whole point of doing a dissertation is to identify a particular question or problem, to collect information and to present some answers or solutions. It is up to you to convince the reader that you have collected information relevant to the question or problem and that you have based your answers and conclusions on the correct analysis of this information. You will need to use some logical argument in order to do this convincingly.

Taylor (1989: 67) offers a useful list of the sorts of argument you might make in your dissertation. You might:

- agree with, accede to, defend or confirm a particular point of view
- propose a new point of view
- concede that an existing point of view has certain merits, but that it needs to be qualified in certain important respects
- reformulate an existing point of view such that the new version makes a better explanation
- dismiss a point of view or other person's work on account of its inadequacy, irrelevance, incoherence, etc.
- reject, rebut or refute another's argument on various reasoned grounds
- reconcile two positions that may seem at variance by appeal to some 'higher' or 'deeper' principle
- retract or recant one's own position in the face of arguments or evidence.

Imagine yourself to be a lawyer making a case in court. You set out to solve the problem (who committed the crime and how) by analysing the situation, collecting the evidence, then making a case for your conclusions about 'who-dunit' and how. The jury will have to decide whether the argument is convincing and the evidence is sufficiently strong. In the case of a dissertation, you will be setting the problem and laying out your case, and the examiner will be your jury.

Just as a lawyer will be careful to make it clear just how he or she has reached his or her conclusions, so must you make it obvious how you came to yours. Always refer to the evidence when you make statements, whether it be by citing some kind of authority or by referring to your data and analysis. Careful cross-referencing is essential here. Always give page numbers of where the evidence is to be found (whether in a reference or in your dissertation), and refer to diagrams and graphs by number when relevant.

It is a good idea initially to set up a skeleton of your argument by making a diagram that starts with the question or problem at the top, then follows logical steps to the conclusions. There may be branches along the way that take in particular aspects of the subject, i.e. subquestions that need to be covered. But all the threads should come together at the end to provide the main answer or solution to the main question or problem. In this way, you will be able to track the route of your argument and spot gaps, fallacies, meanderings or dead-ends. The examiner should be able to draw a similar diagram from reading your completed dissertation.

Obviously, before you have completed the work, you will not be able to finalize the argument. But it is important to have a clear 'route map' so that you can check your progress and fill in gaps. Expect to change some components of your argument as you get further advanced in your work. When you have completed the first draft, consciously check, by scanning through your main sections, that you have clearly stated the question or problem, that you have explained how you will tackle it, that the data collected are relevant, the analysis produces good reasons for your conclusions, and your conclusions actually address the question or problem stated at the outset. It is surprising how often students get somehow lost in the process and come to conclusions that do little to

FIGURE 15.9   A lawyer making a case in court

217

address the initial problem. If you do this preparation and checking, you won't be one of them.

15.9 Gathering your results

Ideally, you will have the research questions at the forefront of your mind throughout your time working on your dissertation. However, this is not always possible as you grapple with the learning of new techniques and methods and the problems of organizing your data collection and analysis. But you must come back to them regularly in order to ensure that you are keeping to the intentions of the project, and will end up with relevant material in order to be able to suggest answers to the questions.

Coming to conclusions is a cumulative process. It is unlikely that the problem you have chosen is simple, with questions raised that can be answered with a simple yes or no. Even if they can, you will be required to describe why it is one or the other and make an argument to support your case. Normally, you will find that the questions have several subquestions, and even these can be broken down into components requiring separate investigation. Throughout the analysis part of your work you will be able to make conclusions about these fragments of the main issues. The skill is to gather these up at the end in the concluding chapter to fit them together into a 'mosaic' that will present the complete picture of the conclusion to the entire dissertation.

Just as you should be able to summarize the main problem that your dissertation addresses in one or two sentences, so you should be able to state the conclusion equally briefly. This belies the complexities that lie in between. You can picture your dissertation as having a continuous thread of argument running through it. The beginning and end of the argument are fat and tightly woven. But in between, the separate strands fan out, become twisted and frayed as different aspects are investigated, but manage to web together before reaching the end.

The secret to success lies in the sound construction of your argument.

FIGURE 15.10

15.10 Chapter summary

The use of language is the main way to communicate research. Argument is used to reach answers to research questions or attain the objectives of the research. Existence and relational statements form the basis of arguments which use logic in order to come to conclusions. The two main forms of argument are inductive and deductive. Simple inductive arguments start with existence statements and derive a relational statement as a conclusion – moving from the particular to the general. Conversely, deductive arguments start with general statements and derive an existence statement as a conclusion – moving from the general to the particular.

Fallacies are arguments that are faulty in some way. There are many kinds, roughly classed as formal or informal. Formal fallacies are based on faulty logic steps, informal are those that use language emotively or make irrelevant assertions. In complicated texts it can be difficult to test the soundness of the arguments presented.

You should clearly use your research aims or questions as the focus for the arguments in your dissertation. The conclusions should be traceable back to the evidence you provide to support them, which in turn should be centred on the issues that you are investigating. You will probably come to several conclusions about different aspects of your research, which should then be combined at the end to form a general overall conclusion.

15.11 What should I do now?

Why not try to construct a diagram as suggested in the second part of Section 15.8? One way to do this is to write all the elements of the argument on bits of paper, and then arrange them on a tabletop until you are satisfied that they follow through logically. You will see where there are missing links, where additional evidence is needed, and what is the shortest route to the conclusions. You can easily reject or add bits of paper. You will also be able to track any parallel arguments that you may need to make when you take several aspects of the problem into account. Do they all add up at the end to form a plausible main conclusion?

When you are satisfied with the framework, you can produce a diagram to record your 'route map'. You could probably also do this exercise on the computer, using a program that is designed to create diagrams of this kind. The next thing to do is to translate how this map will guide the structure of the written work. Does it fall neatly into chapters? Ensure that the steps in the argument remain clear. It is also a good idea to explain the structure of your argument in the introductory chapter. This not only forms a useful guide to the reader, but will impress the examiner with your lucid thinking and organization.

15.12 References to more information

You can quickly get into deep water on the subject of thinking and argument. I would recommend Brink-Budgen to start with, and perhaps follow up the references in there if you want to find out more on specific issues. The other books I have listed, easiest first, require either that you have a special interest or that you have chosen a dissertation topic that focuses on aspects of these subjects.

Further reading

Brink-Budgen, R. (2010) *Critical Thinking for Students: Learn the Skills of Analysing, Evaluating and Producing Arguments*, 4th edition. Oxford: How To Books.

Schostak, J. and Schostak, J. (2012) *Writing Research Critically: Developing the Power to Make a Difference*. London: Routledge.

Wilhoit, S. (2009) *A Brief Guide to Writing Academic Arguments*. London: Longman

Kuhn, D. (1991) *The Skills of Argument*. Cambridge: Cambridge University Press.

If you really want to get into more depth about logic and argument the following are reasonably approachable books, listed in order of easiest first.

Salmon, M. (2012) *Introduction to Logic and Critical Thinking*, 6th edition. Boston: Wadsworth.

Gensler, H.J. (1989) *Logic: Analyzing and Appraising Arguments*. London: Prentice Hall.

Fisher, A. (2004) *The Logic of Real Arguments*, 2nd edition. Cambridge: Cambridge University Press.

These are three books about fallacy that might interest you; see the comments I have made for more guidance.

Pirie, M. (2007) *How to Win Every Argument: The Use and Abuse of Logic*. New York: Continuum.

Pirie, M. (1985) *Book of the Fallacy: A Training Manual of Intellectual Subversives*. London: Routledge and Kegan Paul. Well written and entertaining.

Thouless, R.H. (1974) *Straight and Crooked Thinking*, revised edition. London: Pan. Old, but still entertaining and thought-provoking.

Worth a look for aspects of writing:

Taylor, G. (2009) *A Student's Writing Guide: How to Plan and Write Successful Essays*. Cambridge: Cambridge University Press.

16

How Can I Manage Such a Long Piece of Writing?

Chapter contents

16.1 When to start writing up

To sit down in front of a blank computer monitor with the task of writing a 20,000 word dissertation is a daunting prospect and one to be avoided. You can easily arrange that you will not be faced with this situation. The trick is to gradually amass a collection of notes, observations and data on the issues relevant to your study, which you can then use as a basis for your first draft. This way, you will have started writing your dissertation without even realizing it! If you have followed the advice in Chapter 9 about organizing your note-taking system, you should have little problem in retrieving the notes in an orderly fashion.

To lessen the anguish of starting to write up later on in the programme, it helps to build up your first draft from an early stage. To be able to do this you will need to prepare a structure for the dissertation as soon as you are clear what you will be doing. You can devise this in outline after you have done some background reading and completed your proposal. The structure will then provide a framework into which you can insert your text. Don't expect either the framework or the text to be the final version. Both will need refining and revising as your work and understanding progress. Luckily, word processors make revision very quick and easy.

The issue of writing style should be considered at this point. As a dissertation is an academic piece of work, generally a more formal style is adopted. At its extreme, this avoids the personal pronoun 'I' altogether. It is a good idea to raise the issue of style when you discuss your work with your tutor. There may be some indications given in the assignment details: you should read these carefully anyway for instructions on what is expected of you.

FIGURE 16.1   A more formal style is adopted

16.2 Frame and fill

The framework for your dissertation is most easily created by making a list of possible chapter or section headings. Consult your proposal and plan of work for indications of what these may be. At the very simplest level the divisions may be like this:

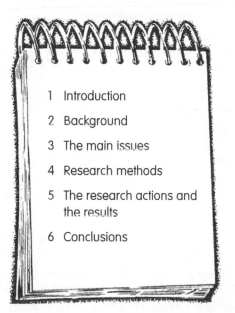

1 Introduction

2 Background

3 The main issues

4 Research methods

5 The research actions and the results

6 Conclusions

This assumes that you will use the background reading to clarify the main issues of your research, often in the form of questions; that you use these questions to select one or several suitable research data collection and analysis methods to delve more deeply into these issues; that this will produce some data or results that you will present and analyse; and that you will be able to draw some conclusions from this analysis in relation to the main issues. This is a conventional format and can be applied to a study in almost any subject. There are other, unconventional, ways of organizing a dissertation. If you do want to use an unusual structure or even want to develop your own, it is best to discuss this with your supervisor to check that it will be acceptable. The main thing is that you can set up a convincing overall argument that leads from your intentions to your conclusions, from your research questions to their answers.

Once you have the main framework, you can elaborate on the contents of each section by inserting subheadings indicating the aspects that you want to cover in each. Just use your current knowledge and a bit of imagination at first to suggest relevant subheadings. This will help to establish the thread of your argument as discussed in Chapter 10. You will be able to reorder, expand or change these as you progress.

An example of subheadings is given below:

1. Introduction.

- The main aims of the dissertation.
- A short summary of the context of the study.
- The main problems or issues to be investigated.
- The overall approach to the project.
- A short description of the structure of the dissertation.

2. Background.

- Aspects of the subject investigated.
- Historical and current context.
- Evidence of problems or contentious issues.
- Current debate – comparison of different opinions or approaches.
- Shortcomings in the level of knowledge.

3. Main issues.

- A summary of the main problem, issue or question, and how it can be divided into different aspects or subproblems or subquestions.
- First aspect/subproblem/subquestion stated and described.
- Second aspect/subproblem/subquestion stated and described.
- Third aspect/subproblem/subquestion stated and described.

4. Research methods.

- General approach to investigation (philosophy?).
- Alternative methods discussed.
- Selection and description of methods related to aspects/subproblems/questions (experiment, survey, modelling, accounts, archival analysis, case study, historical, etc.).
- Selection of samples or case studies (if you are doing a survey or choosing particular examples for detail study), and pilot study.
- Methods of presentation of results (e.g. charts, graphs, diagrams, spreadsheets, mathematical calculations, commentaries, etc.).
- Analytical methods used (statistical tests – specify which ones, comparisons, coding, systems analysis, algorithms, models, diagramming, etc.).

5. Research actions and results.

- Description of actions taken (use a heading for each type of action, e.g. questionnaires, interviews, observations, textual analysis, etc.), possibly related to the different aspects/subproblems/subquestions.

- Results of actions (give account of data collected from each of the actions above), again possibly related to the different aspects/subproblems/subquestions.

6. Conclusions.

- Conclusions drawn from sets of data in relation to the main issues (this can be separated into sections for each aspect/subproblem/subquestion).
- Overall conclusions of the dissertation addressing the main issue/problem/question.

FIGURE 16.2 Once you have the main framework, you can elaborate on the contents

I have kept the subheadings as general as possible so that you can possibly apply these or something equivalent in the context of your subject. You will have to use your imagination and judgement to assess if this arrangement actually suits what you want to do. Devise your own sequence if you like, but note the overall pattern of identifying issues from background study, the definition of how you will investigate these, how you will present the information gained, and how this will be analysed to enable you to come to conclusions.

You don't have to start writing your text at the beginning and continue to the end. Use what notes you have got so far and insert them where they are relevant in order to fill in the framework. If you have the notes already written on your computer, then you can simply copy and paste them in a rough order under the appropriate headings and subheadings. Use the key words that you have appended to your notes to help you make the selections. If you have recorded them on paper, now is the time to transfer them into the word processor. You will thus quickly have several pages of (very) rough draft.

However, be warned. Even though it might look pretty impressive, the text will be no more than a series of raw notes, completely unedited, disjointed and incomplete. But it will provide a solid basis for working on in order to produce a first draft.

FIGURE 16.3   Use what notes you have got so far

16.3 Marshalling your notes and drafting your text

You will probably be told what the overall length of your dissertation is required to be. If not, find out by asking your tutor, or consult previous dissertations written in your course. You need to know this in order to determine how long each section should be to get a balanced result. As a guide, 5000 words are equivalent to about 25 pages of double-space type. Taking the above six-chapter arrangement, a balanced proportion of content might be as follows:

1. Introduction – 5 per cent. This serves as a guide to the dissertation for the reader.
2. Background – 20 per cent. A review of the literature and information about the context of the study.
3. Main issues – 10 per cent. The main points or problems arising from the background that your research will tackle.
4. Research methods – 10 per cent. A description of the steps you will take and techniques you will use to actually investigate the main issues. Reasons for using these methods must also be included.

226

5. Research actions and results – 35 per cent. A record of what you did and what results came out of your investigations. You might split this into two or three sections if you are investigating two or three different issues.
6. Conclusions – 15 per cent. An interpretation of the results in light of the main issues.
     The remaining 5 per cent will be ancillary matter such as the abstract or summary, list of contents, bibliography, etc.

Now you will be ready to start inserting your notes into your structure. How do you get the right notes in the right place? This is where your retrieval techniques will be put to the test. Assuming that your framework gives you enough indication of what you are looking for, search through your notes by key word or subject. If you do this on the computer, you will be shown a selection of relevant notes, from which you can choose what you think is suitable for that section. You can do this manually with notes on paper. Other useful search parameters may be date or author.

For the introduction, just insert your proposal for now. You will be able to use this, suitably edited, when you have finished the rest of the writing, to explain the nature of the dissertation. More will be added later to explain the structure of the dissertation.

Your proposal will indicate the sort of areas that your background study will need to cover. There are likely to be several aspects of the subject that need looking at, e.g. historical precedents, conflicting opinions, political, financial, organizational and social aspects, etc. At this stage you will need to clearly define the limits of your study: you only have a short time to complete it, so keep it manageable.

16.4 Revisions

The nice thing about using a word processor is that you can easily change things after you have written them. This takes away the pressure of getting everything right first time – something that is impossible to do anyway. Once your work is written down, then you can review it, get a second opinion on it, and discuss it. You cannot do these if it is still all in your head. Hence the importance of getting on with writing as soon as possible. Regard the making of revisions as an integral part of the process of doing a dissertation. You will of course have to include some time for this in your time plan.

You don't have to finish the dissertation or even a section of it before you revise it. You can use the process to accumulate your written material, adding to the latest version as the information comes in or as you get the writing bug. Regularly reviewing what you have done so far and to what quality will keep you aware of how far you have progressed and what still needs to be done. It also enables you to break down the work into small sections, revising, altering and expanding sections as your understanding develops. The text will thus evolve as a series of small steps that should need no drastic revision at the last moment.

Revising can be done at different levels. The more general levels are concerned with getting the structure and sequence right. Revision might entail moving around headings and blocks of text. Apart from the content of the text, you may want to try out different page layouts and formatting. At a more detailed level, you might look at the sequence of paragraphs: does each concentrate on one point? Do they follow each other in the right sequence? At the most detailed level you will be looking at grammar, punctuation, vocabulary and spelling.

I find that it is much easier to review what I have written when it is printed out on paper rather than still on screen; I can get a better overview of the layout, length of sections, and line of the argument. If your eyesight is good, change the font to really small (perhaps 8 point) before printing, both to save paper and to make it easier to have an overall view of the work. You will quickly spot gaps, dislocations in the sequence and imbalances in the length of sections. Alternatively, reduce the line spacing instead of the font size in order to maintain the line justification and familiar appearance of the script. Do remember though, that you are only doing these adjustments to make it easier to review your draft. Normally, the final version must not be submitted in less than 11 point font size (check with the submission details for your dissertation, see Chapter 18).

FIGURE 16.4   Getting everything right first time

It is important to keep track of your revisions: make sure you know what the latest one is! The best way is to save each revision as a new file, clearly labelled with a revision number (e.g. Chapter 3/rev1, Chapter 3/ rev2, etc.) You will thus be able to go back to a previous revision if you change your mind or want to check on some detail. Most word processing programs also provide a facility for keeping track of revisions, such as 'track changes' in Word.

16.5 Tops and tails

Particularly if you write your dissertation over a longish period and produce sections based on your notes, thoughts, blocks of data, etc., it is difficult to get smooth continuity in the text. This is really needed in order to make the dissertation clear and easy to read. You cannot usually do this completely as you are building up the text, so one aspect of your revisions should be to check this. As is usual with most things, continuity can be considered at different scales. You can check on the following aspects in scales of descending order.

Scale of the whole dissertation

- Introduction – gives a brief guide to the reader about the content and structure of the whole work. It should be a separate chapter or section at the beginning of the dissertation.
- Conclusions – draws together the main results of the discussion in the chapter; the finale of your dissertation. One should be able to read this section separately as a full account of the results of your investigations.
- Links and cross-referencing – the issues studied should arise out of the background; the methods used in the investigation should relate to the types of questions/issues studied; the actual fieldwork or personal research work should follow the methods described; the data should arise from the fieldwork or personal research; the conclusions should be produced from the data and encapsulate the answers to the questions or issues raised at the beginning of the work. In this way you will complete the circle: problems raised, answers found.

Scale of the chapters or sections

- A final sentence or two of a chapter should form a bridge to the next chapter.
- Cross-references citing page or section numbers are usefully added to link to specific information in other chapters.
- Paragraphs – make one overall point or deal with one topic. The first sentence introduces this, subsequent sentences develop this, the final sentence possibly forms a conclusion and leads to the next paragraph.

- Sentences – best to keep these short and clear.
- Consistent use of terminology. There are often several words that can be used with roughly the same meaning. To avoid confusion, define your terms and abbreviations the first time they are used and use exactly the same terms throughout.

FIGURE 16.5   Complete the circle

Apart from the main text, you will need to add several other sections that help the reader to navigate your dissertation. These are the title page, abstract, acknowledgements (to thank those that have inspired or helped you in any way to do the work), the list of contents with page numbers, lists of figures and tables – all at the beginning; and a list of references and possibly some appendices of related material (such as questionnaire forms, raw data, supplementary information) – all at the end. Do allow time to do these in your programme, as it will take some effort to get them all right.

16.6 Coming to conclusions

The whole point of collecting data and analysing them is so that you can come to some conclusions that answer your research questions and achieve the aims of your dissertation project. The trouble with this part of the dissertation is that it inevitably comes near the end of your project, when you are probably tired from all the work you have already done, when your time is running out, when you have pressures from other commitments such as revision and exams – let alone all the other things you want to get in before your undergraduate days are over.

To compound it all, the coming to conclusions is a quite demanding and creative process that requires a lot of clear thinking, perception and meticulous care. All the previous work will be devalued if you do not sufficiently draw out the implications of your analysis and capitalize on the insights that it affords. You cannot rely on the reader to make inferences from your results. It really is up to you to vividly explain how the results of your analysis provide evidence for new insight into your chosen subject, and to give answers to the particular research questions that you posed at the beginning of the dissertation. The main point I want to make is that you should programme some time for this process, and not under-estimate its importance. Refer to section 15.9 in the previous chapter for more detailed advice on how to formulate your conclusions.

16.7 Don't forget your grammar and punctuation!

Grammar

The principles of grammar are too complicated to outline here. If you have forgotten the principles of grammar, or never learned them, don't worry. Use your own 'voice' as you write, and explain everything as clearly as you would if you were talking to someone. However, do make sure about any particular requirements of academic writing style; certain subjects may demand this. Generally, as long as you are consistent in developing your argument by using straightforward sentences to build up well-formed paragraphs (as explained above) you will be able to communicate effectively. If you are writing in a foreign language, it is worth getting a native speaking colleague to check through a section of your work to see if you are making any recurring mistakes.

Punctuation

There is some flexibility here. A good guide to the use of punctuation is to read the text aloud, and fit the punctuation in where the natural pauses occur in speech, for example: commas for short pauses, semi-colons for greater divisions, colons preceding lists. Commas or spaced dashes (often typed as spaced hyphens) should be used both before and after an aside or additional piece of information within a sentence, just as you would with brackets. Direct quotations must always be within quotation marks (now

FIGURE 16.6   Use your own voice

usually only single inverted commas), unless they are lengthy, in which case they are best presented as separate indented paragraphs.

One of the most common punctuation errors concerns the apostrophe with 's' when noting possession, e.g. 'the animal's face'. With 'it', only use the apostrophe when you can read 'it's' as 'it is'; for the possessive, e.g. 'its face', no apostrophe is needed. As the style of writing a dissertation should not be too conversational, it is better anyway to avoid using abbreviations such as 'it's', 'don't', or 'couldn't'.

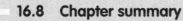

16.8   Chapter summary

Prepare an outline of chapter headings and subheadings before you start to write up your dissertation. This gives you a framework into which to insert your notes, extracted from your note recording system. The main headings for most dissertations will be the introduction; background to the study; the main issues to be addressed in detail, including the research questions; the research methods used to investigate these – including data collection and analysis; the report on what was done and the results of the investigation; the conclusions that can be drawn from the findings – particularly relating back to the research questions and the main issues. Subheadings are inserted as appropriate for the subject.

Keep an eye on the maximum permitted word count of the dissertation by allocating a share of the words to each section. Insert your notes where applicable to form a very rough first draft. You can then build up the text as more information becomes available from your data collection and analysis. Revise the text both as you go along and in response to feedback from your tutor and others. Check for the lines of argument to ensure that they lead to the conclusions, and keep focused on answering the research questions. Back up your work regularly! Add the tops and tails when you are finished. Also check the spelling, punctuation and grammar. If you are writing in a second language, get a native speaker to help you with this.

16.9 What should I do now?

Get started, is the simple message! If you have not yet formulated an outline of your dissertation, then this is probably the best place to start. This framework will allow you to painlessly insert any notes you have, thus providing a first body of written work.

It is worth checking your word processing program for the spelling and grammar features mentioned above. They may need to be activated in order to work.

If you feel that there is not enough information or prompts in the text above, read other books that are more specialized on aspects of dissertation production, such as the process of writing, specific subject-oriented dissertation guides and study guides. See the references below for some suggestions.

16.10 References to more information

Here are three books that deal exhaustively with the art of writing, both the technique and practice. I have noted their particular strengths to help your selection.

Further reading

Woods, P. (2006) *Successful Writing for Qualitative Researchers*, 2nd edition. London: Routledge. Really thorough on all aspects of writing – getting started and keeping going, organization, alternative forms of writing, style, editing, etc.
Mounsey, C. (2002) *Essays and Dissertations*. Oxford: Oxford University Press. A compact, easy-to-read guide to writing; in the 'One Step Ahead' series. Other titles in the same series might also be useful: *Editing and Revising* by Jo Billingham, *Punctuation and Spelling* by Robert Allen, and *Words and Writing Reports* by John Seely.

Greasley, P. (2011) *Doing Essays and Assignments*. London: Sage. Provides students with an insider's view of what tutors and professors are looking for when they set essays and assignments.

The following are two examples of books that specialize in writing about particular subjects. I suggest you do a search for similar books in your own subject, easily done using key words (such as 'writing' and 'geography').

Jay, R. (2003) *How to Write Proposals and Reports That Get Results*. Harlow: Pearson. Really aimed at managers, but we all have to manage! Good practical advice on all aspects of writing.

Fabb, N. and Durant, A. (2005) *How to Write Essays, Coursework Projects and Dissertations in Literary Studies*, 2nd edition. Harlow: Pearson. Especially for those who specialize in writing about writings.

And here are three books to help you sort out the finer points of writing in English:

Evans, H. (2000) *Essential English*. London: Pimlico. Get your spelling and grammar and construction right with this.

Trask, R.L. (2002) *Mind the Gaffe: The Penguin Guide to Common Errors in English*. London: Penguin. See whether you make common mistakes.

Bailey, S. (2011) *Academic Writing: A Handbook for International Students*, 3rd edition. Abingdon: Routledge. Aimed at students with English as a second language.

17

What About Referencing?

Chapter contents

17.1 Why should I bother about references?

Writing a dissertation is not an exercise in creative writing. You will not be relying on your imagination as a source of your text. Almost everything you write will need to be based on the work of others and on your own research work. At this level you will not be required to produce an original contribution to knowledge. You might generate some new data if you do some fieldwork, e.g. surveys, experiments, etc., and you will certainly have to express opinions and judgements that are genuinely your own. Your input will primarily be the building up of an argument or discussion from existing material, collected and organized by yourself. To do this you will need to read quite widely in order to study the background to your subject and to investigate what work has already been done in your chosen field. You will also need to consult textbooks about research methodology, and possibly track down relevant statistics and other data.

In order to record the sources of this information, and also to substantiate facts and claims that you make in your text, you must include citations within the text of your dissertation and make a list of references. The use of a sound referencing system is essential. It is also good academic practice, and if properly applied is bound to impress your examiner. Not only does it demonstrate your high ethical standards, but it also gives a very good record of the number and type of books and other publications to which you have referred during your study. Expect the examiner to know who the important writers are in the subject you have chosen, so you need to ensure that you have consulted the appropriate books.

From the ethical point of view, correct referencing ensures that you do not pass off as your own any ideas, writings, diagrams or information created by someone else. In academic writing there is absolutely no shame associated with referring to, using or manipulating other people's work. In fact, much time is spent by academics doing just this. As long as you are 'up-front' and acknowledge your sources, you cannot be criticized. If you are reviewing existing ideas and knowledge on a subject, your text could legitimately be riddled with acknowledged excerpts and quotations. If, however, you are sloppy and forgetful, even unintentional borrowings are regarded as theft of intellectual property, commonly referred to as plagiarism. As you will see from your university or college regulations, penalties for plagiarism are stiff, and rightly so. It is not at all difficult to conform to the accepted standards of referencing, it just needs a bit of care and forethought.

Not only is referencing used to acknowledge the contribution of others to your text, it is also very useful as a guide to the reader to check on the quality

FIGURE 17.1   Penalties for plagiarism are stiff

of the sources and perhaps to acquire more detailed information. The best test of a referencing system is to try to find the original information, opinion or idea referred to from the reference information given. For example, if you quote that 23 per cent of school leavers cannot read and write sufficiently to fill in a job application form, can the actual published statistic be tracked down from your reference?

17.2 Keeping track

There are several established systems for achieving this task. What you need for all of them is a full record of the source of your information. This is why I stressed very strongly in Chapter 4 that you should always attach details of the author, publication, page number, date of publication and publisher to each note that you have taken from your reading sessions. Without this information you will be at a loss to provide a full reference; many wasted hours can be spent trying to track down the source of a really useful quotation or a relevant theory or opinion, perhaps months after you have read them. Using a computer-based note-taking and referencing program such as Endnote will make life much easier for you in this respect (see Chapter 9 for more details about note taking).

It is the best idea to incorporate all the referencing details while preparing your drafts. This will prevent the references from becoming 'detached' from the relevant text and will save much time later on in the production of the finished script. The citation is the acknowledgement within the text to indicate the source of the opinion or information. This is expanded to the full details in the reference found in the list of references at the end of the chapter or dissertation. Don't confuse this with a bibliography, which is a list of books you have referred to or which expand on the subject, but which may not have been actually cited in your text. Correct referencing can quite easily be done if you use one of the systems I suggest below.

17.3 Right ways of doing it

Here are two alternative systems that you can use. There are actually many alternative systems on offer that differ in detail, and publishers usually stipulate which one should be used if you publish your work with them. These two commonly used systems – the British Standard (numeric) system and the Harvard (author–date) system – are explained in some detail to show the principles of referencing.

British standard (numeric) system

This is ideally used for shorter pieces of text, or for separate chapters, articles or papers. It is suitable for use in your proposal. The citation is simply a number in brackets at the appropriate spot in the text (i.e. after the statement or piece of information to which it refers). You can include several numbers or a range of numbers to refer to several publications. Note, the punctuation is always after the brackets. Use the same style of brackets throughout – square or round. For example:

The order came from the king who was at Gloucester at the time (1). Although, according to traditional views, 20,000 troops were in readiness (2), Jones and Eldred (3) estimated only 5000 on the basis of the latest evidence discovered in a contemporary journal (4). Morton et al. described the state of the troops as 'full of confidence and ready for battle' (5). There are varying assessments of the readiness of the opposing forces (6–9).

Note that 'et al.' is used when there are three or more authors.

The reference gives the full details of the publication and is placed in number order in the list of references. The sequence of information for books is: author, title, edition (if not the first), place, publisher, date, relevant pages. Books containing the work of several authors put together by an editor need details of the author cited as well as the editor, so lists: author, title of his or her chapter, editor, title of the book, place, publisher, date, relevant pages. Journal references are slightly different: author, title of article, title of journal, volume/issue or part number, date, relevant pages. See also examples below of newspapers, Internet sites, etc.

Here are some examples that show the details in different cases. Take particular care to be consistent with the punctuation, spaces, use of capitals and italics. Instead of italics you can use underlining or bold, as long as you are consistent.

1. Jacob, J.R. *The king's commands in battle*. Cambridge: Jason, 2001, p. 78.
2. Hendred, R.S. Common 19th century myths. In Bracknell, L.S. (ed.), *History in turbulent times*. London: Stolls, 1998, pp. 45–47.
3. Jones, A.H. and Eldred, K.Y. *Readings in cathedral archives*, 2nd edn. Oxford: Boles, 2000, p. 138.
4. Ponsford, S.J. *Diaries of a journeyman*. British Museum Manuscript, 1345, p. 13.

5. Morton, R.M., Smith, J. and Rogers, D. The battle of Coombe Hill. *Journal of Studies in Medieval History*, 51 (3), 1998, pp. 48–63.
6. Daly, G.S. Controversy reigns about historic battle. *Daily Express*, 24 June 2001, p. 3.
7. Gloucestershire Past Website. No date. Retrieved 25 May 2003 from: http:// glospast.gobenet/views.htm.
8. BBC History. *Medieval battles*. Produced and directed by James Notts, 1999, video-cassette, 30 min.
9. Open University. *Texts in medieval history*. 2002. Retrieved 24 June 2003 from: www.open.ac.uk/history/resources.htm.

Harvard (author–date) system

This is used internationally. It has the advantage that brief details of the publication are given in the citation in the text and the list of references is arranged alphabetically. This eliminates the need to synchronize the order of citations and references, so easily disturbed if you rearrange the text. Another advantage is that the basic information supplied by the citation remains with the relevant text wherever you might move it. It is therefore ideal for using in extended texts, such as dissertations, theses and books, subject to several drafts and revisions.

FIGURE 17.2   So easily disturbed if you rearrange the text

Below is the same text as above, but using the Harvard system:

The order came from the king who was at Gloucester at the time (Jacob, 2001, p. 78). Although, according to traditional views, 20,000 troops were in readiness (Hendred, 1998, pp. 45–47), Jones and Eldred (2000, p. 138) estimated only 5000 on the basis of the latest evidence discovered in a contemporary journal (Ponsford, 1345, p. 13). Morton et al. described the state of the troops as 'full of confidence and ready for battle' (1998, p. 57). There are varying assessments of the readiness of the opposing forces (Daly, 2001, p. 3; Gloucestershire Past Website, no date; BBC History, 1999; Open University, 2002).

Note that the names of the authors mentioned in the immediately preceding text do not have to be repeated in the citation. The references are given in alphabetical order in the list of references. Note the different order of the items and use of punctuation. The date is given in brackets after the name of the author, rather than near the end. This is useful, as there may be several works by one author but of different dates. List these in date order. If there is more than one reference of the same date, then letter them, e.g. (1999a), (1999b), (1999c). Use the same lettered date in the citation.

BBC History (1999) *Medieval battles*. Produced and directed by James Notts. Video-cassette, 30 min.
Daly, G.S. (2001) Controversy reigns about historic battle. *Daily Express*, 24 June, p. 3.
Gloucestershire Past Website (no date) Retrieved 25 May 2003 from: http://glospast.gobenet/views.htm.
Hendred, R.S. (1998) Common 19th century myths. In Bracknell, L.S. (ed.) *History in turbulent times*. London: Stolls, pp. 45–47.
Jacob, J.R. (2001) *The king's commands in battle*. Cambridge: Jason.
Jones, A.H. and Eldred, K.Y. (2000) *Readings in cathedral archives*, 2nd edn. Oxford: Boles.
Morton, R.M., Smith, J. and Rogers, D. (1998) The battle of Coombe Hill. *Journal of Studies in Medieval History*, 51 (3): 48–63.
Open University (2002) *Texts in medieval history*. Retrieved 24 June 2003 from: www.open.ac.uk/history/resources.htm.
Ponsford, S.J. (1345) *Diaries of a journeyman*. British Museum Manuscript.

Other reference systems differ in detail. If you use a reference database program such as Procite, Endnote or Citation, the program will automatically draw up reference lists correctly in a choice of many referencing systems on the basis of the details you entered on the database.

17.4 How many references do I need?

There is no simple answer to this question. It all depends on the type of dissertation you are writing. Also, some sections of the dissertation will have many more references than others. So where and when should these references appear? Here is a list of these instances, some more obvious than others:

- In a general description of the background to your chosen subject. This will appear in your proposal and in the introduction to your dissertation. What are the main factors, ideas, approaches in the subject?
- In a literature review of the particular issues raised by your research question or problem. Just about every dissertation will have one of these reviews. Who wrote what – state-of-the-art information and comparisons?
- In the descriptions of the methodology you have used to do your research. Again, every dissertation should contain some of these. What are the sources of your information on research methods?
- Appealing to higher authorities as a way of justifying your arguments. The opinion of an expert usually carries more weight than that of an undergraduate student. Who said it, where?
- Using secondary data sources. You might use government or other statistics. Where do they come from?
- Inserting quotations, diagrams and illustrations. Always a useful and attractive feature. You must acknowledge the sources. Where did they come from?

You will see from the above that the type of dissertation that will be full of references is one that reviews the work of others – for example, in a critical analysis of historical interpretations, an evaluation of economic theories, or a review of different practices. Where most of the writing describes your actions and your own collected information, – for example, in carrying out an experiment or survey – then references will rarely be required. But every dissertation will need to refer to ideas, information, methods and material produced by others: nothing is new, everything comes from somewhere.

Given that some dissertation subjects will automatically require more references than others, how can you judge for yourself, apart from the material you have collected anyway, how many references will be enough, or even too many? The latter is easier to answer. Don't bolster your list for the sake of trying to impress. Adding spurious or irrelevant references will actually count against you.

As to the question of how many is enough, this is a matter of both knowledge and judgement. If you are a particularly keen and effective sleuth, you will unearth more relevant secondary material than if you are a reluctant

241

searcher. What you must ensure is that you have included the essential references to the most important work in your subject. You will not know what these are unless you find out! After having done your searches, if you can, check with your supervisor or a specialist in your subject whether you have missed anything important. Swapping information with your fellow students can also help at this stage.

Assuming you have included the basic minimum of references, your method of enquiry and style of writing will influence how you use references. Be alert to making unsubstantiated statements: add a reference or give some supporting information. In the end, you will have to judge what you are comfortable with.

FIGURE 17.3   A particularly keen and effective sleuth

17.5   Chapter summary

Referencing is an essential part of any academic writing. Your work will always be founded on that of others, and this should be acknowledged as a matter of course. This forms the main defence against accusations of plagiarism. It is a virtue to refer to the work of others – it demonstrates that you are widely read and familiar with the current thinking in your subject. However, don't add irrelevant references just to pad out the list!

It is important that you keep track of your sources when you are compiling your notes by appending all the necessary bibliographic data to each note. Check in the instructions for your dissertation what type of referencing system is required – there are several. The numeric system numbers the citations and references, while the author–date system uses the author name and year of publication as a guide, listing them alphabetically in the list of references. An exact and consistent order of information and punctuation is required. Computer-based referencing programs make this easier to manage.

17.6 What should I do now?

If you haven't been systematic in recording your references in your notes, now is the best time to go back and do it. The later you leave it, the more likely you will have forgotten the sources of your information and quotations.

If you have been meticulous in keeping the references with the notes, then whatever note taking and storing system you have used, you will manage the referencing without problems. When you prepare a draft of a chapter or section, include the citations and references straight away. I know that it is tedious and tends to break up your flow of thought, but if you don't do it immediately it will take much longer to go back and do it later.

Do check through your drafts to spot any assertions, quotations, descriptions or other material that are not purely based on your own individual work.

17.7 References to more information

First, consult your own library to find any guidance handouts they might produce. These should be ideally suited to your needs. If you really need more information, then here are some books, easiest first, but check that the style conforms to your own regulations. You might have noticed that the reference style I have used in this book differs slightly from the above models.

Further reading

Pears, R. and Shields, G. (2010) *Cite Them Right: The Essential Referencing Guide*, 8th edition. Basingstoke: Palgrave Macmillan.
Neville, C. (2010) *The Complete Guide to Referencing and Avoiding Plagiarism*, 2nd edition. Maidenhead: Open University Press.

British Standards Institution (1990) *Recommendations for Citing and Referencing Published Materials*. BS 5605. London: BSI.

University of Chicago Press (2010) *The Chicago Manual of Style*, 16th edition. Chicago: University of Chicago Press.

Sunderland College (2010) *Harvard Referencing: Student Style Guide*. Sunderland: City of Sunderland College.

18

How Can I Make My Work Look Interesting and Easy to Read?

Chapter contents

18.1 Presentation ideas

Unless you are particularly design oriented, you have probably not spent much time thinking about just what your dissertation will look like. After all, there are many more important things to occupy your time while trying to get it finished. However, a dissertation is as much an exercise in communication as one in research, so time spent in production design pays good dividends. When your examiner is faced with a pile of dissertations to mark, it is obviously those that are attractive, clear and easy to read that will be the most welcomed. Although there are many possible styles of presentation, a few basic guidelines should be followed. These relate to the actual design of the publication as well as the organization of the material contained within it. The best way to success is to devote some time in forethought and preparation, as it is very frustrating, time-consuming and risky to work by trial and error. A good place to start is to look at the submission requirements for your dissertation, these might be quite specific as to what is acceptable.

As you will be only one of many students at the university or college with the same deadline for submission, the pressure on printing and binding facilities will become greater as the date approaches. Delays will increase just as you are running out of time. I know it is easy to say 'get your work finished early' but you will be doing yourself a favour not to have to join in the last minute scramble. In fact, giving yourself enough time can result in you actually enjoying putting the finishing touches to your 'masterpiece'.

18.2 Cover design and binding

Let us start with the first impressions from the outside. Ideally, you should keep the whole work in one volume. This may be difficult if you are, say, presenting large format graphical work as well as written text. Although A4 size is the most common for text-based dissertations, if your subject demands considerable graphic work, consider A3 size. You can still easily and economically photocopy in this format, and printers coping with this format are not uncommon. Text can also be comfortably integrated in columns on the page. The larger formats tend to be more expensive to reproduce and it is difficult to design the text elements in such a way that they are comfortable to read. If you do have to produce your work in two sizes, it is worth devising a way of connecting the two physically, so they do not drift apart – a common source of problems. If only a few large pages are needed, perhaps you can stay with the A4 or A3 format and arrange the larger sheets to fold out.

There are several ways of binding your work. It is important that pages cannot become separated, so a folder of loose sheets or slide-on plastic holders will not do. Even the clip-type ring binders are vulnerable to coming undone or the pages being pulled out, with disastrous results. Ring binding with plastic 'comb' rings can cope with almost any number of pages, and they also allow the pages to be opened right up so that they lay flat. You need to have access to a special machine for slotting your paper and inserting the binder; these should be available to you somewhere in your department, so it is worth finding out in good time.

The cover should have the title of the dissertation, your name, a date and details of the module or course number. Check with the official instruction for

FIGURE 18.1   What does 'well arranged' mean?

any stipulations on this. Get some good quality coloured card for the front and back covers. You can print on these to good effect. For an even more glossy finish, you can add a piece of transparent plastic to the front and back. Especially if there is a design element in your course, it is worth spending some effort in making the cover distinctive, particularly if the result can be related to the contents of the dissertation. Even if you keep it very simple, ensure that the typography is well arranged and easy to read.

What does 'well arranged' mean? There are no hard and fast rules on this: you will need to rely on your aesthetic sense and on any ideas gleaned from the layout of other publications that you admire. Aim to get a certain logic and consistency in the layout, so that it expresses a distinct style. Decide whether you want to centre the text, or if you want to align it to the left or right. Usually, it is wise to keep to the same typeface, altering the size to suit the importance of the text. Using a large font for the main title aids legibility, as does leaving plenty of empty space around the lettering. Avoid having a strong picture as a background to the text.

18.3 Title

The title of your dissertation has undoubtedly been the focus of your work for many weeks or even months, but now that you have virtually completed the dissertation, it is worth reviewing it in the light of what you have actually done. Does it still accurately and succinctly sum up the nature of your study?

As briefly stated in Chapter 3, the title must contain the crucial terms related to the work; after all, this is what will be listed in any reference to it. Keep it as short as possible.

A useful way to review your title is to check the following points:

- Are the one, two or perhaps three main concepts or issues mentioned? For example: sport and fitness; learning difficulties; road layouts for traffic calming; wealth, influence and power.
- Are these then located into a context to focus and limit the study? The context might be sector of society, time period, location, etc., e.g. sport and fitness for disabled people; learning difficulties in first-generation ethnic minorities; road layouts for traffic calming in mixed use suburbs; wealth, influence and power of eighteenth-century Spanish industrialists.
- An indication of the main methodology or philosophical stance might also be usefully added, e.g. a case study approach, a feminist perspective, an archival analysis, etc.

A common way of forming the title is to state the main concepts, then add the detail as a subsidiary phrase, e.g. 'Health and efficiency: naturist philosophy in Germany, 1920–40'. Beginning phrases like 'A study of' or 'A comparison between' can generally be omitted.

On the title page, you should also add your name and the date. You might also add a description of what course or module the dissertation is set to fulfil. Check the assignment details for any specific instructions.

18.4 Acknowledgements

These are short expressions of thanks to people or organizations that have been particularly helpful in your work. The relatively small scale of an

FIGURE 18.2   Thanks to people who have been helpful in your work

undergraduate dissertation makes this an optional feature, but you may feel particular gratitude that you want to express to someone. If you have been funded by an organization, you may be obliged to acknowledge this by the terms of the agreement.

18.5 Abstract

You have probably realized by now that you do not have time to read whole books or even journal articles in order to find out if they are of interest to you. You have also probably noticed how useful the abstract, list of contents and introduction are as shortcuts to finding out the content of the text. The index is also useful in this respect. In order to provide a guide to the reader of your dissertation, you should also provide these features. Seeing it from the point of view of the reader will help you to make these features really useful.

The abstract (or résumé, often called the executive summary in reports) is a compact summary of the whole dissertation, usually not more than 150–200 words long. It is placed right at the beginning of the dissertation, usually after the acknowledgements (if any) and before the list of contents. Despite it being at the beginning of your document, you can only write it, for obvious reasons, when you have completed the rest. This will be at a time when you are under stress to complete, so it is worth allotting some time for its production in your programme. It should not take too long, but is really worth the effort from the point of view of impressing your marker. Because it must be so short, it is not so very easy to write: you will need all your skills in summation to make it read well (this paragraph is already 150 words long!).

Start with a statement of the main aims of the project. Then add a bit of background to give the context in which it was carried out. Follow with the specific questions or problems that you posed, and then with the principal methods you used to investigate them. End with the main conclusions and perhaps a note about their significance.

For examples of abstracts, see any thesis, journal paper, conference paper, or a journal of abstracts.

18.6 Contents list

The list of contents is much easier to devise. All you have to do is make a list of all your chapter headings, subheadings and even sub-subheadings, together with their page numbers. Put this just before the main text. You can automatically generate the list of contents with your word processing program if you do not want to do it manually. To be really professional, you can also add lists of figures, charts and illustrations, either separately or altogether on one list. Just make a list of the titles and page numbers in order of appearance. Insert this after the list of contents, starting on a separate page. A list of appendices, if you have any, should also be added.

18.7 Introduction

The subject matter of the introduction has been mentioned in the previous chapter. Just to remind you, here it is again: the main aims of the dissertation, a short summary of the context of the study, the main problems or issues to be investigated, the overall approach to the project, and a short description of the structure of the dissertation.

This lead-in to the main body of the work will be just a short chapter, the main function of which is to provide a guide to the reader about the subject and structure of the dissertation, and to point out its main features. It should whet the reader's appetite to read on, but not give away the conclusions – just as a detective novel will create a certain suspense from the start but not say 'whodunnit'. As your work is unlikely to go exactly as originally planned, it is not feasible to complete the introduction before the main part of the study is completed. Hence, allow yourself some time near the end for finishing this writing.

FIGURE 18.3   Unlikely to go exactly as planned

18.8 References and bibliography

What is the difference between these two? A list of references mentions all the publications that have been referred to in the text, but nothing else. A bibliography lists also other publications that are useful or related to the subjects covered.

You definitely need to include a list of references. Normally, and most conveniently, the list is put at the end of the dissertation. Alternative locations, which are more difficult for your marker to review, are at the end of each chapter, or as footnotes to the relevant pages. If you are using the British Standard (numeric) system (see Chapter 17), make sure that the numbers follow correctly in sequence and tally with the references. These may have been shifted when you made revisions to the text. If you are using the Harvard (author–date) system, check that the references are in alphabetical order. You should also scan through all the citations in the text to ensure that they are detailed on the reference list – a tedious task, but one that can save you losing marks.

The order and punctuation in each reference should accord with the standard requirements and be consistent throughout. Mistakes are easily made here, so a thorough check is required. You will save yourself time and trouble if you have used a bibliographic database program, as the list can be generated automatically. Even if you have not, you have probably made a list of references as you went along, so paste this in and revise it rather than attempt to type it all out again from scratch.

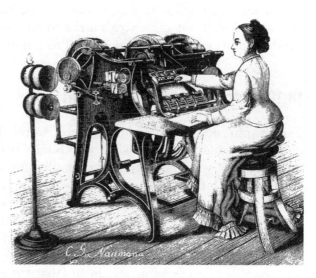

FIGURE 18.4   The list can be generated automatically

If you want to indicate that you have read more widely than just those publications cited, it is best to add a bibliography as a separate list. The intention might be to show that you have consulted supplementary information, e.g. on writing skills, research methods, project organization, etc. Don't overdo it though; it is obviously easy to list whole sections of the library catalogue, but this will convince no one of your extraordinary diligence.

18.9 Appendices

These are additional sections added at the end to supplement the main text, and are generally to be avoided. The main argument for this is that either the information is relevant to the subject and therefore should be included in the main text, or it is not directly relevant and should therefore not be added at all.

I believe that there are certain exceptions to this. If you have done a survey, a copy of the questionnaire or interview questions should be included as an appendix, perhaps also with a copy of a typical response. Similarly, a typical data sheet of observations could be shown. Copies of letters of permission or other crucial correspondence might also be included. Other bits of information that will illustrate how you did the work might also be usefully added, if these are really informative but would disrupt the flow of the main text. You should refer to the appendices where appropriate in the main text.

To be avoided is inclusion of lengthy articles on related subjects, full survey responses, elaboration or discussion of important issues, etc. What is certain is that you will not get extra marks by padding out your dissertation with sundry additional information added as appendices.

18.10 Internal layout and design

Typographic design and layout is a profession of its own. But even without the help of an expert, it is possible to produce really smart results with a computer. Unless you are a student in publishing or a related subject, it is probably not worth the time and effort to learn a specialized publishing program. Word processing programs bristle with features to help you write and compile reports (and dissertations) so that they are clear and easy to read. It will take you some time just to exploit all the features if you have not done so already.

There will probably be stipulations about font choice, minimum font size, line spacing and margins, etc. in the instructions for your dissertation, so it is worth checking before you spend much time experimenting.

Page layout and margins

A bit of design input should be used here. The page layout and margins determine the overall appearance of the content of the dissertation. You only have to look at a few books of different types, e.g. art books, novels, textbooks, etc., to see what a range of options there are. Once you have set up a page layout style, make sure that you are consistent in its application. One choice is whether to mirror the layout of left and right pages, or to keep the design the same orientation on all pages. If you are only allowed to print on one side of the paper, which is normally the case, this problem does not occur. As with most issues of design, a few experiments to try out and compare different options will help you to make decisions.

A balance should be achieved between white paper and printed areas; very full pages are tedious to read. Wide margins, as well as being left blank, can be used as an area to place key words, and small illustrations or diagrams. Leave plenty of space at the hinge side of the pages, especially if the pages can-not be folded flat when opened. If you are

FIGURE 18.5   Very full pages are tedious to read

using A3 format you will almost certainly need to set your text in columns. You can determine the position and width of these.

Typography

Here you have a range of choices to make, but this might be limited by your dissertation regulations. First, you should decide on the typeface (font). There is a wide choice of these with a range of fanciful names, most used only for billboards or advertising copy. However, even among the 'standard' fonts there is quite a choice. The main distinction is between 'serif' and 'sans serif' designs. Serif designs have the little tails at the ends of the letters, derived from the stonemasons having to start the incision when carving the letters. This text now is in a serif font. Times New Roman is one of these. Sans serif fonts, without these tails, look more modern (see the figure captions as an example). Arial is also one of these. Funnily enough, it is not always the simplest font that is easiest to read – perhaps because the lack of subtlety makes letters and words less instantly recognizable. The choice of font will determine the overall stylistic appearance of your text. It is easy to try out different ones to see what they look like.

Font sizes

For easy legibility use a font size of 11 point or more for the general text. Large fonts make reading slower and take up lots of room (this can be used to your advantage if your content is rather meagre). Normally, keep to one font for the text. Exceptions can be for quotations, headings, labelling of diagrams and tables, etc. If the text is divided to serve two different purposes, for example, as an extract from literature and as a commentary on that extract, then you could use two different fonts to make this obvious.

Line spacing

A normal requirement for work that is marked is that the lines should be double-spaced. This provides room for the marker to add comments and corrections. Check on any official requirement in this respect. If you need to stretch your work a bit, then increase the spacing marginally. Quotations, if in a separate paragraph, are normally single-spaced (i.e. should not need correcting). The quotation should also be indented on both sides.

Paragraphs

You have the choice of indenting the first line to show the beginning of each paragraph. However, this is not necessary if you leave a blank line between paragraphs (which I personally prefer).

Bold, italics and underlining

These should be used sparingly within the text. They can be used to good effect to accentuate particular words when they are used for the first time (e.g. specialist terminology), and to highlight crucial sentences (e.g. statement of the main research problem). Be consistent in their use, and it is best not to combine styles (e.g. underlined italics). Another common use of a style change is italicized quotations within the text, and within the references in the list of references and bibliography.

Headings

This is where a change of font, size and/or style can be used to emphasize the different levels of heading. The most important thing is not to get too complicated and to be consistent – not always easy in a long text. The placing of headings on the page can be varied. It is normal to keep them aligned to the left. Centred headings tend to look very formal, and headings aligned to the right are rather modern. Indenting subheadings is common.

FIGURE 18.6   Not to get too complicated

The 'styles' command gives you a choice of types of text – body, title, heading 1, heading 2, etc. These can be formatted to your own liking. Use these, with numbering if required, as they will be useful for compiling the list of contents (and for viewing a navigation pane for quick overview).

Section numbering

Section numbering helps the reader to navigate the dissertation, so it should be consistent and easy to follow. The features that need numbering are: chapters, sections, possibly subsections, figures, diagrams, charts, tables, graphs, appendices and, most important of all, pages (see below).

There are several styles of numbering of chapters and sections, all of which you can generate automatically. However, these formatting aids are not foolproof and sometimes come up with unexpected results, so checking is always necessary. Consistency is what is looked for. The simplest form of numbering and the most commonly used for lengthy reports is that each chapter is numbered in succession (1, 2, 3, etc.), each main section of the chapters is numbered within that chapter (1.1, 1.2, 1.3, etc.). Subsequent subsections follow the same pattern within the main sections (1.1.1, 1.1.2, 1.1.3, etc.). Three levels of numbering are usually quite sufficient; you may find that two are enough. Make sure that the table of contents corresponds with the actual numbering in the text.

Bullets can be used when you are providing a list where the sequence of items is not significant. Bullets can be generated automatically.

Page numbering

This is an essential feature. If you have saved your text as several different files, you will have to ensure that, once combined, the page numbers follow

255

through correctly from beginning to end. There is a choice about the location and style of page numbers that will be dictated by your overall presentation. Choose what you think is the best position for your page layout (top, bottom; centre, left or right), making the numbers easy to find when flicking through the pages. To aid easy finding, keep the numbers near the outside edge of the pages rather than in the centre. Automatic page numbering is a standard feature of word processors.

Headers and footers

These are the zones at the top and bottom of the page that are repeated on every page, often containing the page number, chapter heading, dissertation title, etc. The headers and footers should be generated using the tool in the word processor; do not try to type them out on each page. You can use different text in the left and right page headers, for example, the dissertation title on the left, and the current chapter title on the right. You can insert a line to separate the headers and footers from the main text.

Illustrations

These can vary so much in size, shape and complexity that you need to make your own judgements as to how you will present them. Colour illustrations require lots of memory, and, of course, colour printing adds to the expense. Always add a caption and don't forget to acknowledge the source of the illustrations if they are not your own. Assume that images on the Internet are subject to copyright legislation and check for terms and conditions of use before copying digital images. Your library probably provides a guide to sources of images, some of which will be copyright free or available for academic use. Numbering of illustrations is an essential feature of academic writing. The normal convention is to distinguish between figures, tables and formulae. Figures are any kind of picture, diagram, graph, etc. that is not a table. Tables are obvious, as are formulae. Each category is numbered separately and consecutively in each chapter (Figure 1.1, Figure 1.2, Table 1.1, Table 1.2, etc.). An index of the figures and tables at the beginning of the dissertation is a useful feature. In all cases, use your judgement to provide maximum clarity and ease in navigation.

Text boxes

These can be used to separate sections of text in the form of vignettes, excerpts, lists, etc. They can be framed with a choice of line styles.

FIGURE 18.7   Clip art

Spelling, grammar and language

Remember to check what language is set (as there are several types of English available). You still need to double check the spelling yourself (or get someone else to do it) as some words spelt right but in the wrong context will not be highlighted. If written in what is not your first language, watch out for the highlighting that indicates faults in grammar. It is a good idea to get a native speaker to check through your grammar before you submit it.

Auto formatting

Word, among others, gives a choice of instantly formatted styles. These arrange the margins, fonts, heading styles and indents to suit a wide range of different types of documents. If you apply one of the options to text that is already written, it shows you instantly in a window just what it will look like.

Table of contents, figures, tables and index

A table of contents can be generated automatically if you have used the headings in the style facility when setting up your text, which gives a range of choices of text style, e.g. normal, heading 1, heading 2, etc. These will be picked up when you use the table of contents tool. Similarly, you can automatically compile a table of figures and tables, but only if you have inserted captions using the tool. These tables should appear at the beginning of the dissertation.

Likewise, if required, an index can be generated if you have marked the works that you want entered into the list. An alphabetical list of the chosen works will appear together with the page numbers on which they appear. This list should appear right at the end of the dissertation, after the list of references.

List of references

A mentioned in Chapter 17, the list of references should be consistent with the style chosen. This list should appear immediately after the main text, and before any appendices. If you have used a note taking and referencing program compatible with your word processing program, then you can easily compile this list automatically from the citations you have inserted in the text (e.g. Word and Endnote). The style can be altered at the touch of a button.

18.11 Avoid the production blues

Take some good advice on organizing your computer-based work.

Saving and backing up

You will be storing months of work on bits of vulnerable magnetic film, so easily corrupted or damaged beyond repair. Ensure against disaster by saving your work regularly and by making backups. Copy your work to two, or better three, different media, e.g. data stick (easily lost), computer hard drives and your university intranet home directory. It is also a good idea to print out what you have done so far; if all else fails, you can scan this with a character/text recognition program. While you are writing, make a habit of saving your work every 10 or 15 minutes so you do not lose too much if the computer crashes. You can instruct your program to make recovery and backup saves automatically at regular intervals.

Large files

Your entire dissertation could, no doubt, be saved as one file. However, the file can become very large and unwieldy, especially if it contains illustrations. One way to get over this is to split it up into sections, perhaps as chapters, and create a file for each. Keeping the files reasonably small can help to speed up the computer and makes it easier to navigate your work. More important, if one file becomes corrupted, at least the other ones are safe.

Printing

Dissertations can be quite complicated to print. It may take some time to get what you see on the screen to print correctly. Different printers have different printable areas, so your carefully arranged pages may not appear as desired. Before printing, check all the pages on the Print Preview. Colour illustrations and other graphic work may need colour printing, perhaps on different size paper. Tables and diagrams might need to be in landscape format, or perhaps you might want to print certain pages on acetate. This all needs some thought and time in order to get it right.

Timing

Remember that you will be one of many who want to use the computers and printers before the submission date, so try to avoid the rush of the last few days. Other equipment, such as scanners and binders, will also be in great demand during this time. If you have problems, even the help desk is likely to be subject to long queues.

FIGURE 18.8   Try to avoid the rush of the last few days

18.12   Chapter summary

A well-designed and presented dissertation will be a clear signal to your supervisor and marker that you have taken care with your work and are keen to communicate your message. Always check with the stated presentation requirements to ensure

(Continued)

(Continued)

that you comply fully. These may cover the format, text size and spacing, order of contents, etc.

The title should be short and contain the main concepts and limitations of the study. Don't forget those that helped you in any way by inserting an elegantly written acknowledgements. The abstract should be a concise summary of the contents of the dissertation, including problem, methods and conclusions. The contents lists provide a quick way to find sections, so page numbers are essential.

The introduction sets the scene and provides a quick guide to the structure of the dissertation. The references are there not only to provide details of cited publications, but also to guide the reader to further information. Generally, a bibliography is not required. Appendices are useful for inserting additional material that is too bulky for the main text and provides additional information.

In designing the presentation of your dissertation, take into account the page layout and margins, the typography, font size, line spacing, use of paragraphs, and use of bold, italics and underling. Important for the structure and reader orientation are the headings, section and page numberings. Enliven your text with illustrations and other graphical work, and use text boxes where they enhance the layout. Your word processing program will have a wealth of features to help you present your work – get familiar with them to make your life easier!

Don't leave production and printing to the last moment as it can be time-consuming to get everything to look right and print correctly. Avoid last minute panics!

18.13 What should I do now?

Make sure that all your work is adequately backed up on two or three different locations. One way to preserve your text against all disasters is to print it out. To do this economically, temporarily reduce the font to 8 point, single-line spacing, when you print it. Not only do you save paper, but it is much easier to swiftly review what you have written, and to check the sequence of subheadings and numberings.

See what others have done in the past. You have surely by now looked at examples of successful dissertations from previous years. Now compare a few, looking at the presentation. You will soon see what is attractive, easy to read and professional looking. Consider the cover design, type of binding and size of paper. Then look at the internal layout and design, use of illustrations and figures. What about the typeface and font size? You will have to make notes and even perhaps sketches of what you think is the most attractive and effective.

This is a good time to check with the official requirements. Is the minimum font size stipulated? Are there instructions about margins, paper size, line

FIGURE 18.9   Looked at examples of successful dissertations

spacing, binding, etc.? If you cannot find the requirements, ask your supervisor for another copy. Better to be safe than sorry!

Play a formatting game. Save one of your chapter drafts to a new file and give it a new label (safest for playing around with) and, with the cursor at the beginning, try out different styles in the style gallery in the format menu. You can also see examples of reports etc. with full formatting. This not only will give you ideas on presentation but can provide a shortcut to the whole formatting process. Do check through afterwards to make sure that the formatting is as you wish throughout.

You can also experiment with generating the contents, fixing the headers and footers, aligning text around illustrations and text boxes, and all the other word processing tricks. Once you have decided what you want and determined how it works, then you can apply it to your proper text.

18.14 References to more information

The first port of call for questions about any aspect of word processing is the help facility in your program. This should answer questions about how to do things, and perhaps suggest things that you had not thought about or did not know. Although time-consuming, just exploring all the menus of any computer program is a good way of learning how they work. As you probably will be short of time at this stage of the project, using an explanatory handbook about the program is another option that might be useful if you are really new to this. See what is available in your library and your computer centre.

There is no point, I think, in me recommending here lots of books about typography, publishing design, layouts, etc., as you are unlikely to want to spend the time now in learning about these subjects in detail. If you are studying an arts subject that involves design issues, then use what you have learned to apply to your presentation work. However, this book might be useful:

Raubenheimers, J. (2013) *Doing Your Dissertation with Microsoft® Word.* Bloemfontein, South Africa: True Insight Publishing.

19

Who Else Might Be Interested in My Writing?

Chapter contents

19.1 Don't waste all your hard work: make it work for you!

As soon as you have submitted your dissertation, I am sure you will sigh with relief and be keen to get on with doing other things. But don't forget, your submission has been the result of a great deal of hard work and has taken up lots of your time. Perhaps you can wring more use out of it than just a mark from the examiners. It is therefore a very good idea to make a copy of your dissertation for your own use, as in most courses you will not receive it back.

It will go into the dissertation collection that you consulted so many weeks ago (well, that is a good start to widening its readership!). Anyway, you will have probably saved an electronic version onto disk.

So what can you do with it so that it produces some more advantages for you? Most people don't bother to do anything, so you will be an exception. Obviously, whatever you do will take time and effort, so it is only worth doing if you get some benefits. Consider the following possibilities. You could:

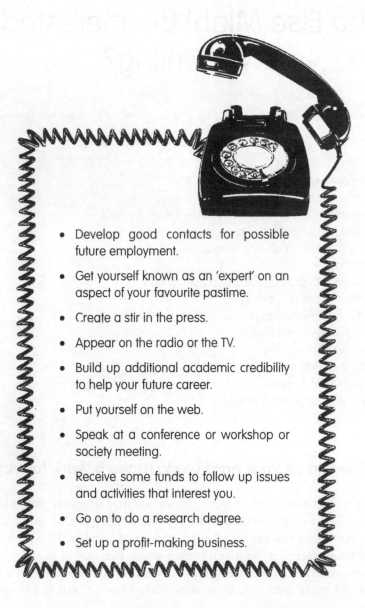

- Develop good contacts for possible future employment.

- Get yourself known as an 'expert' on an aspect of your favourite pastime.

- Create a stir in the press.

- Appear on the radio or the TV.

- Build up additional academic credibility to help your future career.

- Put yourself on the web.

- Speak at a conference or workshop or society meeting.

- Receive some funds to follow up issues and activities that interest you.

- Go on to do a research degree.

- Set up a profit-making business.

It is pretty obvious that you might get several benefits at once if you work things out in the right way. So, how can you go about it? For a start, in order to be motivated and successful, you need to remain really interested in the subject of your dissertation, as you will have to spend some time revising the length and format of what you have written. If you chose your title wisely right at the beginning, you might have developed even more interest now that you know so much more about your subject.

I will suggest, below, the different formats suitable for the different beneficial goals listed above.

19.2 Feedback to subjects and participants

If you have used a real-life situation for your dissertation research, e.g. in case studies or surveys, you have probably received plenty of help from several people. These may be managers, organizers, specialists, etc. If you were finding out about aspects of their organization, they may be very interested to know what you wrote. They are unlikely to want to read your whole dissertation, but the parts that deal particularly with their organization, perhaps in comparison with others, and the conclusions you have drawn, will certainly be of interest to them. You could cut and paste sections of your work to provide them with a short report, tailored to their particular interests. You could also investigate whether they have an in-house newsletter to which you could contribute a short article.

This will certainly get you noticed; your following up will impress both for the gratitude that you show and for the perhaps useful feedback that is usually the reason for getting involved in a research project. Not only does this provide a nice 'thank you' for their help, it might also be a good step towards getting some work in their organization, if that is what interests you. Even if you are not angling for a job, having contact with the movers and shakers in your particular field of interest is an asset that may be useful in the future.

It is more difficult, and probably not worth your effort, to provide feedback to a large number of interviewees or respondents to questionnaires. However, if you were investigating a community or some kind of an interest group, their leaders might appreciate it if you gave a short presentation of your study at one of their meetings. You might be treading on delicate ground, so make sure that the leaders are aware of the contents of your presentation. Assess how this exercise might be useful to you. It will certainly be a plus for your CV, and might also lead to useful contacts and recommendations. It also might be a stimulating experience and end up in

FIGURE 19.1 A good step towards getting some work in their organization

a lively discussion – or worse! If a face-to-face session seems rather daunting see if they produce a newsletter or discussion board, perhaps even a website to which you could contribute.

If you have done your dissertation work in connection with your pastime (as in some of the suggested examples given in Chapter 3), you may be able to channel your newfound knowledge back into the activity or hobby. For example, an easy-to-read article in a surfing magazine about the physics behind surfboard size and shape for different waveforms and height could be appreciated, or a talk at the local dog fanciers' club about the fashion and utility dogs of the aristocracy might go down well. You have done the work, so why not use it in such a way as to promote your own interest. You might make interesting contacts and get useful feedback.

19.3 Newspapers, journals and magazines

Getting into print is always a good idea, though quite a challenge. You will be well aware of the huge variety of daily, weekly and monthly periodicals on offer at newsagents. Every one of them must fill their paper with articles and advertisements, so they are always looking for material. However, they must be selective – and therefore so must you! How do you target the right publication? It depends on what you write about. Consider the nature of the report you could submit.

If your research has come up with really surprising results, that could have a serious or wide significance, i.e. something that could be considered newsworthy in a general sense, either locally or nationally, then you could devise a press release and submit it to the local or national paper. A press release is only two or three paragraphs long, and provides the essential details of the 'story', the what, where, how, when, who information. Address it to the editor and don't forget to add the date and your contact details. If someone on the editorial team is interested, they will contact you for more information. Obviously, local newspapers are easier to get into, particularly if the story is based in their area. Something along the lines of 'A study at our local university has recently revealed that ...' might be a good way to start. The national tabloid press will be most interested in sensational (and bad) news – but don't get carried away. You could land yourself in hot water if you exaggerate or falsify your report.

If your research is of interest only to a specialist readership because of its particular subject, then you should look for publications that are focused on this subject and cater for the people with this interest. Niche market magazines have proliferated in recent years, not only those that are publicly available at the newsagents, but also subscription magazines and professional papers and journals. You will probably be already aware of those catering for your particular interest. If there are several publications catering for the same interest, note that each will have its own character, and aim at a particular level of understanding. Gauge the level at which you will be most comfortable: will it be a more popular article for the interested, or a technically detailed one for the experts? Make your choice, keeping in mind the motivation for writing the article in the first place. You normally have to write the whole article first and then submit it to the editor of the chosen publication for consideration. Even so, it is a good idea to make a preliminary enquiry first by telephone to find out what they prefer and what your chances are of being accepted.

Academic journals are really aimed at publishing the work of professional researchers. There is little chance of you getting an article into one of these, unless it specializes in student dissertations.

19.4 Radio and TV

Some people will do anything to get onto TV! You won't have to, as you have already chosen your own reason for appearing on the radio or telly. How you persuade the programme makers is another question. And you will have to ask yourself what advantages you will get from being successful. Let us consider radio first.

The advantage of radio is that there is a multiplicity of stations ranging from the local hospital radio to national networks. My local area has at least three radio stations that feature all sorts of local news, characters and events. Listen in on the programmes for a few days, if you haven't already, and you should soon see whether you could compile something that would interest one of them. Obviously, if your work has revealed some attention-grabbing information about the locality you will have a good chance of being asked to make an appearance – vocally, that is. National radio is a different matter. Apart from taking part in a phone-in discussion, many of which are of questionable quality and will definitely not get you any kudos, you will probably struggle to find acceptance. Only if your dissertation has produced really important or surprising information on a topic of national concern will you have a chance

FIGURE 19.2   Some people will do anything to get onto TV

of interesting programme makers on national radio. Again, you need to be familiar with the format of the station output to spot the chance of getting on. Some stations do rely on audience input in some of their programmes.

Local television, apart from the regional news, is virtually non-existent, so you need to try a different approach. You are far more likely to appear on the TV if you have committed an 'orrible murder' and got caught than if you have done sterling work to help your community. I have been invited several times to appear in top entertainment programmes just because I featured in a small book about weird hobbies as someone who played the Swiss alphorn. No one ever asked me to talk about my research projects! So unless your findings are shocking, amazing, amusing or damning, you will have difficulty in making your break on the small screen. Look out for feature programmes that draw on local knowledge or specialist expertise. One problem is that most serious programmes are planned well in advance, so you do not know what is being looked for. Personal contacts in the TV world will be an invaluable asset in this respect.

19.5 Conference papers and poster presentations

There are numerous conferences that are organized for information, training and mutual contact on every subject and at every level of sophistication. There are some that are specifically aimed at the student level, while others sometimes have a student section in them. Find out from your university department and your older student friends what is on offer. Some conferences are an annual event and it is likely that previous students have contributed a paper or poster presentation at one of them. One thing is certain, you will not be paid for doing these.

A paper is presented as a short talk of about 15–20 minutes, usually supported by some visual matter on overheads, slides or a PowerPoint presentation. A poster is an information panel about your work that is hung up in the conference area. You will normally have to respond to a call for papers by sending in a short summary (abstract) of your intended paper or poster months before the planned event. If accepted, you may have to submit the full paper or poster shortly before. If the conference is far away, perhaps even abroad, see if you can get some financial support for travel and accommodation from your university; they usually have a fund for this. Your presentation at a conference will be a good addition to your CV particulars.

19.6 Grants, awards and prizes

There are several schemes and competitions that give awards on the basis of undergraduate dissertations. If you have done particularly well you might have a chance to cash in on your work. Again, you will have to find out what is offered in your particular subject. Ask your supervisor, your department and your university information centre. The scheme may be awarded by your university, a professional body, a commercial company or another institution. You could win a grant to travel and widen your studies, win a cash award or prize, or win a place for work experience at a specialist institution or a foreign university. Whatever it is, it will be another good addition to your list of achievements on your CV, as well as an enjoyable reward for all your hard work.

19.7 Publishing on the Internet

Anyone can put a web page or add to information on the Internet. What good it will do is another question. But perhaps I am being cynical. It really depends on just how you design and locate your presence on the web. Make a search to see what there is on your subject interest; you have probably done this already during your background research. The main question to ask, whatever you do, is: how will it benefit you?

Having a personal website has advantages if you have something to sell or you need to provide information about yourself and your activities. The contents of your dissertation are unlikely to be an important element of this. However, you might be able to use your newfound knowledge and skills to contribute to existing sites on your subject, or if you are particularly impassioned, to set up a new site or blog dedicated to your interest. The main advantage of doing either of these is that you will be able to network with others with similar interests. Make sure there is a facility to contact you or contribute to a discussion forum on your site. There is plenty of online advice available about how to set up and design web pages – it is getting easier all the time. And you probably know much more about blogs, tweets and social networking than I do!

19.8 Setting up your own business

This is probably a long shot in this context. But setting up a business does not necessarily mean hiring a suite of offices and getting yourself a PA. You may be able to exploit your acquired knowledge or skills to earn a bit of money in a more informal way.

It is pointless for me to write loads of advice about what kinds of business you could start and how it is done; the possible options are too wide. But do spend some time considering whether you could offer some kind of a service that you could charge for. Have your added knowledge and skills in research and writing provided you with something other people need? If so, is there a way that you can convince them it is worth hiring you to do the work? Using personal contacts will inevitably be the easiest way to find work of this kind. You will probably have made quite a few during your dissertation work and

FIGURE 19.3   An enjoyable reward for all your hard work

also have found out what the needs are. All it needs is some thought and imagination, then some skills of presentation and persuasion, and then some sound work to deliver the goods in order to earn perhaps a very useful addition to your income.

19.9 Ethics reminder

It is particularly important when you publicize your research work in any form that you carefully follow the ethical guidelines. Make sure that where confidentiality has been assured, it is strictly adhered to. The last thing you will want is to cause damage to people or organizations, or get yourself landed in legal troubles.

The two main aspects you should consider are privacy and commercial/organizational sensitivity. Just because people have been willing to provide you with personal and company/organizational information for your university study, it does not mean that they would be happy to see that information in the public domain. Get specific written permission from the sources of information to ensure probity. If you are at all uncertain about any aspect of this, get advice from your supervisor, the ethics experts in the university, or in really delicate situations, legal specialists.

FIGURE 19.4   It does not mean that they would be happy

Watch out too for copyright issues on illustrations and copies of newspaper articles or headlines. Any pictures, diagrams, graphs, tables, etc. copied from published sources are covered by copyright. You need to have written permission from the copyright holder to reproduce them, and they sometimes charge for this. Look at the publishing details at the beginning of the book or journal to find out whom to apply to. Alternatively, only use your own figures and illustrations.

You should also be careful not to make claims that you cannot back up with sufficient evidence. You might not automatically get enough feedback from the marking of your dissertation to see if your arguments were really convincingly based on the supporting data. If in any doubt, you should consult with your supervisor, and even better, the internal examiner who marked your dissertation, and raise the relevant issues to gain his or her opinion.

19.10   Chapter summary

Exploit all the hard work you have done to complete your thesis by using it, or what you have learned, to extend beyond your university studies. You might gain useful contacts for your future career from the people you met doing your studies. Your detailed investigations have made you something of an expert in that field, so you can use this knowledge to your advantage. Let people know by publishing an article in a journal or magazine, or even get yourself onto the local radio or television. If you want to advance your academic credentials, aim at getting a conference paper or poster accepted. You may even apply for a grant, award or prize on the strength of your dissertation.

Publishing on the Internet is getting easier all the time. Design yourself a website that includes details about your new expertise. You could even set up a blog on the subject of your dissertation if your think people might be interested. You might even be able to earn a bit of money using your new skills and expertise.

Keep in mind the ethical issues of privacy, confidentiality and anonymity with regard to organizations and individuals who have been involved in your research. Check on copyright of materials used – the conditions are much more restrictive outside of the academic field.

19.11 What should I do now?

Only go back to exploiting your dissertation work when you feel ready and motivated. I hope that this chapter has given you some interesting ideas of what you can do. As any of these options requires quite a bit of time and effort, make sure that you have clear reasons for doing what you have chosen and that you will reap sufficient benefits.

Most research work becomes quickly out of date, so the longer you leave it the more difficult it will be to successfully exploit your work. Also, you will quickly lose contact with people you have consulted during the process and you yourself will have moved on to doing other things. So, strike while the iron is hot, make hay when the sun shines, and ... well, you can probably think of a few more proverbs in this vein.

19.12 References to more information

I should think that the last thing you want to do now is to read more books. However, you may need to get some advice on writing press releases, articles and papers or designing a website. Here are some suggestions on different aspects of getting published – the titles speak for themselves.

Further reading

Murray, R. (2009) *Writing for Academic Journals*, 2nd edition. Maidenhead: Open University Press.

Becker, C. and Denicolo, P. (2012) *Publishing Journal Articles*. London: Sage.

Day, A. (2008) *How to Get Research Published in Journals*, 2nd edition. Aldershot: Gower.

Ruberg, M. (ed.) (2005) *Handbook of Magazine Article Writing*, 2nd edition. Cincinnati: Writer's Digest Books.

Baverstock, A. (2002) *Publicity, Newsletters, and Press Releases*. Oxford: Oxford University Press.

Bartram, P. (2006) *How to Write the Perfect Press Release: Real-life Advice from Editors on Getting Your Story in the Media*. London: New Venture Publishing.

Darkin, C. (2011) *Designing a Newsletter: The Really Really, Really Easy Step-by-Step Guide for Absolute Beginners*. London: New Holland.

McManus, S. (2011) *Web Design in Easy Steps*, 5th edition. Southam: Easy Steps.

DISSERTATION

References

Broadbent, G. (1988) *Design in Architecture: Architecture and the Human Sciences*. London: David Fulton.

Bromley, D.B. (1986) *The Case-Study Method in Psychology and Related Disciplines*. Chichester: Wiley.

Collier, A. (1994) *Critical Realism: An Introduction to Roy Bhaskhar's Philosophy*. London: Verso.

Copi, I.M., Cohen, C. and McMahon, K. (2010) *Introduction to Logic*, 14th edition. Harlow: Pearson.

Davies, P. (2002) *Get Up and Grow: How to Motivate Yourself and Everybody Else Too*. London: Hodder Mobius.

Fearnside, W.W. and Holther, W.B. (1959) *Fallacy*. Englewood Cliffs, NJ: Prentice Hall.

Fine, K. (1970) 'Propositional quantifiers in modal logic', *Theoria: A Swedish Journal of Philosophy*, 36 (3): 336–346.

Freeman, R. and Meed, J. (1999) *How to Study Effectively*. Cambridge: National Extension College Trust Limited.

Kerlinger, F.N. and Lee, H.B. (2000) *Foundations of Behavioral Research*. Fort Worth: Harcourt College Publishers.

Leedy, P.D. and Ormrod J.E. (2010) *Practical Research: Planning and Design*, 9th edition. London: Collier Macmillan.

Lofland, J., Snow, D., Anderson, L. and Lofland, L.H. (2004) *Analysing Social Settings: A Guide to Qualitative Observation and Analysis*, 4th edition. Belmont, CA: Wadsworth.

McLuhan, M. and Fiore, Q. (1976) *The Medium Is the Message*. Harmondsworth: Penguin.

Miles, M.B. and Huberman, A.M. (1994) *Qualitative Data Analysis: An Expanded Sourcebook*, 2nd edition. London: Sage.

Pinter, H. (1998) *Various Voices: Prose, Poetry Politics 1948–1998*. London: Faber and Faber.

Pirie, M. (1985) *The Book of the Fallacy: A Training Manual of Intellectual Subversives*. London: Routledge and Kegan Paul.

Preece, R. (2000) *Starting Research: An Introduction to Academic Research and Dissertation Writing*. London: Continuum.

Renoir, J. (1952) Filmed interview about his 1930s film *Une Partie de Campagne*. BBC, programme no longer available.

Reynolds, P.D. (1977) *A Primer in Theory Construction*. Indianapolis: Bobbs Merrill Educational.

Robson, C. (2011) *Real World Research: A Resource for Social Scientists and Practitioner-Researchers*, 3rd edition. Chichester: Wiley.

Taylor, G. (1989) *The Student's Writing Guide for the Arts and Social Sciences*. Cambridge: Cambridge University Press.

Woods, P. (2006) *Successful Writing for Qualitative Researchers*, 2nd edition. London: Routledge.

Index

978-1-4462-0325-5

978-1-4462-0287-6

978-1-44620-710-9

978-0-85702-932-4

978-1-84920-562-7

978-1-84920-794-2

978-0-85702-928-7

978-1-4462-0932-5

978-1-4462-0143-5

For more study skills information, multimedia resources
and special offers visit **www.uk.sagepub.com/studyskills.sp**

SAGE STUDY SKILLS - GIVING STUDENTS THAT EXTRA EDGE!